POSTCARD HISTORY SERIES

# *Lake Elsinore*

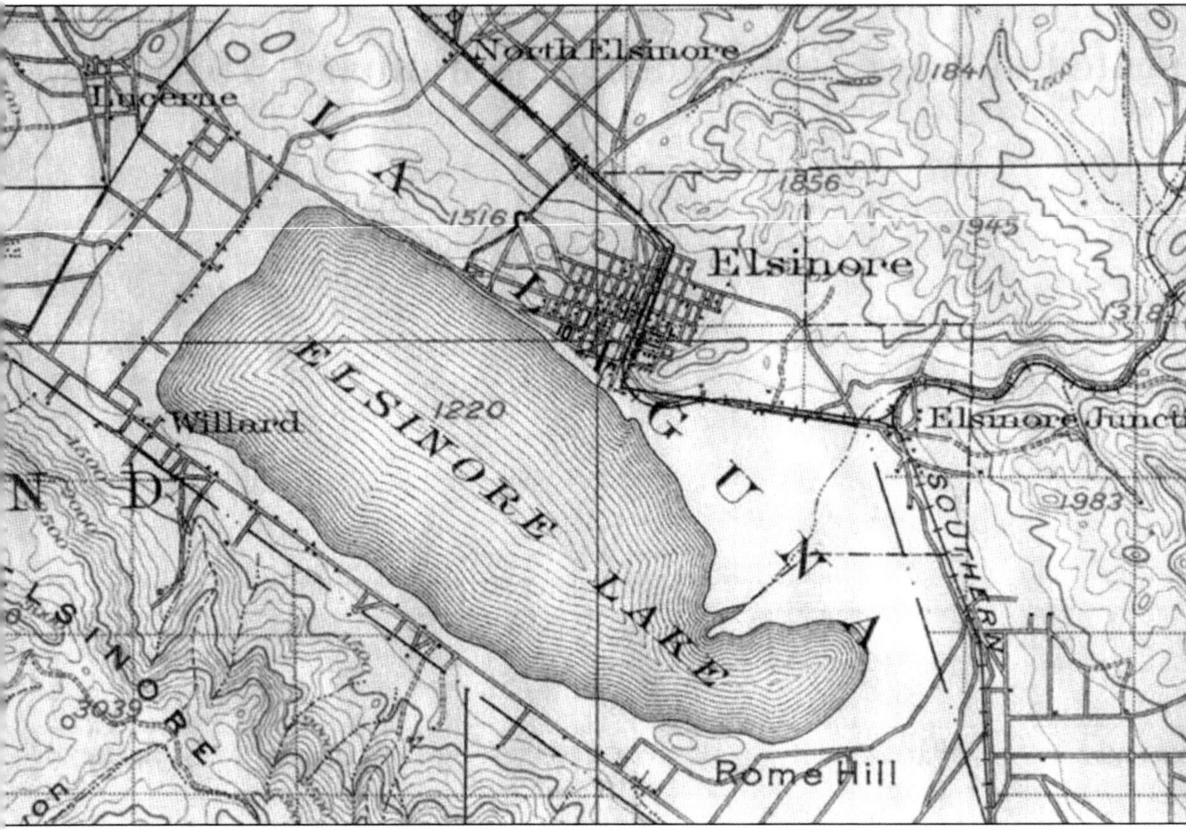


This 1901 U.S. Geological Survey map showing Elsinore and the surrounding area bears the names of communities that existed at the time. Elsinore Junction was the site of the railroad station before 1896, near today's Railroad Canyon and Diamond Drive. North Elsinore, Lucerne, and Terra Cotta did not survive as communities. Rome Hill is a large hill on the southeast side of Lake Elsinore.

The Lake Elsinore Historical Society hopes you enjoy this book about the sights and history of the city of Lake Elsinore.

**ON THE FRONT COVER:** A band consisting of local young men prepares to perform at one of many local functions. *Elsinore History Vignettes*, compiled by Elizabeth James, includes diaries of the social events that took place from the 1880s to the 1900s. Music was important at public functions, picnics, weddings, and parties held in the area. (Courtesy of the Lake Elsinore Historical Society.)

**ON THE BACK COVER:** The Aloha Pier was the recreational hot spot, with swings and playgrounds for the children on the beach, a pavilion constructed for dances on summer nights, and boat races where speed records were set. Huge crowds thronged to the pier, and parking was at a premium. Visitors ate their lunches seated on the car running boards. (Courtesy of the Lake Elsinore Historical Society.)

POSTCARD HISTORY SERIES

# Lake Elsinore

*Lake Elsinore Historical Society*

ARCADIA PUBLISHING

ISBN 978-0-7385-5588-1

Published by Arcadia Publishing
Charleston SC, Chicago IL, Portsmouth NH, San Francisco CA

Printed in the United States of America

Library of Congress Catalog Card Number: 2007931275

For all general information contact Arcadia Publishing at:
Telephone 843-853-2070
Fax 843-853-0044
E-mail sales@arcadiapublishing.com
For customer service and orders:
Toll-Free 1-888-313-2665

Visit us on the Internet at www.arcadiapublishing.com

# Contents

# ACKNOWLEDGMENTS

Because of a person's desire to have a place to collect and preserve artifacts, the Lake Elsinore Historical Society was founded in 1995 by Donna Morin and a couple of friends. Thank you to Mrs. Morin for her vision and her work to create this worthwhile endeavor.

There are many people to acknowledge for their support and advice. First the society would like to thank the members for authorizing our participation in the project and the officers for supporting it. Thanks to Linda Compos and Claudia Goldberg for their generous donations of postcard collections. Other members and friends who have shared their rare cards with the society include Jeanie Corral, John Gonzales, and Cynthia Graves. We are indebted to these individuals. Thanks also to Jerry and Nadine Harmatz, Gene and Linda Ridenour, Mike Norkin of Cherished Memories Photography, and Cori Loria for their support and assistance.

Our beloved historian, Lilah Merrifield, was a supporter of the formation of this society and continued to assist us. Her files have been donated to the society by her family. The family has also donated three volumes of 3-inch-thick files from Altha Merrifield Cauch, Lilah's aunt. The notes and files of Altha and Lilah have been useful research material.

The society appreciates the efforts of Hermann Dreier, Jeanie Corral, Joyce Hohenadl, and Ruth Atkins. These members have spent many hours locating postcards, researching, consulting, organizing, proofreading, and scanning. The Lake Elsinore Historical Society would like thank the City of Lake Elsinore for sharing its new brand, "Dream Extreme." Lastly, the society appreciates working with editor Debbie Seracini of Arcadia Publishing. Her professionalism and guidance have been invaluable.

All images used in this book come from the archives of the Lake Elsinore Historical Society, unless otherwise noted.

# INTRODUCTION

The Luiseño Indians, who first occupied the land around Lake Elsinore, knew the water by the musical name *Etengvo Wumoma*. When the Spaniards came, they gave to the lake the name "Laguna Grande," or Big Lagoon. The first American settlers changed the name to Elsinore.

Elsinore Valley, its lake, hot springs, and surrounding hills were well-known to the Native Americans and featured largely in their legends of the beginning of man on earth. It is possible that Juan Francisco Ortega, who accompanied Portola on his northward march in 1769, sighted the valley from the summit of the Elsinore Mountains; however, there is more reason to believe that the first Spaniard to see the valley was Pedro Fages, who explored the inland part of Southern California in 1772. For certain, the valley was visited in 1797 by Father Juan Santiago, for whom Santiago Peak, northwest of this lake, is named. The Elsinore Valley is surrounded by the San Jacinto and San Bernardino Mountains to the north and east, the Palomar Mountains to the south, and the Elsinore Mountains to the west.

In 1844, Julian Manriquez was granted by the king of Spain the lake and surrounding valley comprising almost 20,000 acres. In 1851, it passed into the hands of Abel Stearns and, in 1858, was bought by Augustin Machado, the Lake Elsinore Valley's first resident. Along with his wife and son, he built a home on the south side of the water. The adobe bricks of their house were barely dry when the U.S. legislature authorized the establishment of the Butterfield Overland Mail stage line. It was created to carry mail from St. Louis, Missouri, to San Francisco, California—the first trip took 21 days. The stage operated from October 1858 until approximately 1862, ceasing because of the Civil War.

The Machado home was a regular stop for stage drivers to eat, relax, and change horses. During the years of Augustin Machado's residence here, his home was also a resting place for military couriers and immigrants passing to and from the East. In the very early days of American occupation of California, Laguna Grande was a campsite for travelers over the southern trail, which was then being carved from the wilderness. Kit Carson visited here a number of times. The largest army of volunteers to leave California for the Civil War camped on the shores of the lake.

Machado's wife died a couple years after he purchased the rancho, and he soon remarried a woman with 11 children. After his death in 1865, his estate was divided between his wife and 12 children. In 1873, Machado's family sold all but 500 acres of the ranch to Charles A. Sumner, an English settler who had recently arrived in San Francisco with his wife, two children, and a maid. Augustin's son Juan retained 500 acres on which the Machado home was located.

Before the property passed from Machado ownership, Juan increased substantially the herds his father had started. He told a visitor in 1872 he had sold 1,800 colts the previous fall for $6 each. He had several thousand sheep, and did not know the precise number of cows until after the rodeo, the annual gathering of cattle when all the owners drove stock onto the plain. Each owner would pick out his own cows and would withdraw them into a separate herd, brand them, and turn them loose again. The Machados liked it when the lake was low because they had good grazing land at the east end and the remainder provided water for the thirsty animals.

Charles A. Sumner had no experience as a rancher and had to learn his lessons the hard way. He treated living on the ranch as a grand adventure rather than a serious business. Extensive descriptions of the Sumner family and their experiences during their 10-year stay are presented by Tom Hudson in his book *Lake Elsinore Valley: Its Story, 1776–1976* and in *Elsinore History Vignettes*, a book of stories compiled by Elizabeth James. Sumner fenced off the mineral springs from the cattle since he thought the foul-smelling water was bad for the animals. When the Native Americans who worked for him saw this, they told him that it was medicine water and would make the cows well.

In 1880, Franklin Heald, originally from Iowa, sighted the lake from the summit of Mount Baldy. In 1883, he purchased the property held by Sumner in partnership with his associates: Donald Graham, a realtor in Pasadena; and William Collier, Graham's brother-in-law and a practicing attorney in Iowa. When the purchase was recorded on October 6, 1883, the men established the town, and Graham's wife, Margaret Collier Graham, selected the name "Elsinore" from *Hamlet*, for the immortality given it by Shakespeare and its pleasant sound. The three men paid $24,000 for La Laguna Rancho, with one-third paid to the bank on September 24, 1883. The balance was to be paid off in three years time; however, records indicate they paid it off sooner. An application was approved for a post office in Elsinore, and it commenced operations on January 2, 1884.

During the latter part of the 19th century, Elsinore experienced its own gold rush. Gold in large quantities was taken from nearby mines, most notable amounts being from the Good Hope Mine about five miles northeast of Elsinore. Madison Chaney and his wife discovered a vein of coal in the hills north of Elsinore in 1883. Today maps show all of the various minerals found in Riverside County.

As Elsinore was growing, other communities were being developed. Wildomar, six miles to the south, was founded about 1885 by William Collier and Donald Graham when they withdrew from the partnership with Heald. This gave Heald control of all of the land surrounding the lake except for the 500 acres owned by Juan Machado. Alberhill, to the north, was established by the Albers and Hill families as a clay and coal mining community in 1886. The town of Terra Cotta was laid out and, in 1887, given a post office, only to fade in 1901. Nearby Lucerne soon became a name to be remembered only by the old-timers, while the clay mines of Alberhill still flourish today.

The need soon arose for a burial ground in Elsinore. Originally, burials were performed on the east side of Highway 71 on a hillside. This location was not considered satisfactory by the Elsinore Cemetery Association, which had been organized to locate a new site. In April 1891, the new association purchased 12.5 acres on Collier Street from Peter Wall for $1,250. This new spot was named Greenwood Cemetery. All of the bodies were moved from the original site to the new one, and the first to be buried here was an 18-year-old boy on January 4, 1892. In May 1926, the property was sold to the Elsinore Valley Cemetery District for $500, and the name was changed to Elsinore Valley Cemetery. With additional purchases of land, the burial ground now covers approximately 14 acres. Adjacent to the Elsinore Valley Cemetery is the Jewish Cemetery. Many original settlers are buried here, including Ida L. Heald, Franklin Heald's fourth wife, who was murdered in her small San Bernardino store and gasoline station in January 1932. The Lake Elsinore Genealogical Society has donated copies of the records of all deceased persons buried in the Elsinore Valley Cemetery to the Lake Elsinore Historical

Society. These records span through 2005 and include hard copies as well as CDs. To date, there are more than 700 veterans interred at this location.

During 1882, railroad tracks were completed on the California Southern's line from National City to Colton. In 1885, it would connect with the Santa Fe tracks to the east. Laguna Grande would then be located on a transcontinental line to San Diego, and Elsinore would be a designated stop. The California Southern Railway brought visitors to the area via Railroad Canyon. The tracks twisted endlessly down the narrow canyon and stopped at the lower end of the lake bed. Visitors were taken into town via horse and buggy. When the rains of 1884 started in January and continued into June, the tracks through Railroad Canyon were washed out, and months passed before they were ready for use.

The coal and clay plant began operations in 1888 in a very convenient arrangement, with both fuel and raw material within a few feet of the kilns. In 1896, a spur track was built from the depot at the east end of the lake through Elsinore, where a new depot had been established, and on to new clay mines being developed in Alberhill.

Still, California Southern Railway had failed to give full credit to the power of nature. When the tracks were washed out a third time, in 1891, the tracks from Temecula to Fallbrook were abandoned for the Santa Fe. A new line had been completed following the coast, more or less, from Los Angeles to San Diego. Elsinore was then located on a branch line from San Bernardino to Temecula.

A few months later, the *Leader-Press* reported that Temescal Water Company was preparing to start work on a $120,000 dam. With the railroad right-of-way doomed to be inundated, trains from Riverside through Railroad Canyon became only a memory. With the dam across Railroad Canyon imminent, it was time for the Santa Fe to carry out its delayed plan to extend the line from Alberhill to Corona.

The route envisioned by the railroad company would become primarily a freight line. This route would transport cattle to and from Vail Ranch; grain and produce from the valley's fields; bricks, tiles, and sewer pipes from Alberhill; and silica sand from Temescal Canyon. For a while, people visiting Elsinore's mineral baths or Wildomar, Murrieta, and Temecula would be passengers on this new line.

For more than 50 years, Elsinore had enjoyed rail connections with Wildomar, Murrieta, and Temecula, but this period suddenly came to an end as highways replaced tracks. In January 1935, Santa Fe discontinued service on the Temecula end of the line, and later that year the tracks were removed. A wye was constructed near the San Jacinto River so that locomotives arriving in Elsinore from Corona could turn around. Just west of the wye, across the tracks from Railroad Avenue, a cattle-loading pen was built, and for years thereafter cows destined for the Vail Ranch were unloaded there and trucked the rest of the way to the ranch.

The first diesel locomotive to visit Elsinore arrived on October 17, 1950, causing quite a sensation. The modern locomotive pulled 27 cars of cattle destined for the Vail Ranch. In July 1951, the last mournful whistle of a steam locomotive was heard in Lake Elsinore Valley.

Elsinore was incorporated as a city in 1888. The lake has consistently attracted visitors, excepting the periods when it was dry. The mineral waters and bathhouses for which Elsinore became famous in the early days of the valley's settlement attracted many visitors. Records indicate the existence of more than 300 wells and springs in town at one point. The mineral waters were a remedy for rheumatism and kidney troubles, and drinking the liquid worked many wonderful cures. People came from far and near (from European royalty to well-known American political leaders) to soak in the baths and improve their health.

Elsinore grew to be the foremost town in San Diego County because of the natural freshwater lake, which lured sportsmen and hunters with its abundance of quail, duck, geese, swans, and wild game. The new town attracted new residents with land for sale for homes and for farms. Until this time, the area we know today as Riverside County was a part of San Diego County. With the population growth, citizens grumbled continuously about the two-day trip to San Diego to transact business. At one time, the idea of Elsinore County was promoted but failed.

After many attempts, the California legislature passed a bill in March 1893 creating the county of Riverside by taking portions of San Bernardino and San Diego Counties. Riverside County officially opened for business on July 1, 1893.

Important steps over the years that have contributed to the growth and development of the valley include the formation of both Lake Elsinore Park and the Parkway District in 1958. This led to the eventual transformation of the lake into a state park and the formation of the Elsinore Valley Municipal Water District in 1950, which brought Colorado River water to the valley. At this time, the Metropolitan Water District deemed the mineral wells illegal because the water turned children's teeth yellow. The wells were capped, and non-mineral water was piped into the homes.

The citizens of Elsinore voted in December 1972 to change the name of the city to Lake Elsinore. One city council member, Cheryl French, had such strong feelings about retaining the name of Elsinore that she resigned from the city council over the change.

During the Clevelin real estate era (from approximately 1923 to 1928), developers installed street lamps along Lakeshore Drive. Some wonder if they were ever lit, and others think they were installed for appearance only. These lamp posts, long an eyesore, stood forlornly along the streets for more than 40 years. In June 2007, the City of Lake Elsinore restored 17 of these lamp posts using the original posts, but with new casts to hold two globes each. Now these street lights shed a lovely golden glow along Lakeshore Drive to recall the grandeur of days gone by.

# *One*

# Early Days in Elsinore

As Franklin Heald was selling lots for homes and farmland, the people came to La Laguna. Glowing letters were written to his family in Iowa telling about the glories of the area, the wonderful climate, and the prosperous future he thought it held for the residents. His sister Ida described her first impression of the valley: The lake was dry and she saw many bleached bones of cattle lying on the lake bed and wondered if her brother had lost his mind. Soon the rains came and the vegetation popped up. Ida Heald then understood what her brother saw with the green pastures, the wildflowers, the majestic mountains, and the beautiful lake.

With new arrivals in the colony, more buildings were needed. Heald sold business lots in town for $45 and up, and farmland sold for $25 and up per acre. Social life was active in the valley. The property we know today as the Santa Rosa Plateau was owned by Parker Dear, whose annual picnics drew as many as 2,000 attendees. James K. Schanck maintained an extensive diary of activities beginning in 1887. His entries include riding around the lake, playing with the band for numerous parties, Sunday school picnics, July Fourth fireworks, a Republican rally, a masked carnival, the high temperatures in September, the cyclone that blew down the Methodist church, ice cream socials, and bicycle races. Schanck maintained his diaries about the valley's activities through 1899.

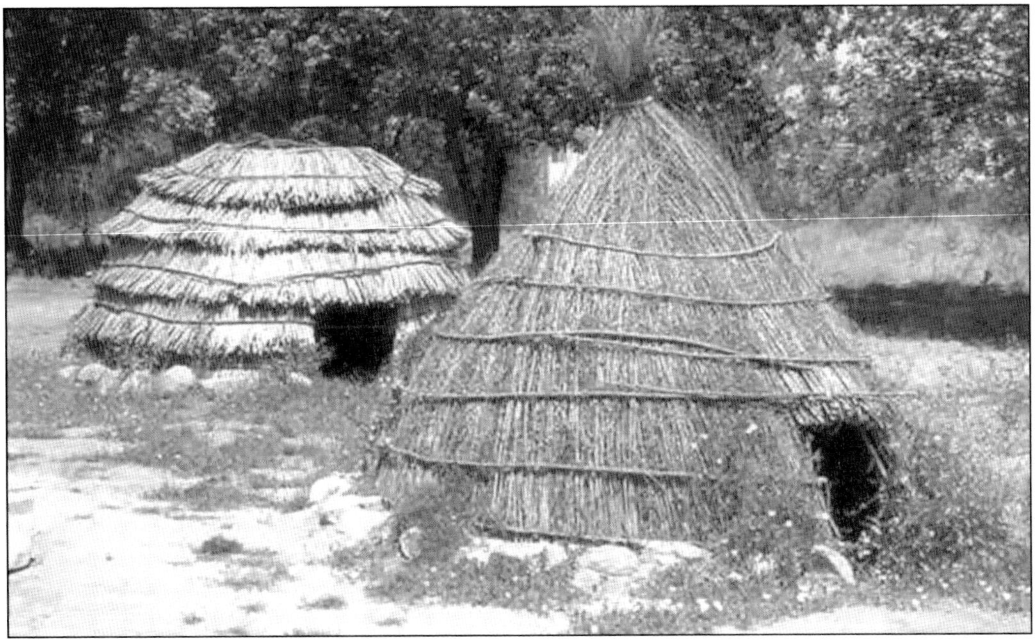

The Luiseño Indians built their homes out of reeds, willows, and other materials they found surrounding the lake. The precisely designed structures were reinforced to keep the wind from blowing them away. Note that the bottom of the huts are secured to the ground with various sizes of rocks. These artifacts, which are very important to Native American culture, tell stories about their owners' nomadic lifestyle.

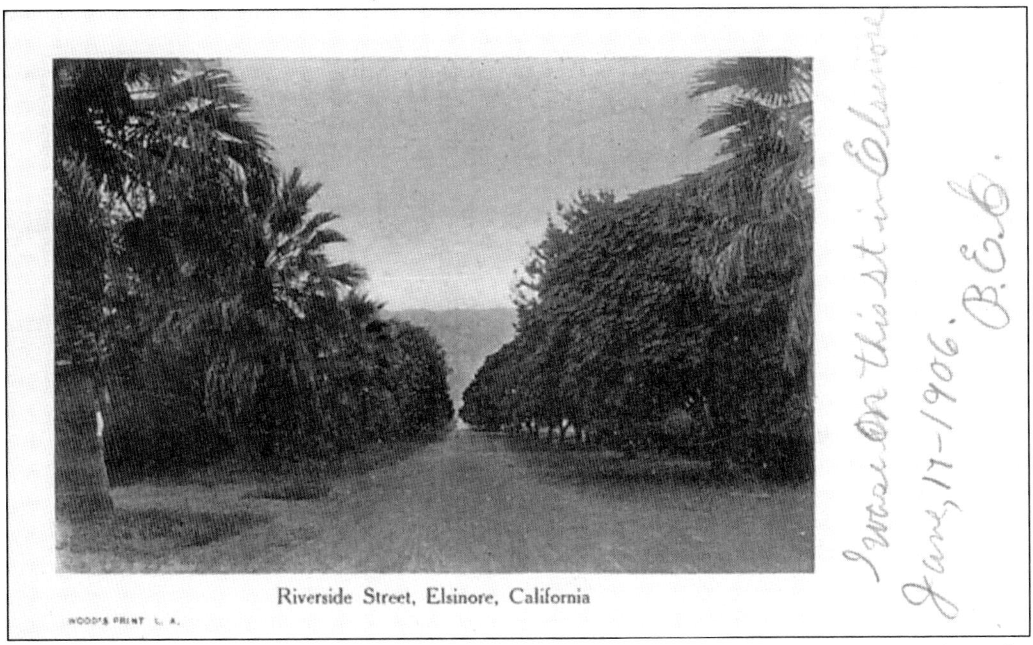


This beautiful street is lined with lovely trees, including palm and walnut. Situated on the northwest side of Lake Elsinore, Riverside is an artery for traveling between Grand Avenue and Lakeshore Drive. Today it is known as Riverside Drive or Highway 74 and acts as one of the main routes between Riverside and Orange Counties.

It is unusual to find a postcard of a house; this one stands at 505 West Graham Avenue. Built by a Mr. Harris about 1887, the residence was later occupied by Mr. and Mrs. W. W. H. Beach. The Century Plant was planted in 1888, and this photograph was taken around 1910. Today it is located across the street from the post office; however, there is no evidence of the Century Plant.

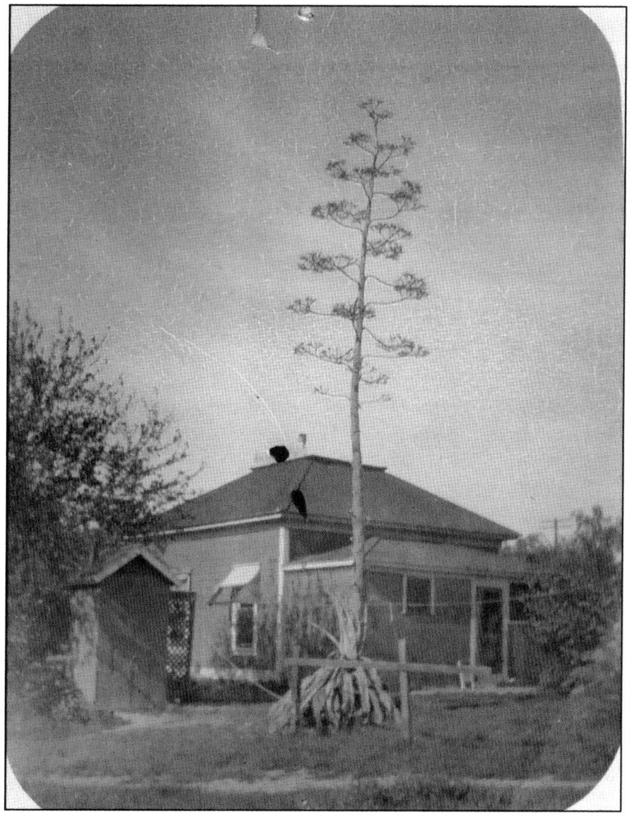

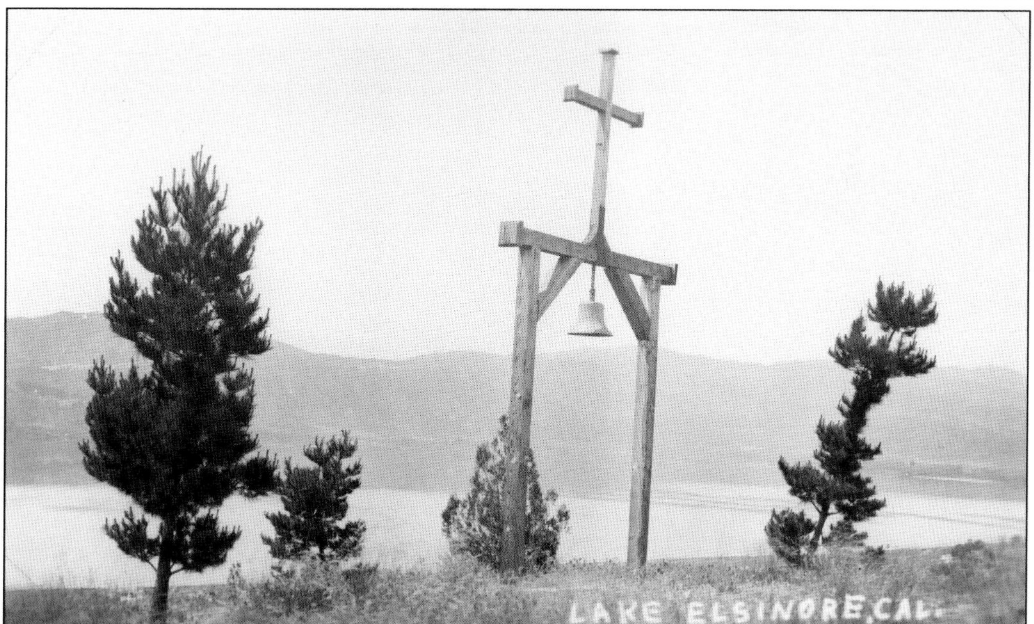


A wood structure to hold the bell was erected on Flagstaff Hill, located overlooking the southeast section of Lake Elsinore. The first Easter sunrise service was held on April 17, 1914. The bell was stolen sometime in the 1940s and never recovered. (APS.)

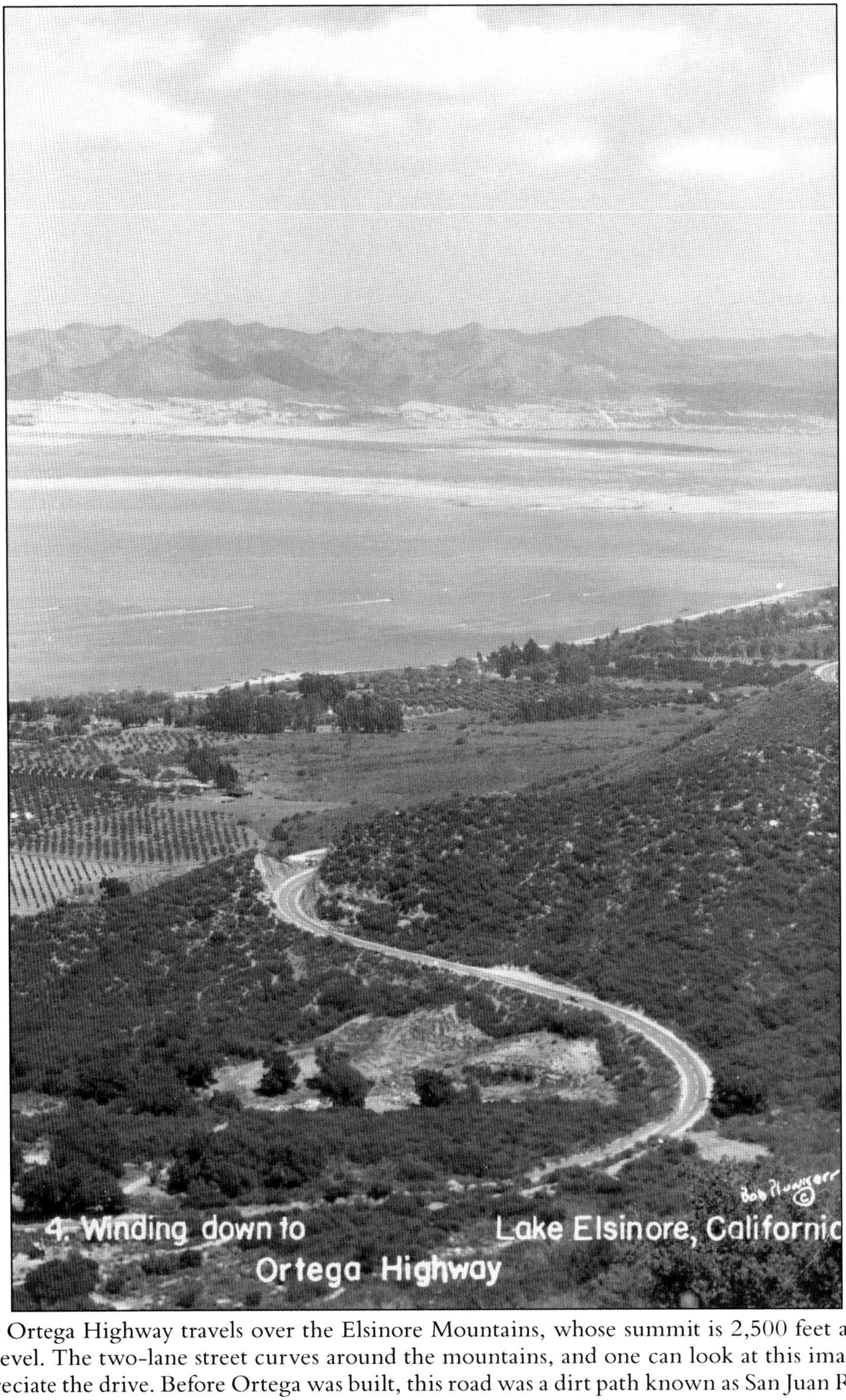


The Ortega Highway travels over the Elsinore Mountains, whose summit is 2,500 feet above sea level. The two-lane street curves around the mountains, and one can look at this image to appreciate the drive. Before Ortega was built, this road was a dirt path known as San Juan Road. In the background are the hills of the Country Club Heights area, dotted with lovely homes.

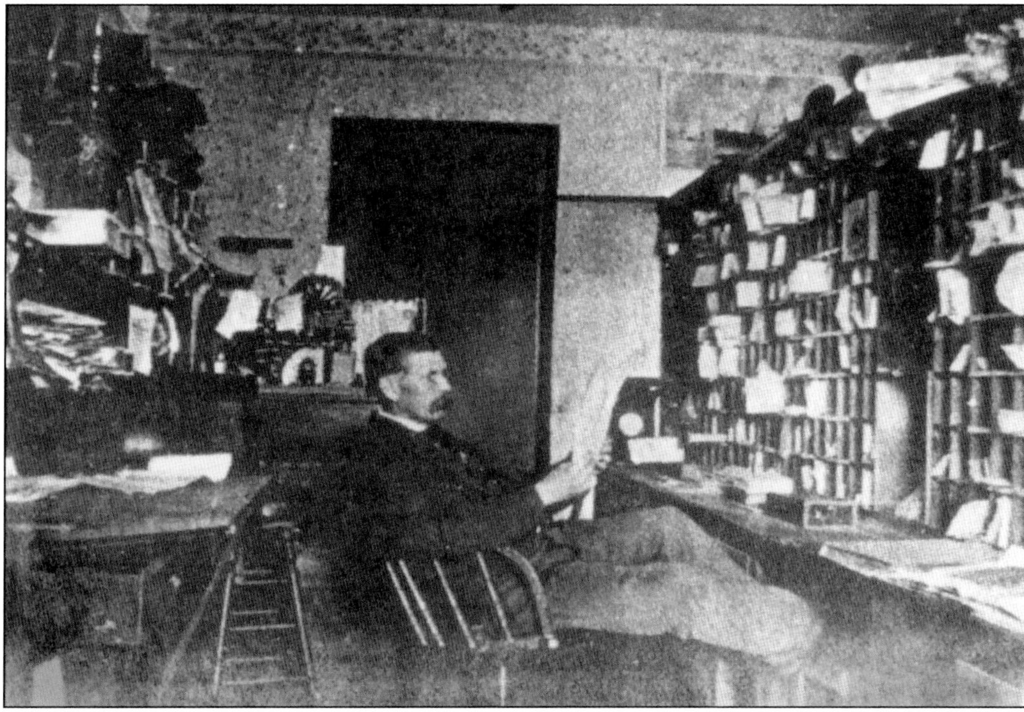

The Elsinore Post Office operated out of J. K. Schank's jewelry store, as he also served as postmaster. The first post office was a box nailed to a willow tree on Spring Street between Graham and Heald Avenues. The mail carrier riding between San Bernardino and San Diego left letters there, and everyone sorted through the pile for his own.

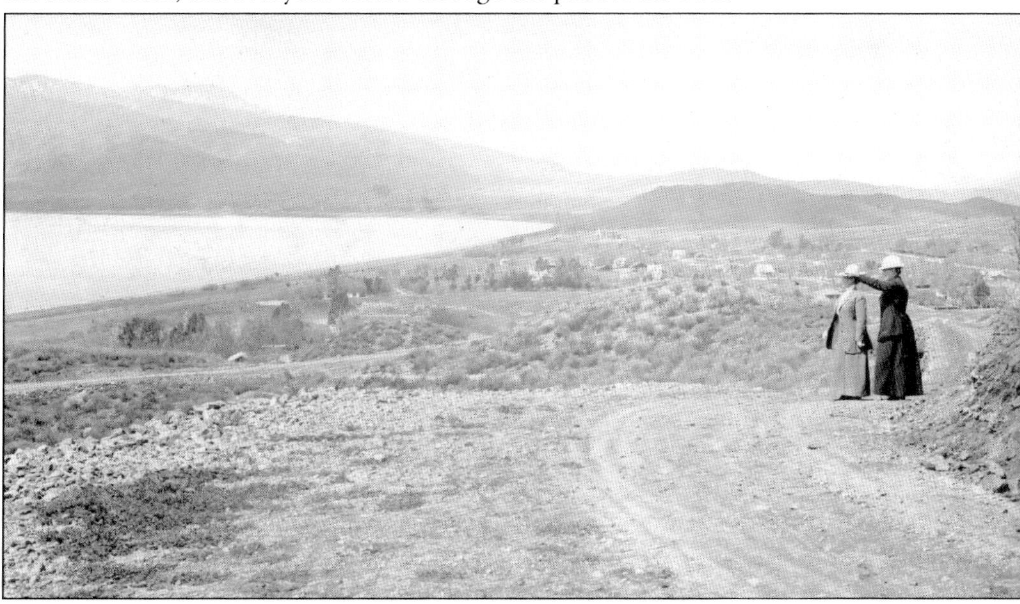

These ladies appear to be surveying the lake and planning for a future home from a point northeast of Lake Elsinore looking toward the Elsinore Mountains. The center of the new community was below the gravel road on which they are standing. Their apparel suggests this postcard was created in the early 1900s. (CyG.)

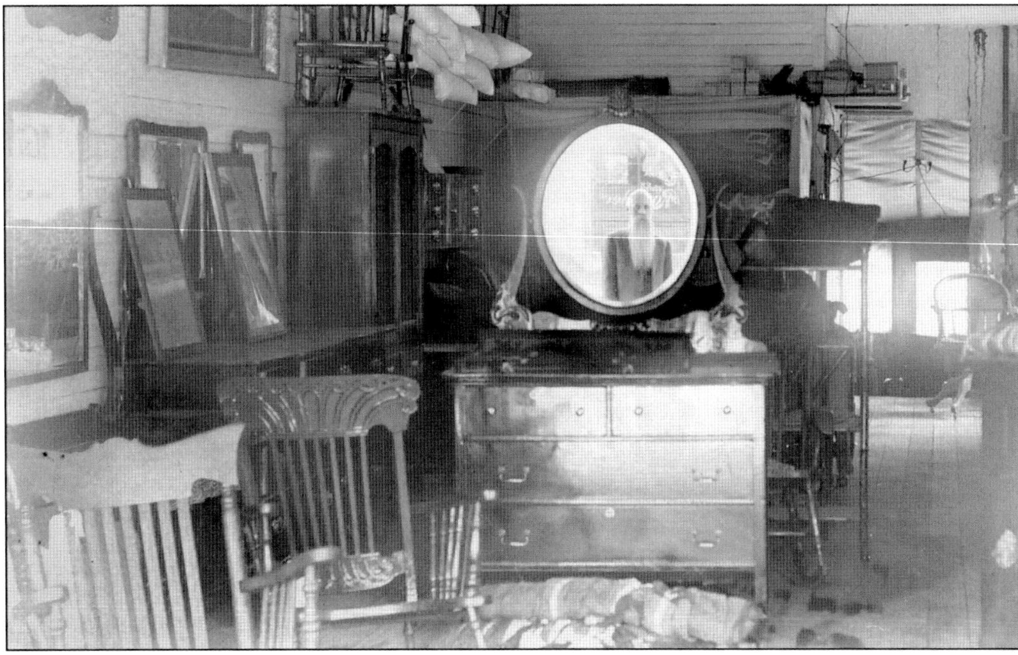

L. D. Clark's Furniture store was located on Main Street. This display shows the availability of the furniture pieces people could purchase. In historical writings, new Elsinore residents stocked up on "buttons and lace" before moving west to ensure they had the best money could purchase. An article in *La Laguna Revue* indicates that Clark was also the town undertaker for 35 years, carrying on that business in the back room of the store.

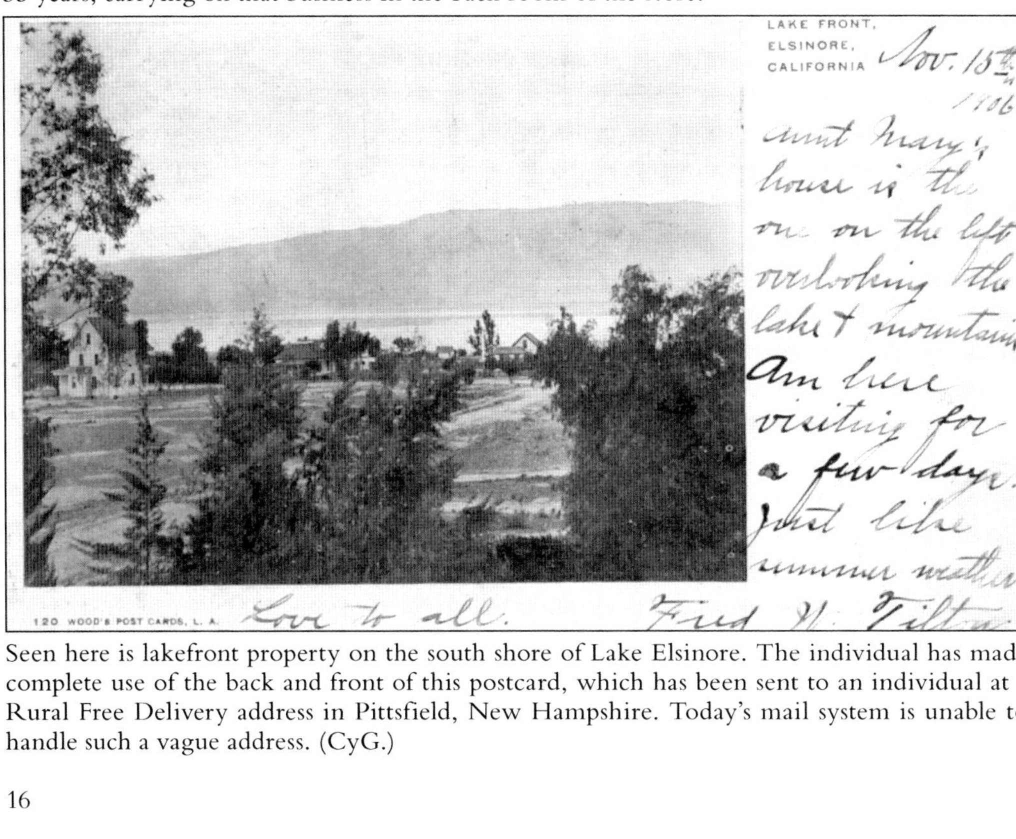


Seen here is lakefront property on the south shore of Lake Elsinore. The individual has made complete use of the back and front of this postcard, which has been sent to an individual at a Rural Free Delivery address in Pittsfield, New Hampshire. Today's mail system is unable to handle such a vague address. (CyG.)

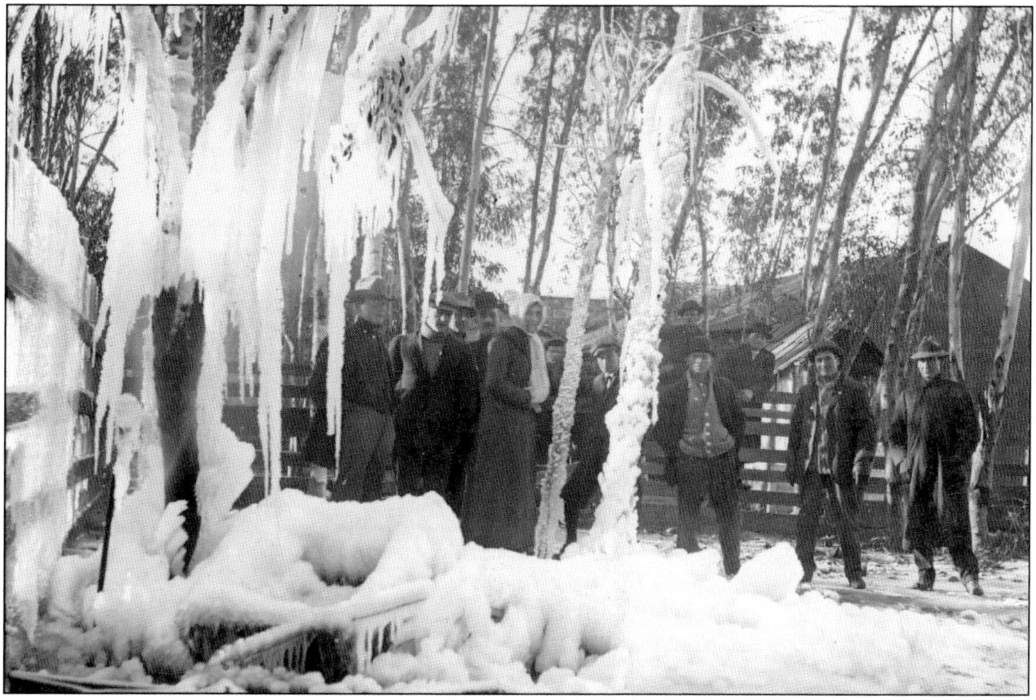

In the late winter of 1915 and continuing into 1916, Lake Elsinore suffered a series of heavy snowfalls that not only covered the mountains but shut down the power and roadways to and from town. The size of the massive icicles from the pig pens demonstrates the effective freeze in the postcard above. These hog pens were located near the other loading chutes that were by the railroad tracks. Snow has fallen in the 1950s, 1970s, and even in the last few years (2005 flurries lasted about five minutes on the ground) on nearby mountains below. However, the snowstorms of 1915–1916 were unbelievable; it took more than two weeks to get the road open to the outside communities of Corona, Murrieta, Temecula, or Riverside. (Both JC.)

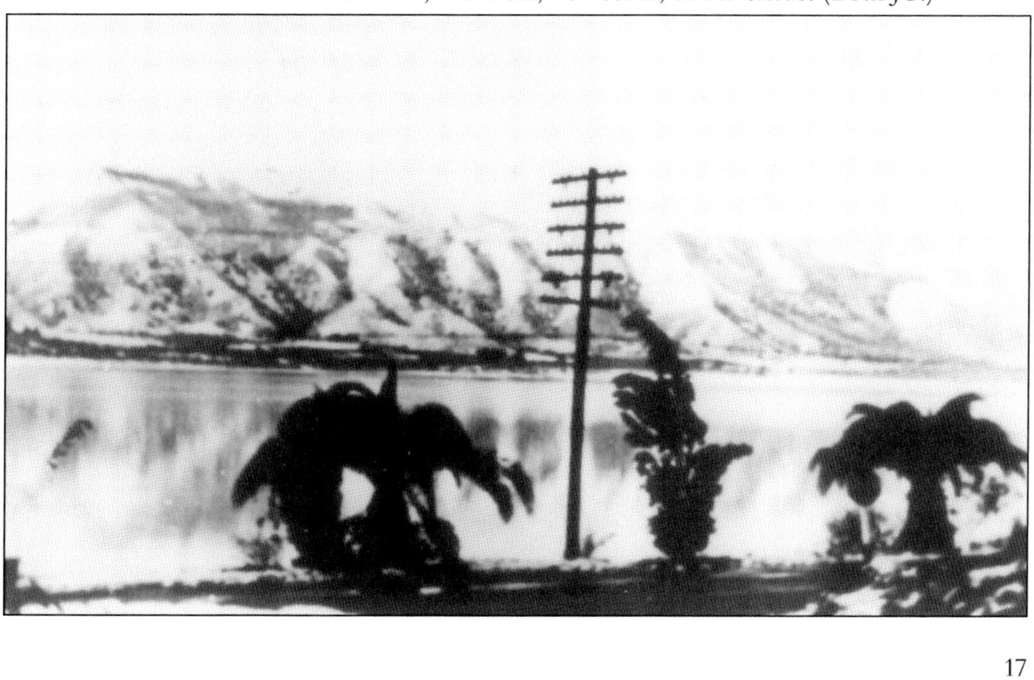

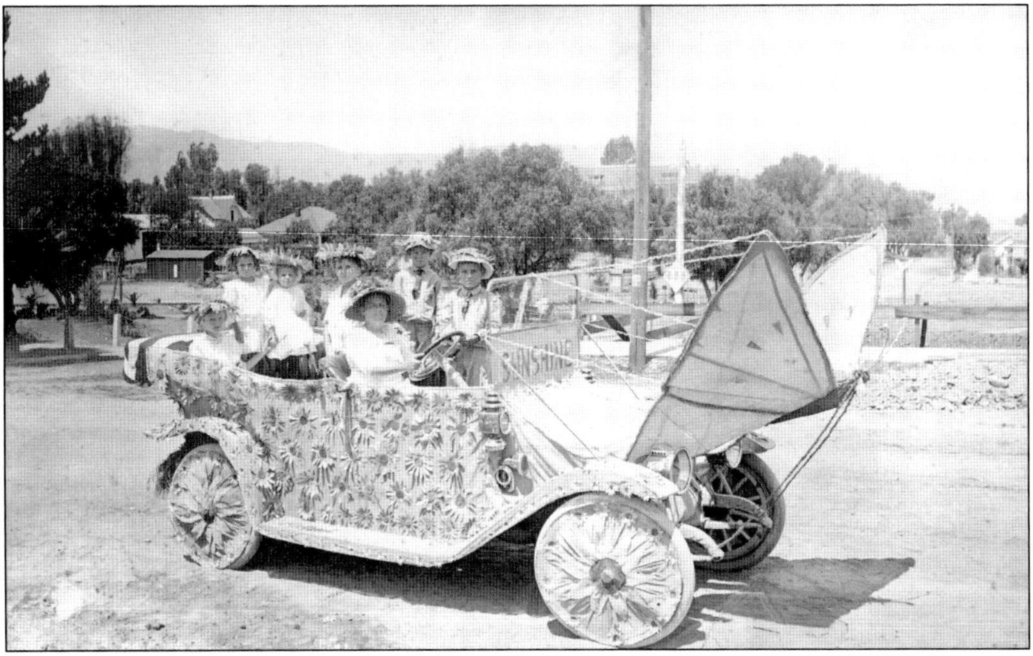

A four-door convertible sedan with a right-hand steering wheel is decorated for the Fourth of July parade in 1912. The item on the front radiator appears to be a giant butterfly controlled by one of the passengers, and even the wheels are decorated. The automobile may have been parked near City Park. The driver was Emma Graham, the wife of Perry Graham. (LC.)

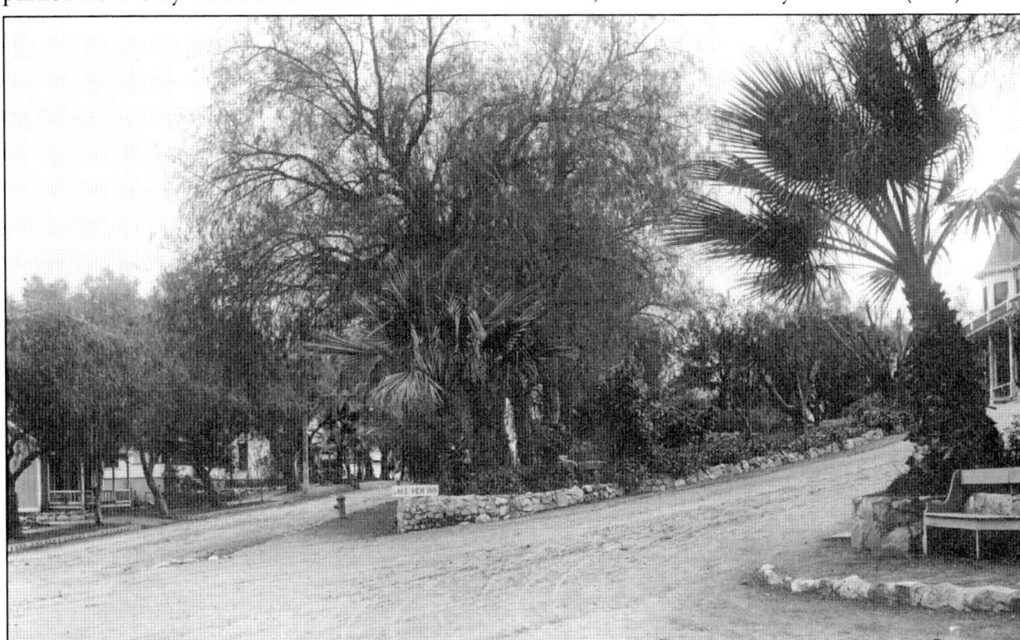

The entry to the Lake View Inn, located at the corner of Limited and Spring Streets, is pictured on the far right of this *c.* 1912 postcard. The structure was built in 1887 as the Lakedale Hotel and burned down in 1894. Immediately rebuilt, it was called the Lake View Inn/Lakeview Hotel and served many guests before being razed in 1970.

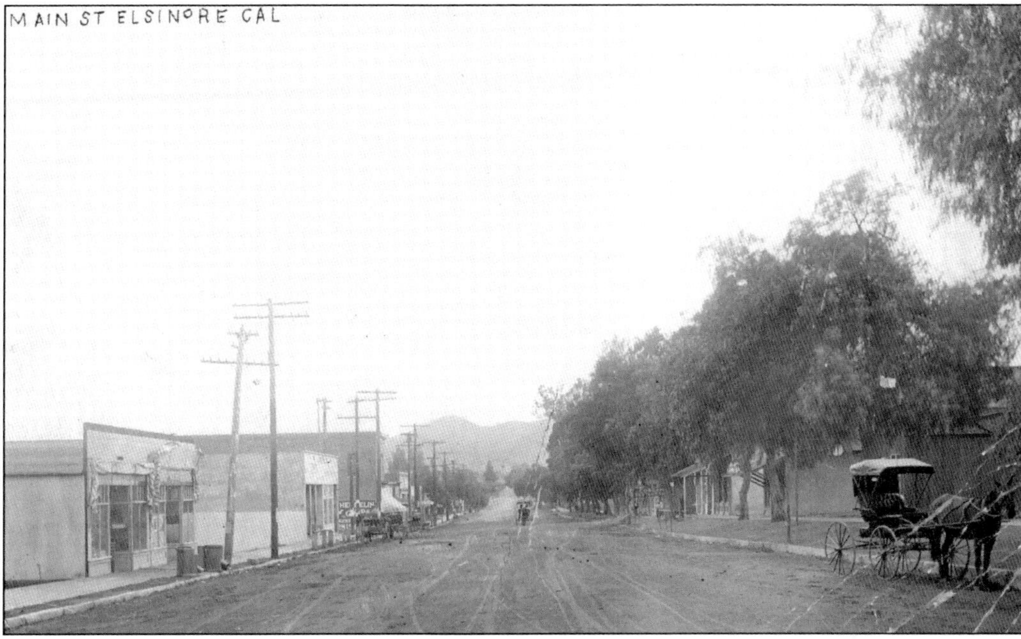


On this postcard of Main Street, the sender wrote, "March 3, 1913—Dear Sis, I got here at 4:05 wasn't that some time." The message was written using a pencil, and parts are illegible. The card bears a 2¢ stamp and was indeed mailed to her sister in Hermosa.

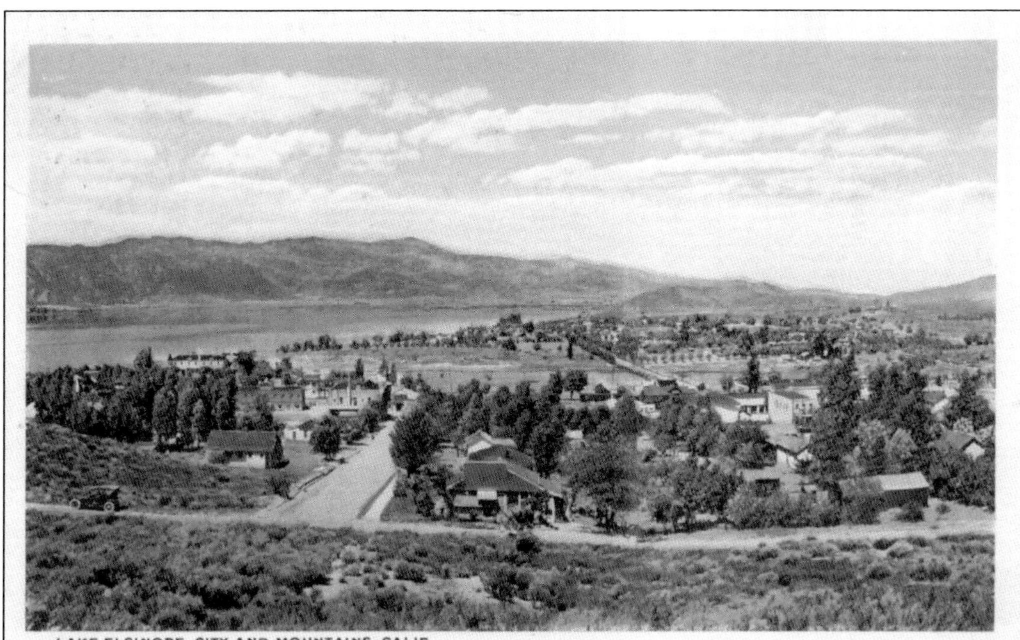


Looking from the hills on the east side of Elsinore, this view shows the city in the foreground and the lake lying peacefully between the city and mountains. No wonder famous people such as Clark Gable, Dorothy Cottrell, Toby Wing, and Bela Lugosi liked to come and relax in the Lake Elsinore Valley. (EP.)

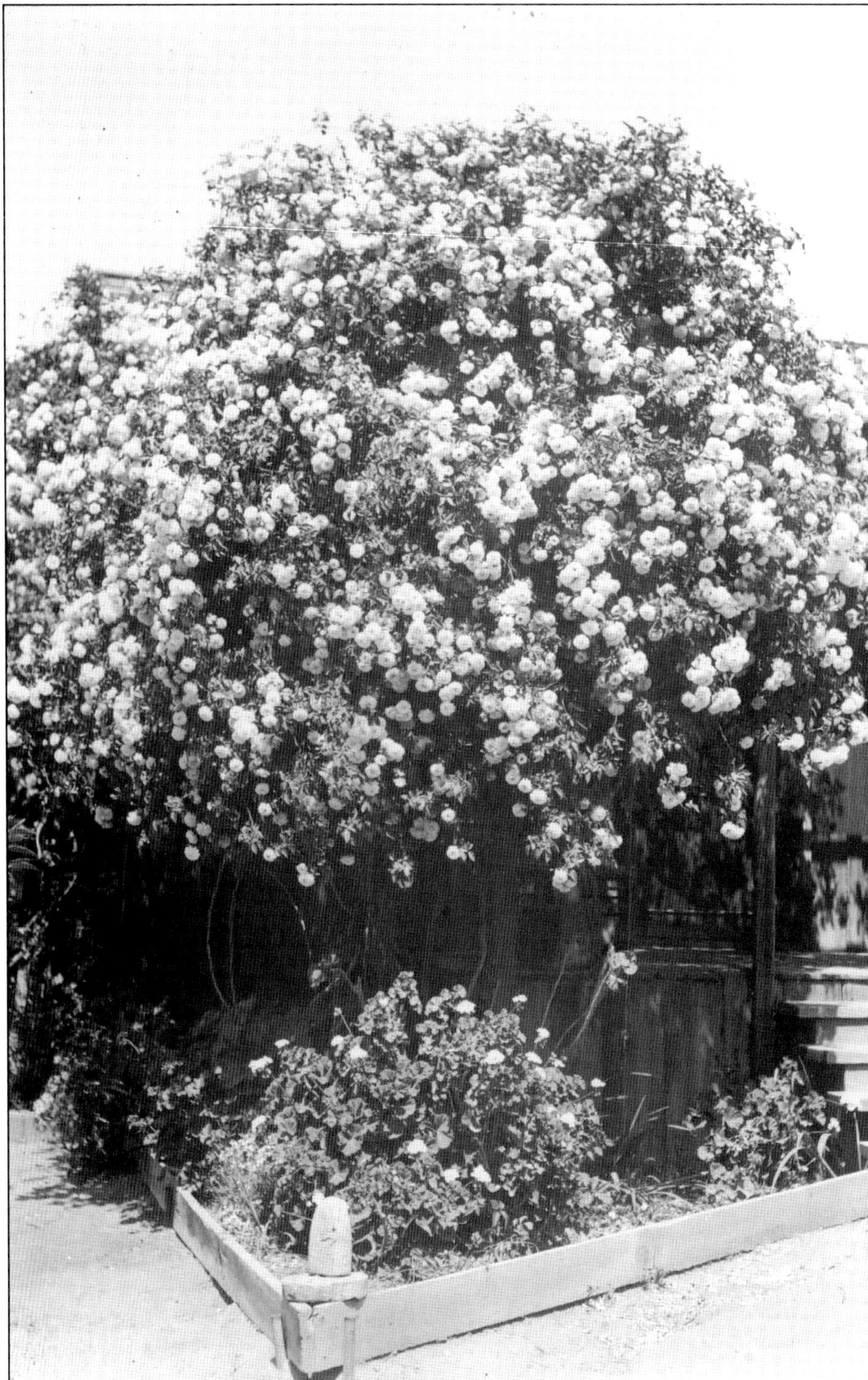

One can only see parts of the roof and the entry steps of the Clark home on Scrivener Street because of the large blooming shrub. The shrub appears to be a rosebush that blooms prolifically with some small plants in front. The back of the postcard bears the notation "c 1920."

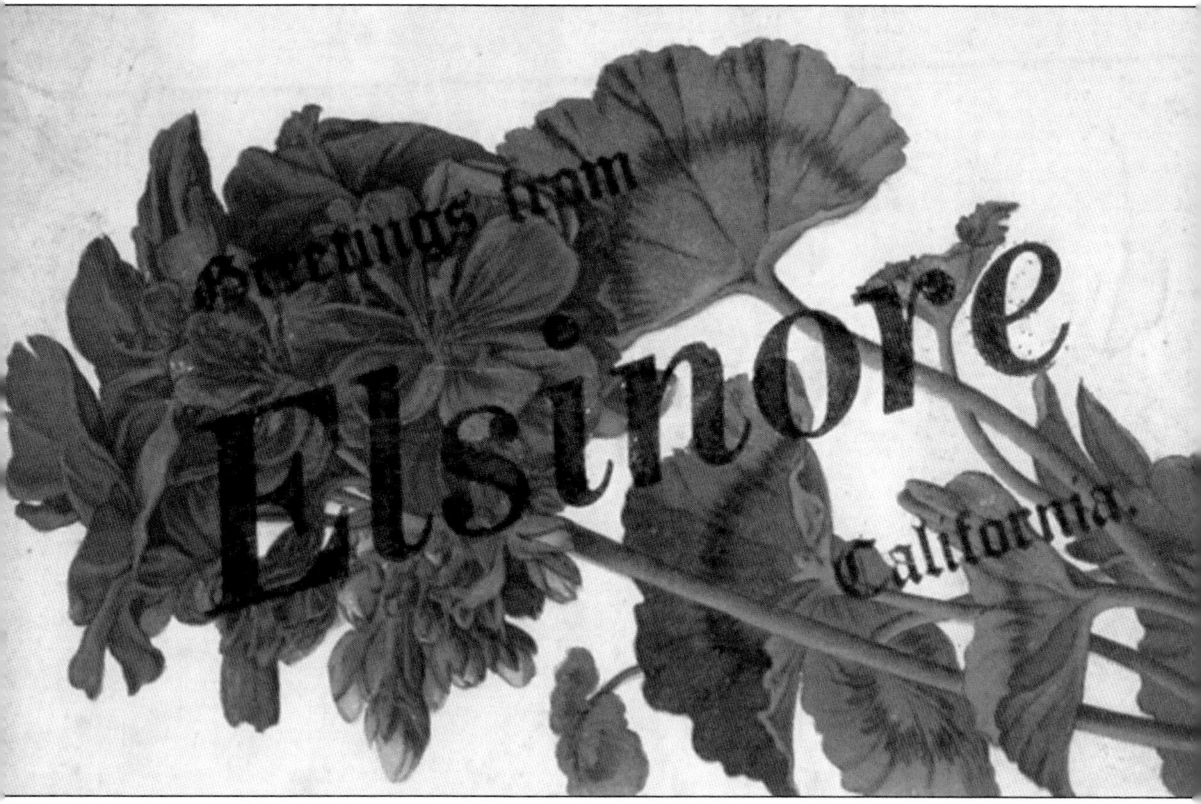


As indicated in the pictures on these two pages, flowers are abundant in Elsinore. The climate is considered high desert, with cool evenings and warm days. The area's rainy season is approximately from November until March. During the winter months, the low temperatures are generally in the 30s and, in the summer, the high temperatures can exceed 100 degrees. The gardens are prolific with roses, annuals—such as petunias, geraniums, marigolds—and other colorful plants, such as bougainvilleas with their profusion of blooms. Residents love the color their gardens provide the community.

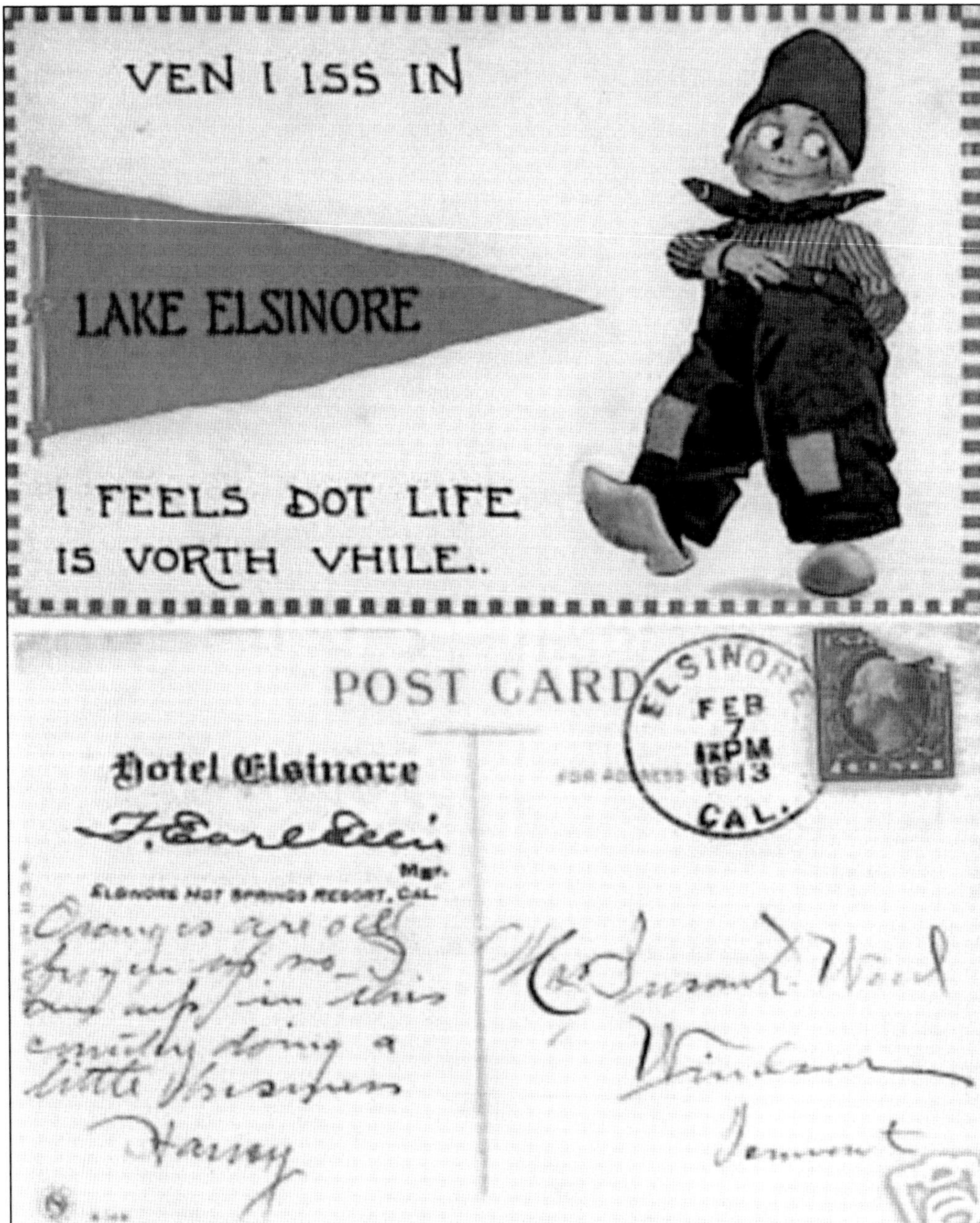


The little Dutch boy is saying, "Ven I iss in Lake Elsinore I feels dot life is vorth vhile." This postcard from the Hotel Elsinore was signed by the manager, T. Earl Ellis, Elsinore Hot Springs Resort, California. It is postmarked February 7, 1913.

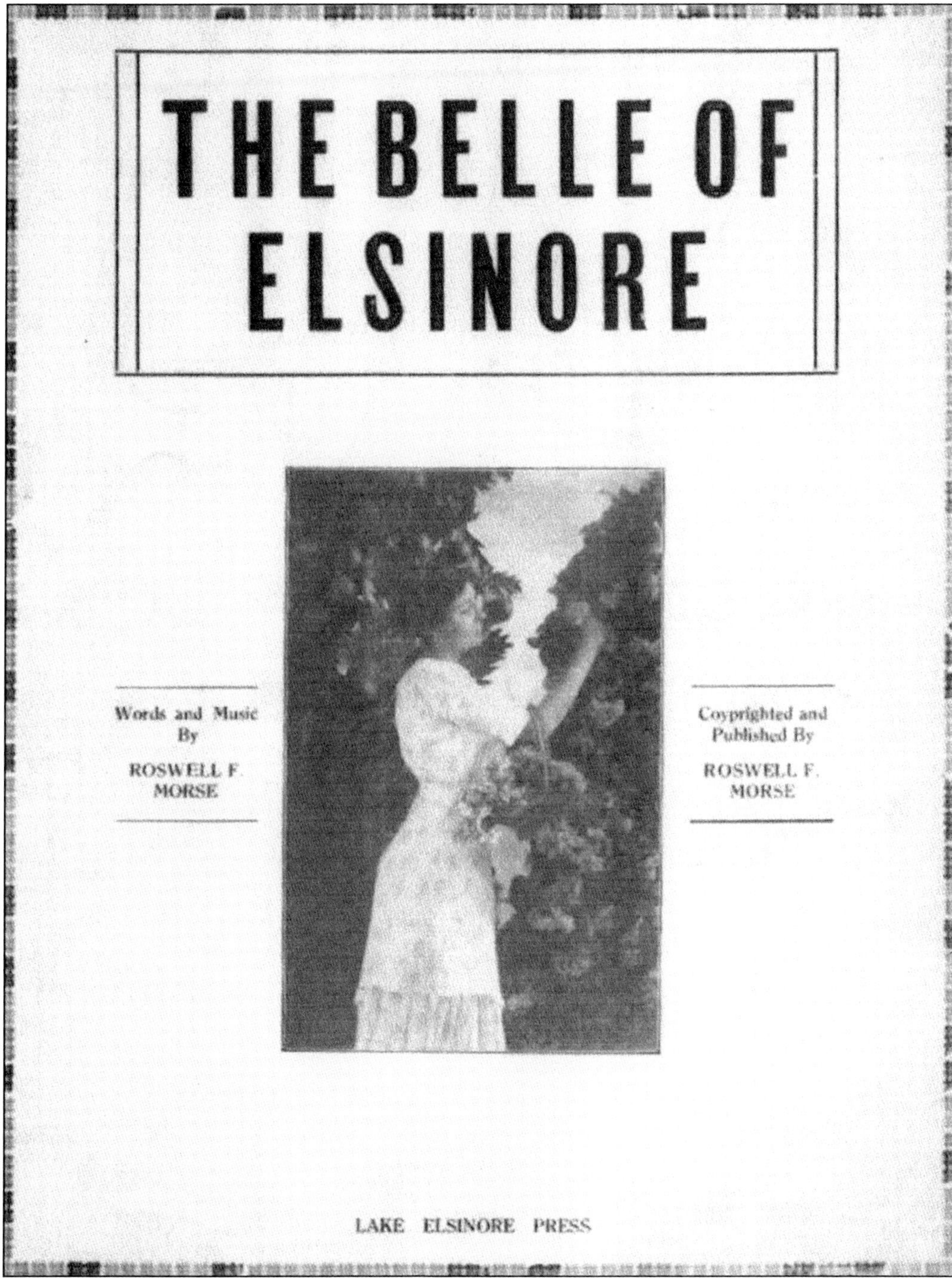


"The Belle of Elsinore" was just one of many songs (and poems) written about the area. The words and music were composed by Roswell Morse and copyrighted in 1910. The first verse is as follows: "In Southern California, where the orange blossoms grow, No stormy winds of winter, nor cyclones ever blow; Where balmy ocean breezes blow softly on the shore; There lives a charming maiden by the lake of Elsinore."

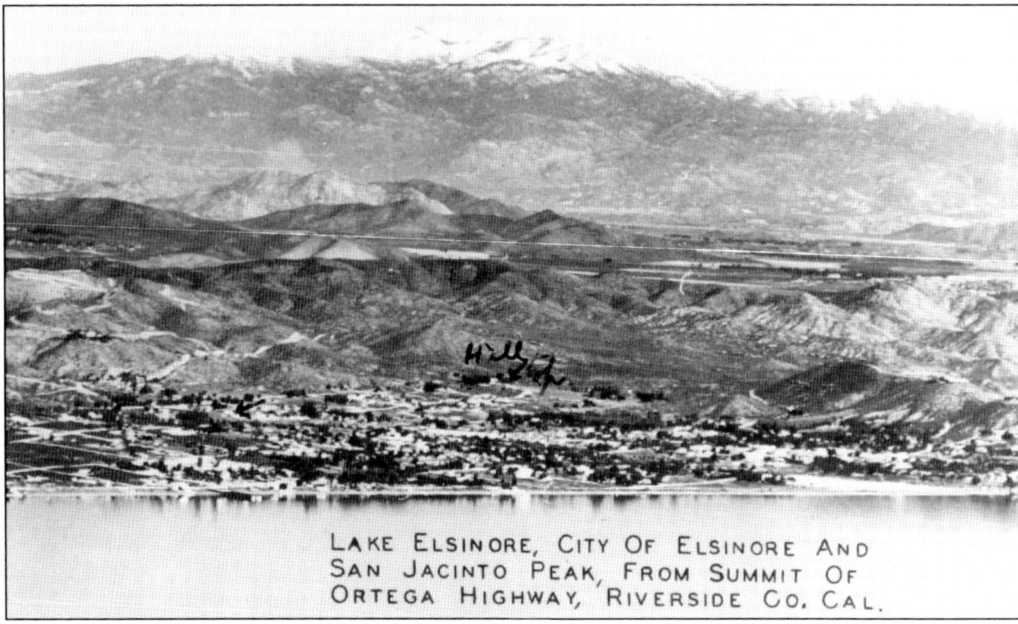


This message reads, "This card is a good one of Elsinore. It shows our house fine and you can see clear up to Hill Top Lodge. You wouldn't know our town. It has been covered with 4 to 6 inches of snow for the past 5 days. I would say that is unusual."

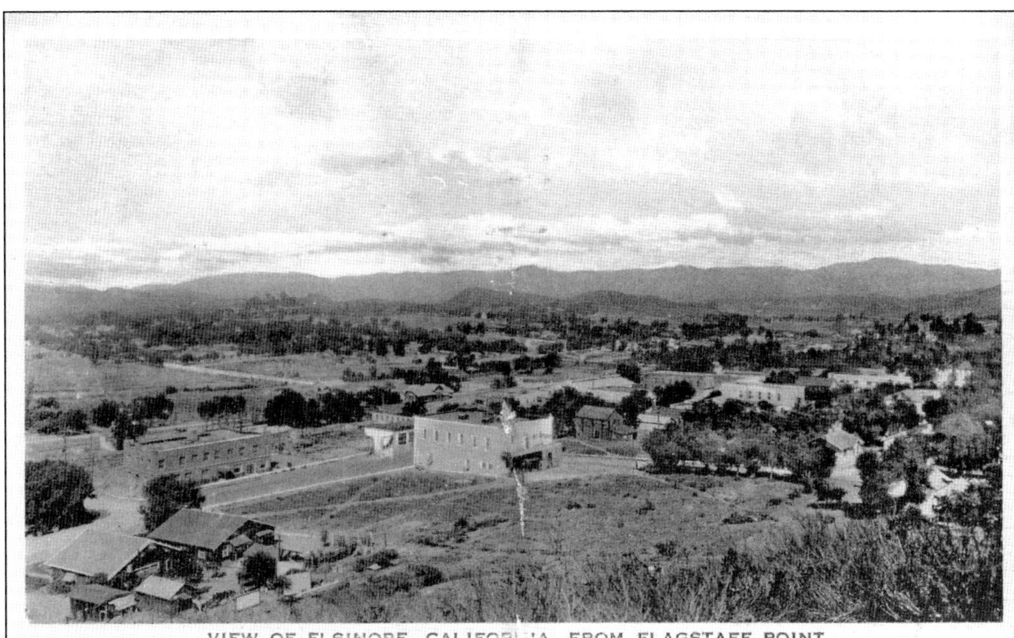


In this view from Flagstaff Point, the white building in the center is believed to be the Ambassador Hotel. The card was mailed from Los Angeles with a 1¢ stamp on August 1, 1924, to the sender's sister in Chicago, Illinois. The written message expresses shock over receiving a telegram. (PCQ.)

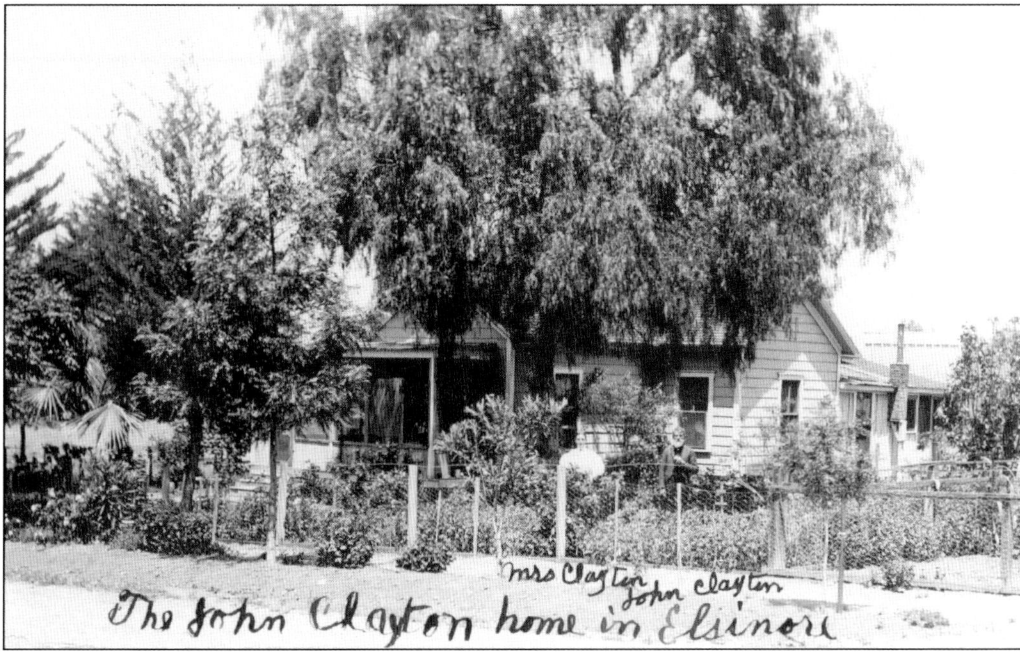


The John Clayton Home was situated among trees, including a palm tree, and lots of shrubs as well as garden crops. Here Mr. and Mrs. John Clayton are in the yard near the front window. The location of the home is unknown, but the house appears to have an addition on the rear to accommodate the Claytons' growing family. With the large garden, the family was well supplied with fresh vegetables.

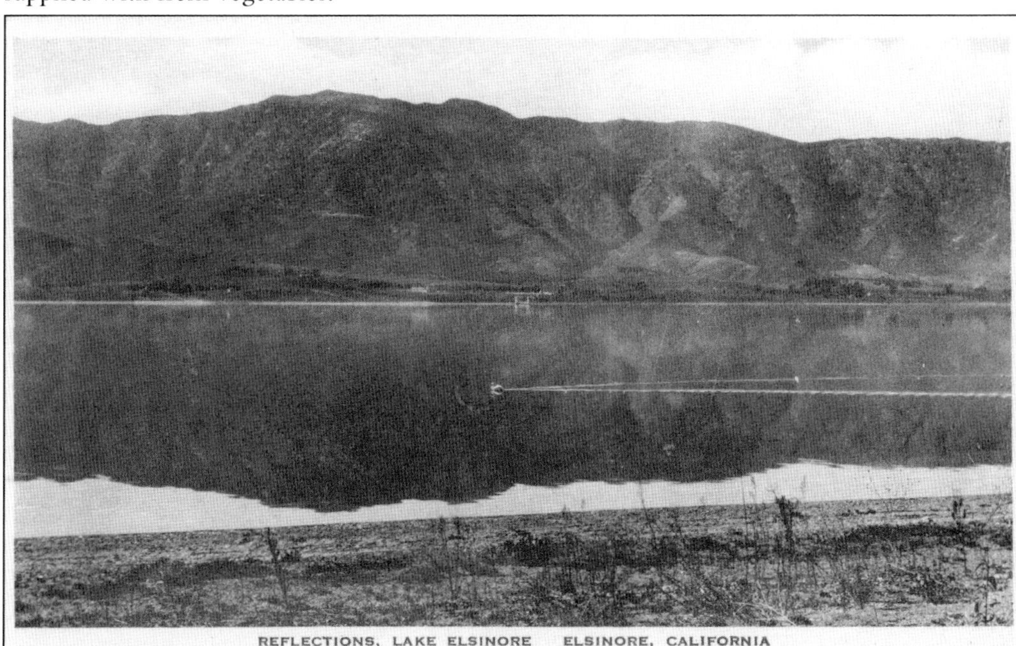


Mountain reflections make a delightful postcard. Nothing in the photograph reveals where or when it was taken, including the weeds along the shoreline; however, it is certain the mountains are the Elsinore Mountains on the south side of Lake Elsinore. (PCQ.)

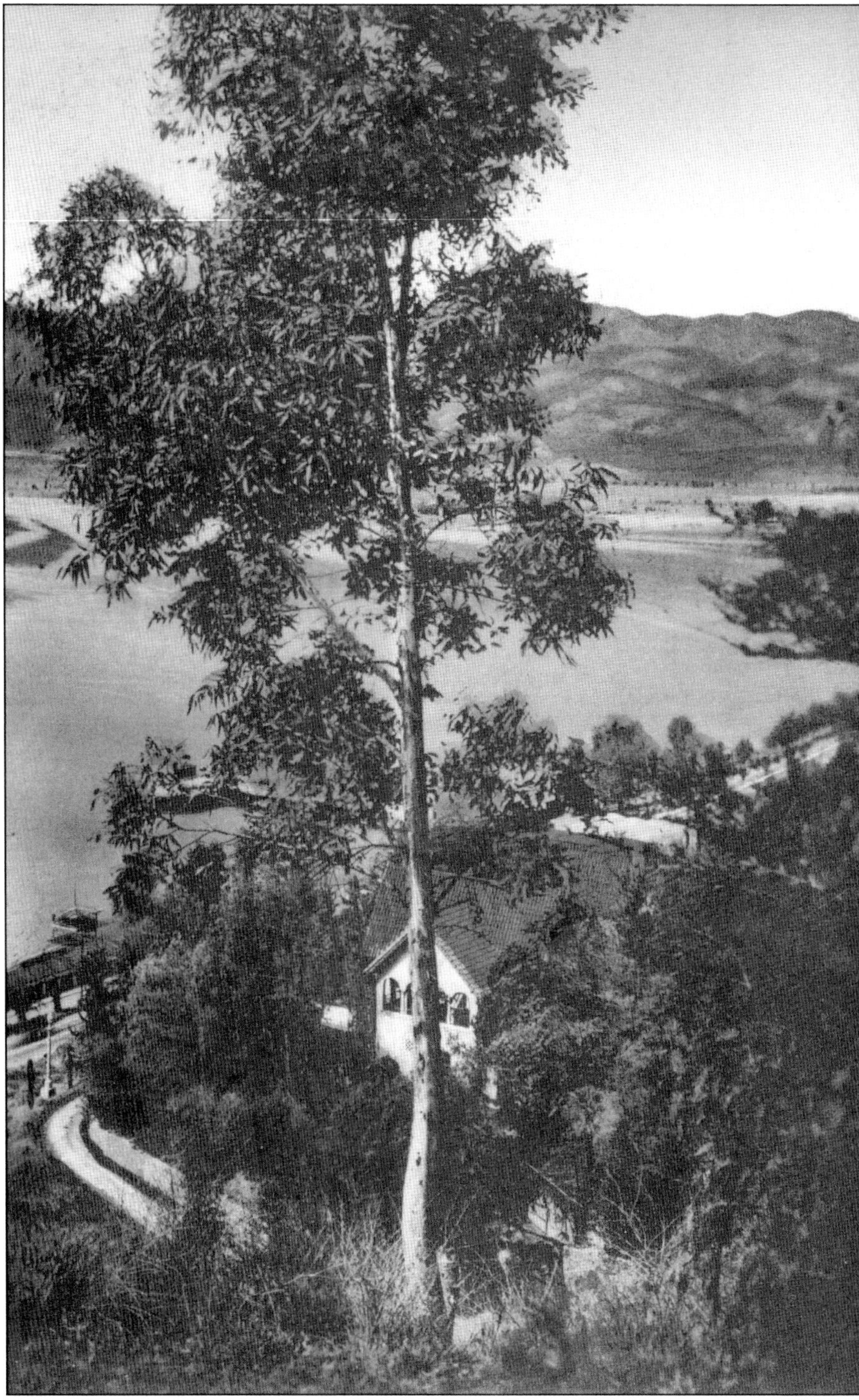

This lovely view of Elsinore, taken from a Country Club Heights home, shows a graceful eucalyptus tree in the foreground and overlooks the lake, looking toward the southwest area of the Elsinore Mountains. Hidden behind the branches is a portion of the Aloha Pier below Lakeshore Drive. (AC.)

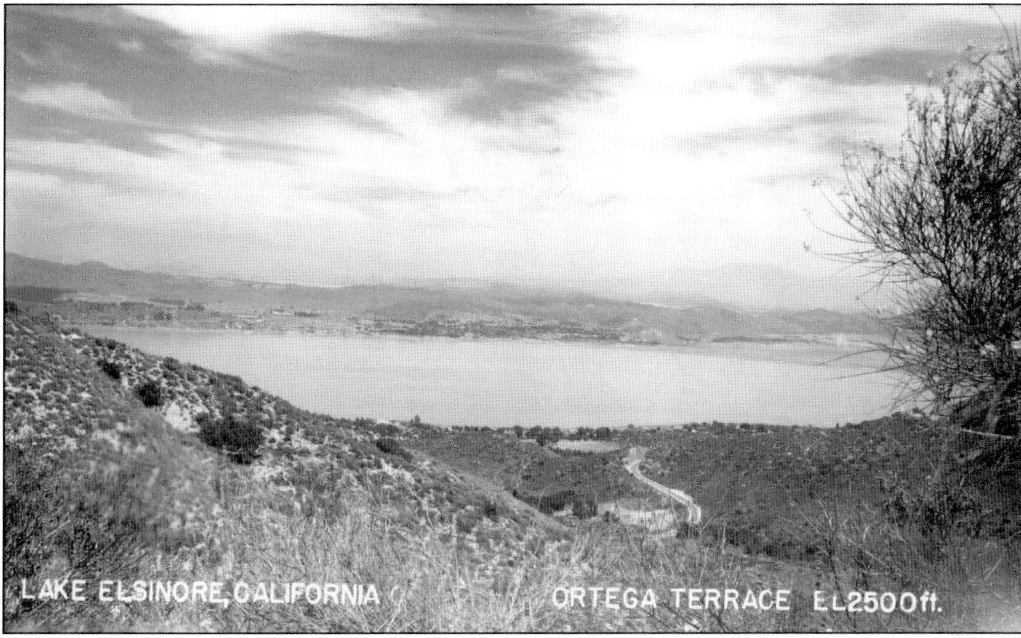


The photographer climbed partway up the mountain to capture this view from the southwest section of the lake. The S above the word "terrace" is believed to be part of the Ortega Highway. On the far side of the lake are the Country Club Heights clubhouse and the Aloha Pier, both of which were situated on Lakeshore Drive.

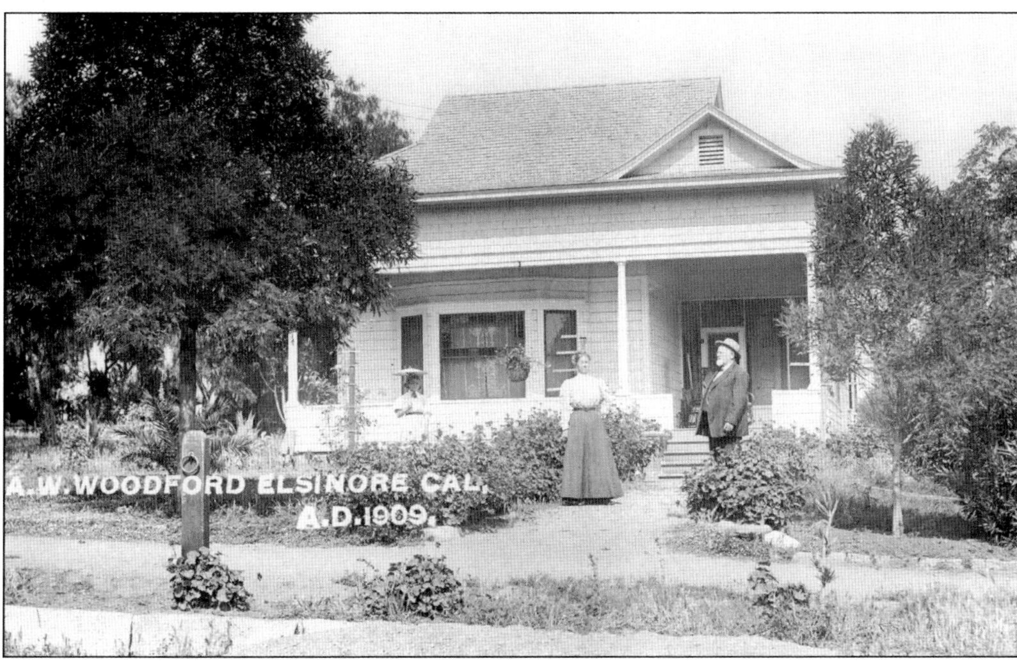


The A. W. Woodford home was built in Elsinore in 1909, when the semi-Craftsman style was popular in Southern California. Woodford was a successful farmer in the area. When guests came to visit, they tied their horses to a hitching post at the curb.

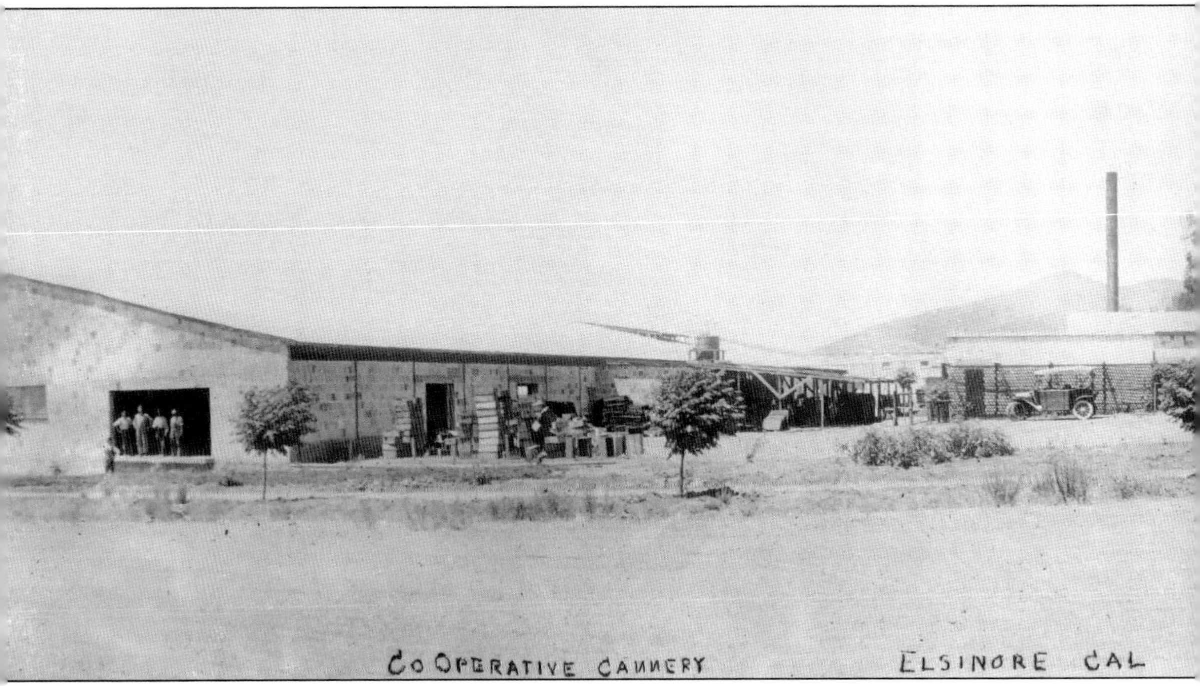


The Co-operative Cannery was located in what was known as the Glo-Fire Building. By 1919, an estimated 2.25 million cans of produce had been packed at the cannery. The products were olives, apricots, and solid-pack tomatoes. During peak periods, anyone available was put to work since the plant was always short of help.

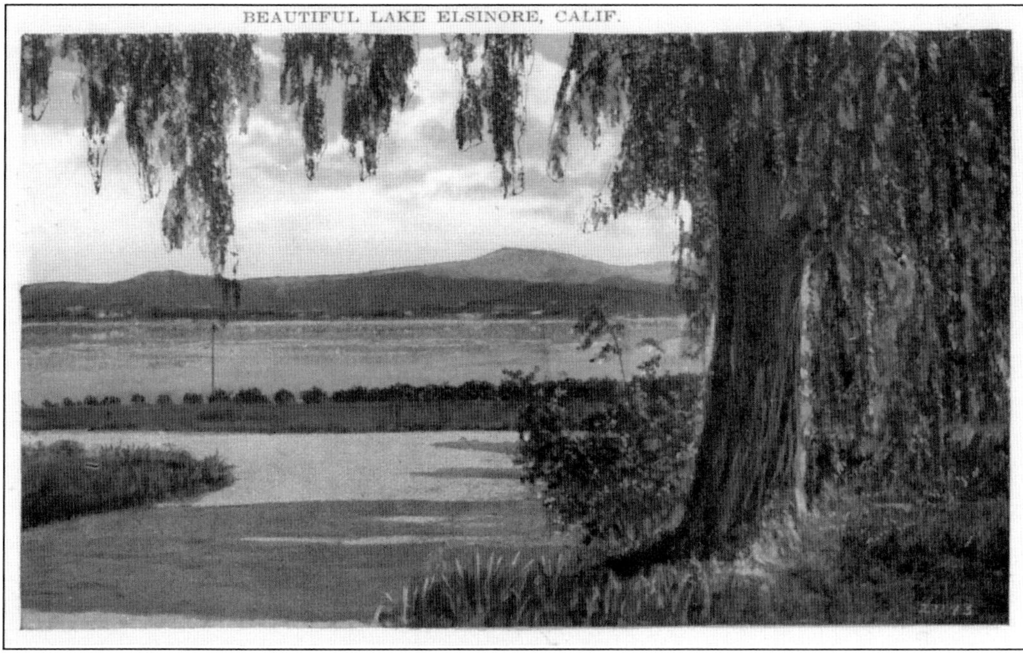


Seen in this view from the Lakeland Village side, the largest natural lake in Southern California covers more than 2,900 acres. The lake level is dependent on the amount of rain received each year. Large eucalyptus trees shade the area, providing a scene of peace and tranquility. (MK.)

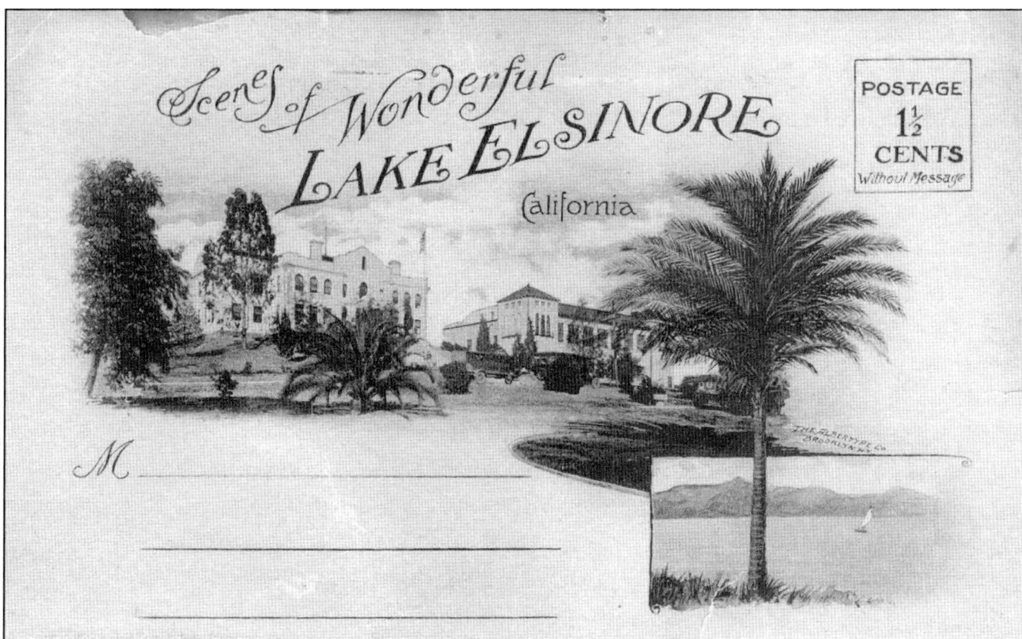


Amongst artifacts, an album of postcards titled "Scenes of Wonderful Lake Elsinore, California" was found. The album states that "Postage [is] 1 1/2¢ Without Message" to mail the bundle of 10 scenic postcards. On the front are images of the Elsinore High School and the Clevelin Country Club.

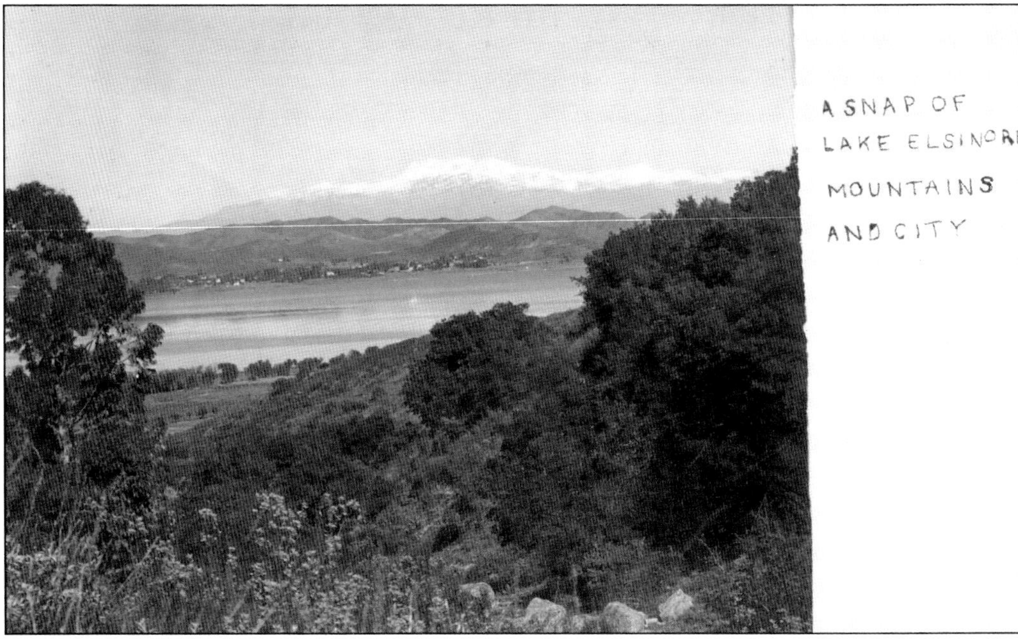


This view looks down the Elsinore Mountains with wildflowers in bloom in the foreground. Beyond the lake are the mountains of Country Club Heights, and in the background are the San Gorgonio and San Jacinto Mountain peaks of the Palm Springs area.

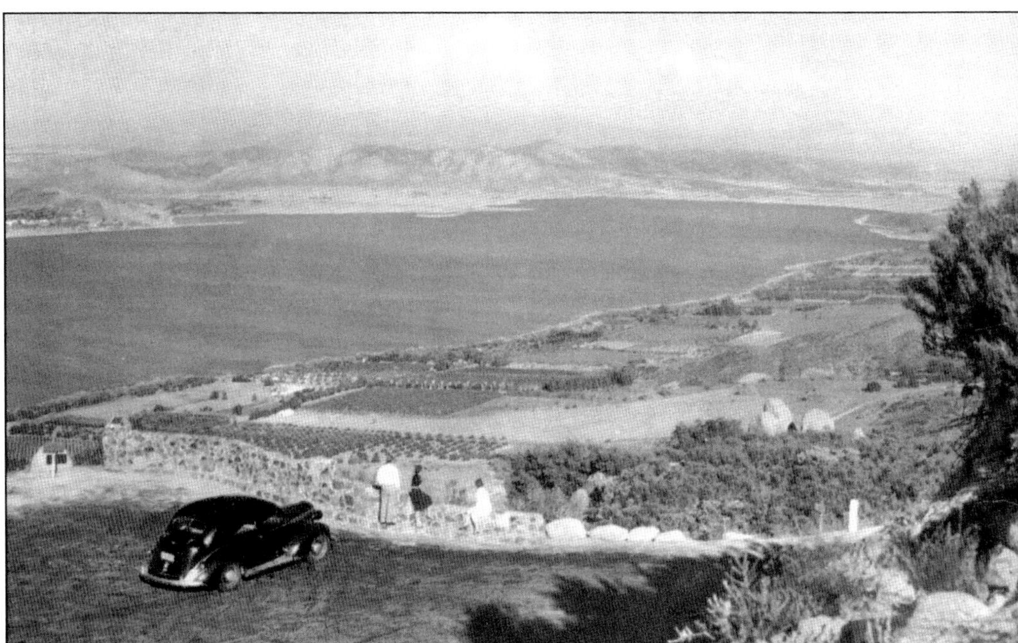

Lake Elsinore, the scene of Southern California surfboard motor races, is viewed from the Ortega Highway in Elsinore Valley. Reached from the inland route between Los Angeles and San Diego, the lake is well-known for its adjacent hot springs. This postcard is No. 6 in the Union Oil Company's *Natural Scenes of the West* series. (UOC-C.)

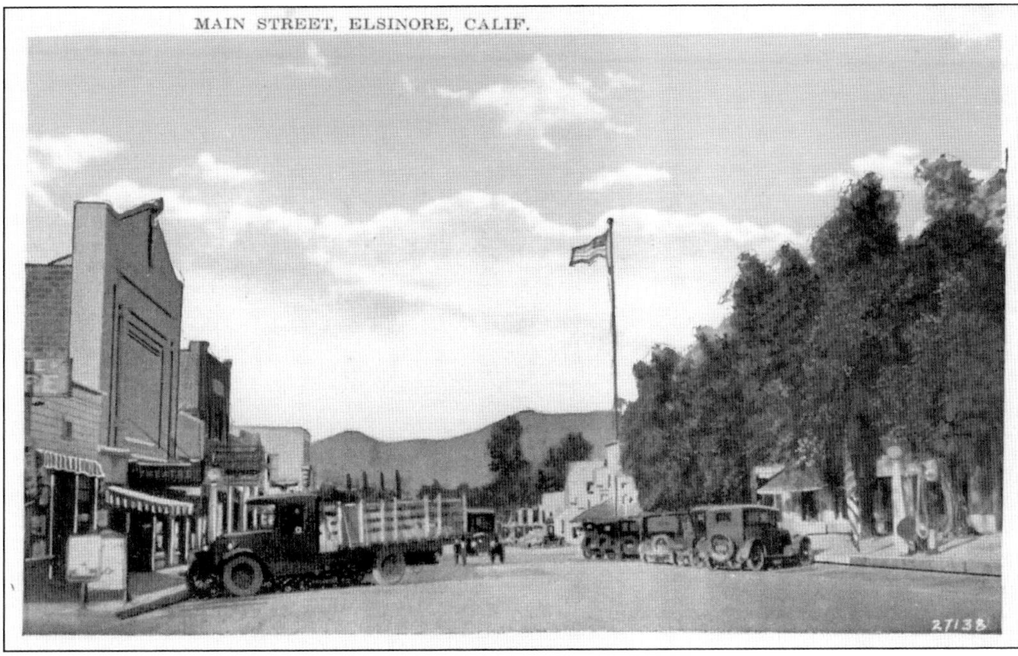


The above postcard, produced in the 1920s, shows Main Street between Graham Avenue and Sulphur Street. The tall white facade on the left-hand side was a theater that opened in March 1925. The structure burned down on February 16, 1962. The site now houses an office building. The flag marks the location of the post office and city hall. The postcard below displays the intersection of Main Street and Graham Avenue, with the Rexall drugstore. As evidenced by both images, people loved to park their cars on Main Street—just like today. (Above, MK.)

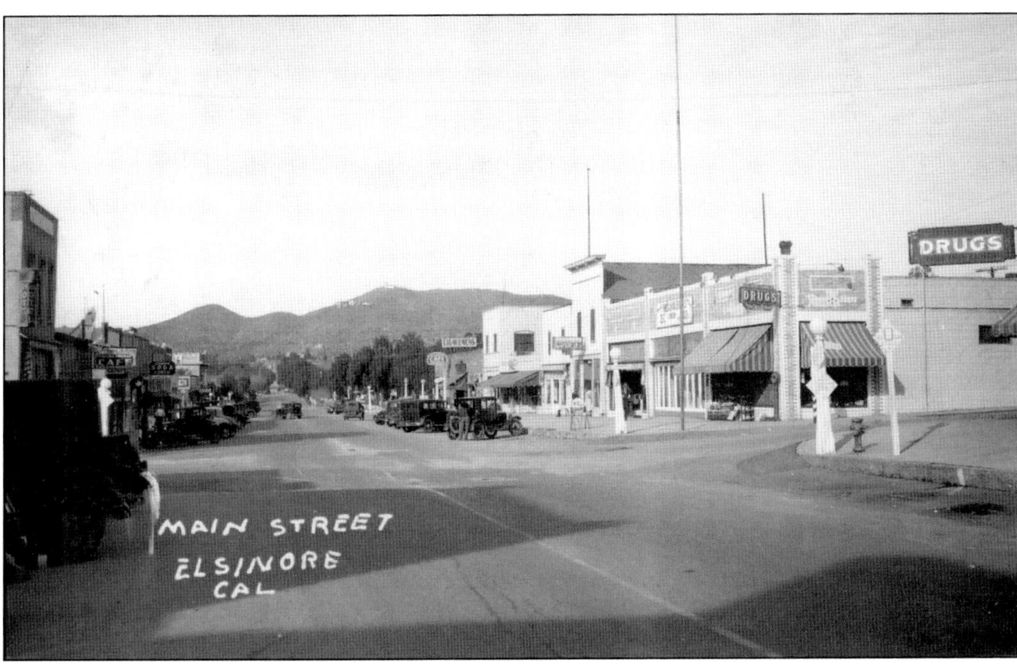

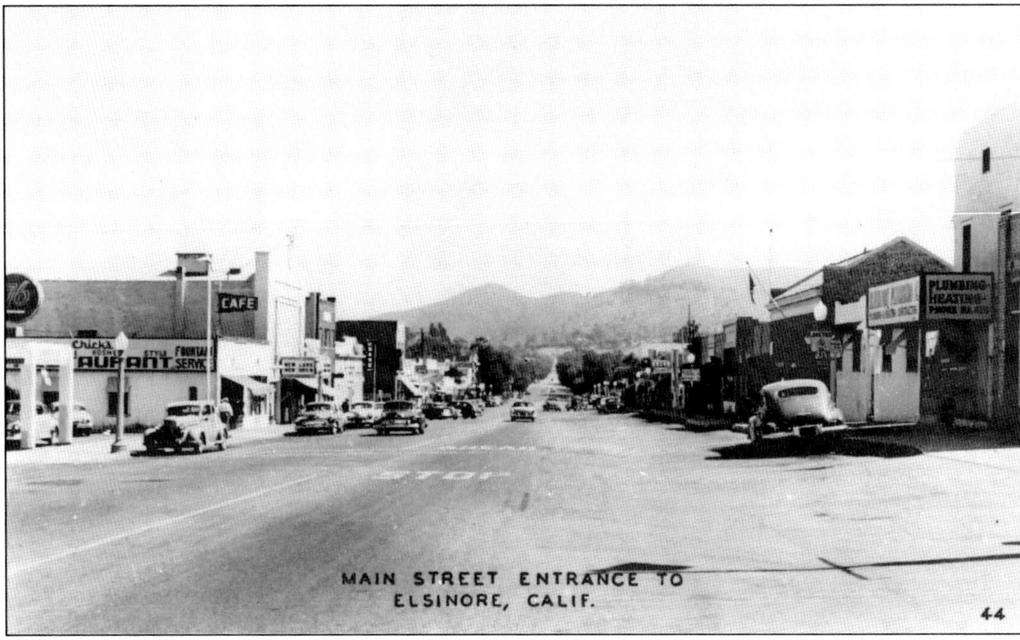


This northward view of Main Street reveals the mountains at the north end of town. On the right side of the image, midway down the street, one sees the American flag where city hall was located during the 1940s.

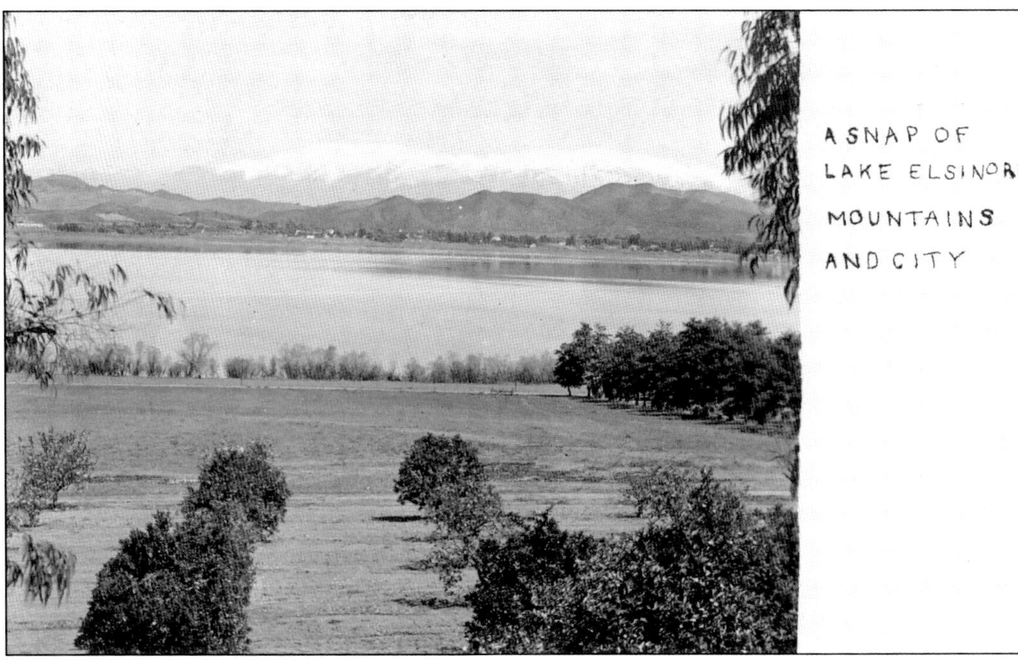


Taken midway down Grand Avenue, this view looks toward Lakeshore Drive and the north side of the lake. The undated postcard is a peaceful and serene view of the area on a clear summer or fall day. Today there are only a few spots such as this where one can relax and enjoy Lake Elsinore.

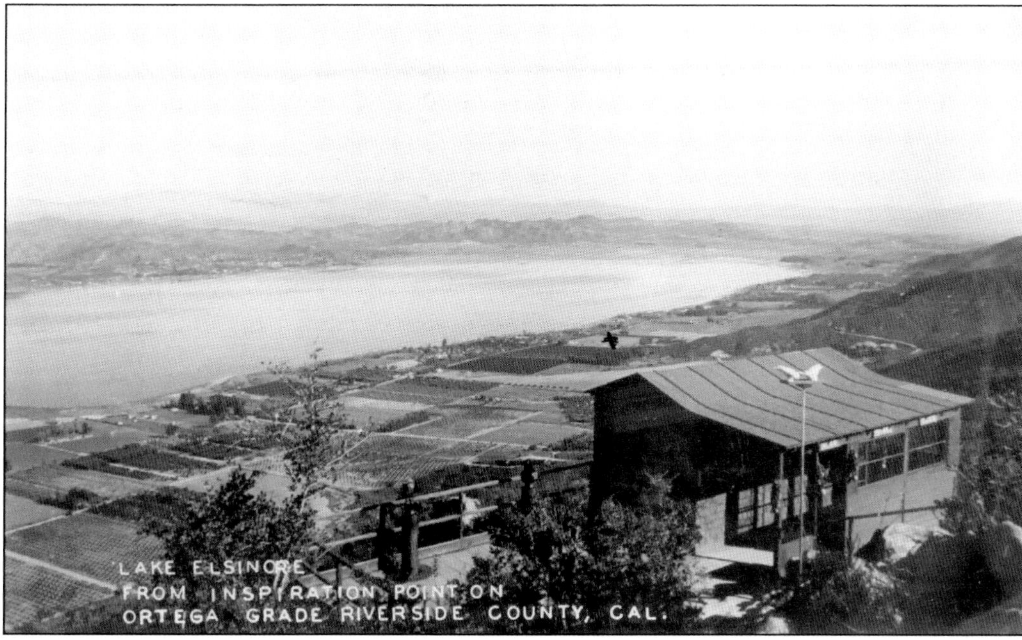


Inspiration Point is also known as Jameson Point. T. C. Jameson was a Riverside County supervisor who worked to get the Ortega Highway built. It is believed that the highway was named for Juan Francisco Ortega, who sighted the valley in 1769. It is appropriate to call this spot Jameson Point since his wife was an Ortega.

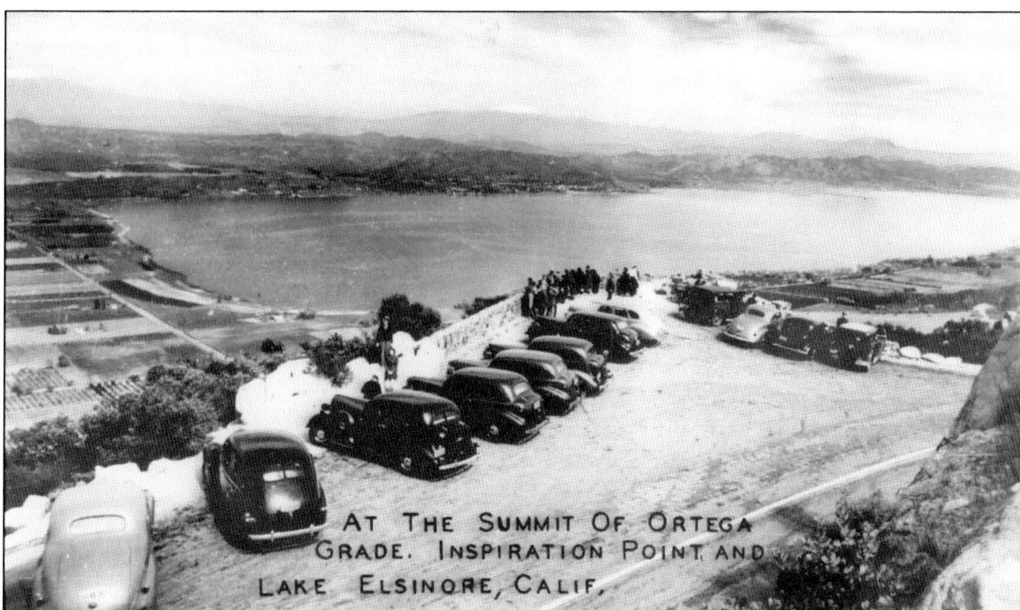


Agricultural fields are visible on the left in front of the automobiles. Across the lake is the Aloha Pier, and above Lakeshore Drive are the homes of Country Club Heights. The mountains in the far distance are those of the San Gorgonio range near Palm Springs.

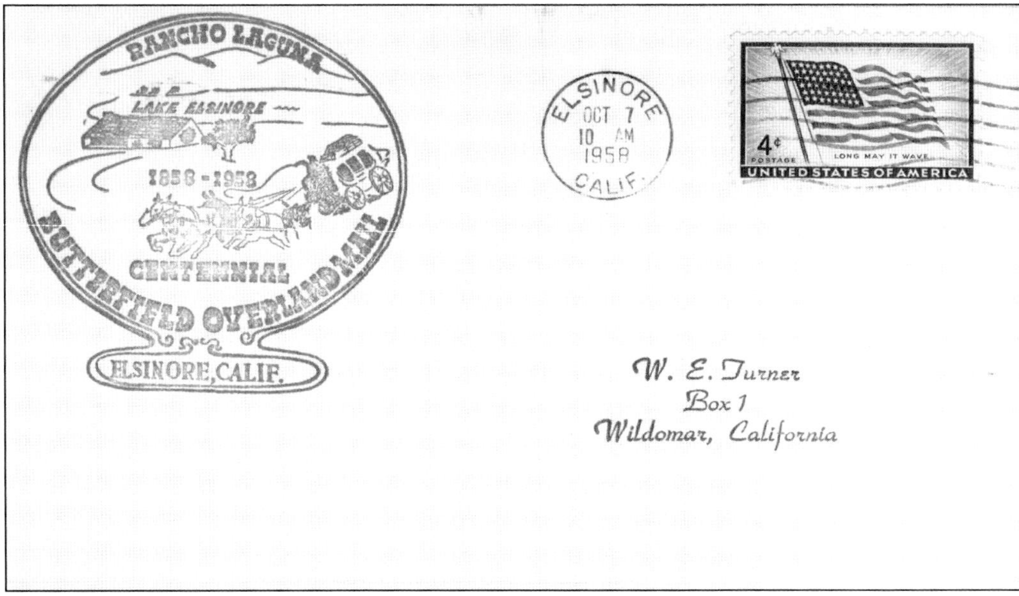


"Rancho Laguna—Celebrating the Centennial of the Rancho Laguna Butterfield Overland Mail—1858–1958—Lake Elsinore." This postcard was sold to commemorate the anniversary of the Butterfield Overland Mail route, in existence for a few years before the Civil War commenced. The stop in Elsinore was the Machado Adobe, which still stands today. (USPS/ JG.)

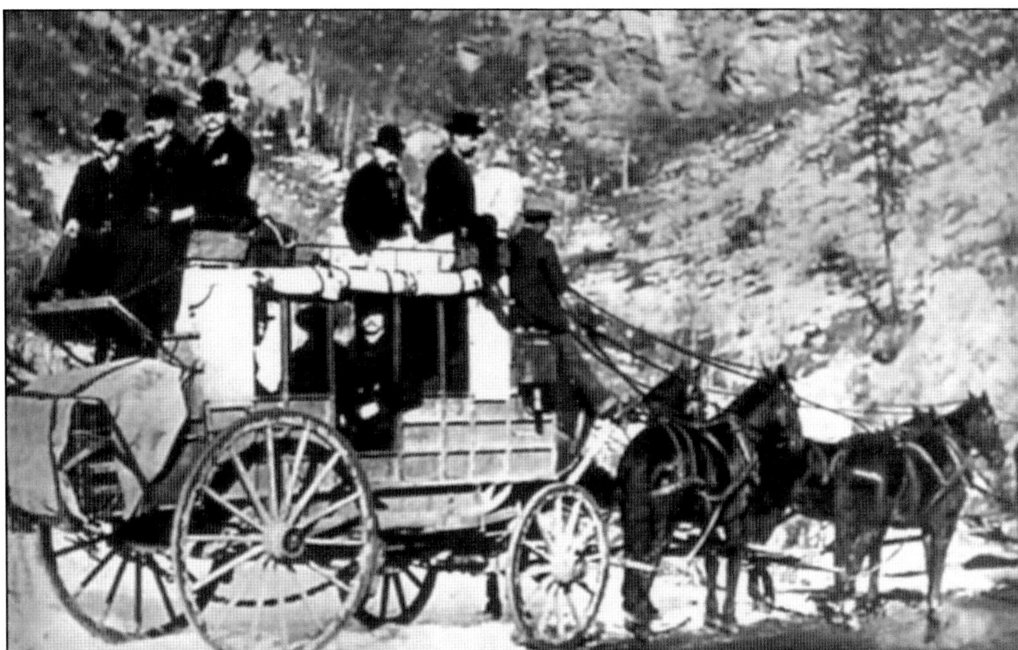

A Butterfield Stage Line stagecoach stops at the Machado Adobe home, belonging to Augustin Machado. Here the coach changed drivers and horses, and drivers partook of food prepared by Señora Machado and rested before proceeding on to the next stop. Nothing is said about passengers on the stagecoach; however, it is assumed they were fed as well.

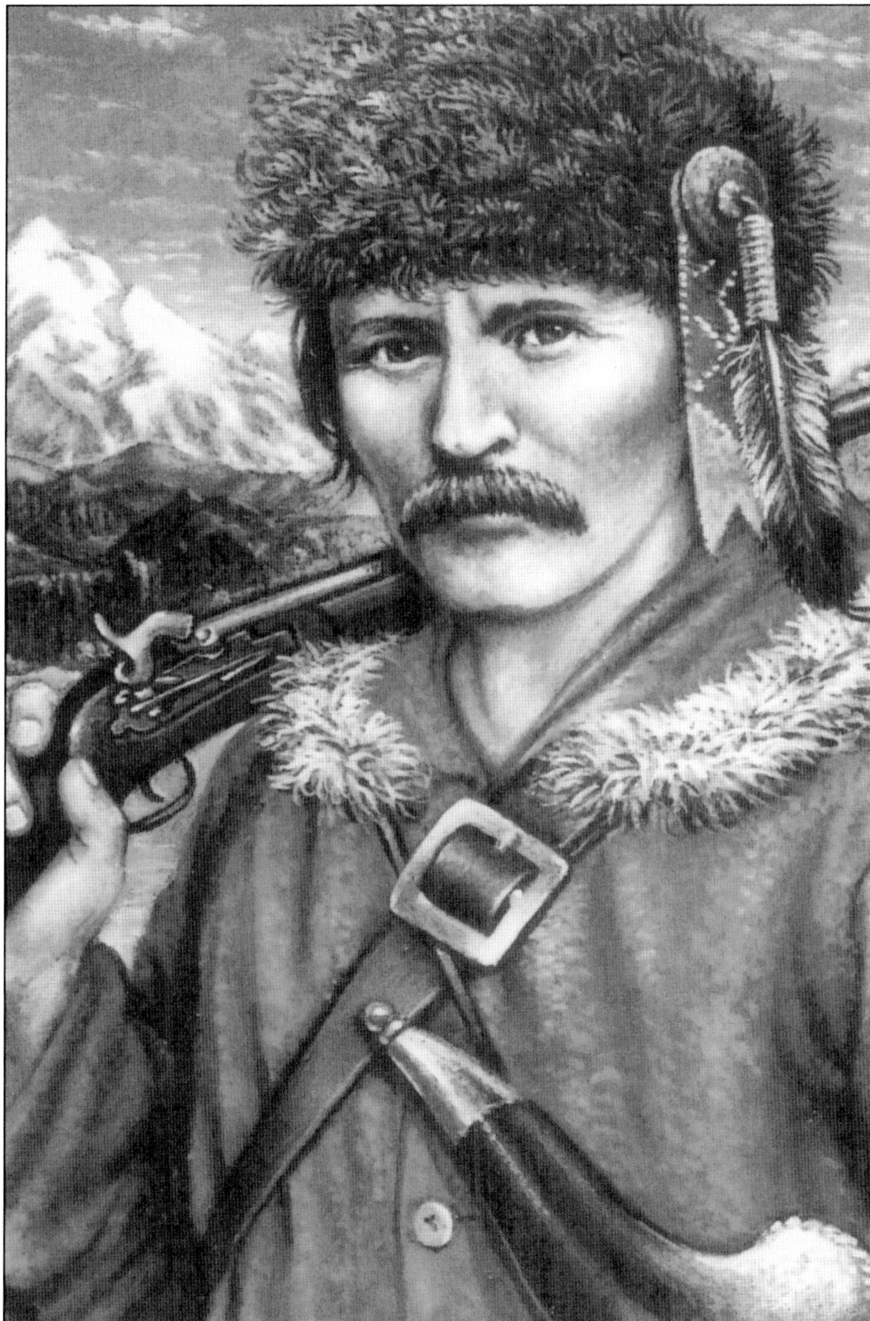

Kit Carson was a scout, and historical records state that on one of his expeditions he rode with his men along the lake's shore. Carson was hurrying east in 1846 with an erroneous report that the war was over. Again in 1848, with news of the discovery of gold on Sutter's Creek, he camped among the lake's cottonwoods. Born Christopher Carson in 1809, he became known as an American frontiersman and guide. Eventually Carson was sent back to California to secure aid from San Diego for the U.S. forces. This postcard was issued by the U.S. Post Office. (USPS/ JG.)

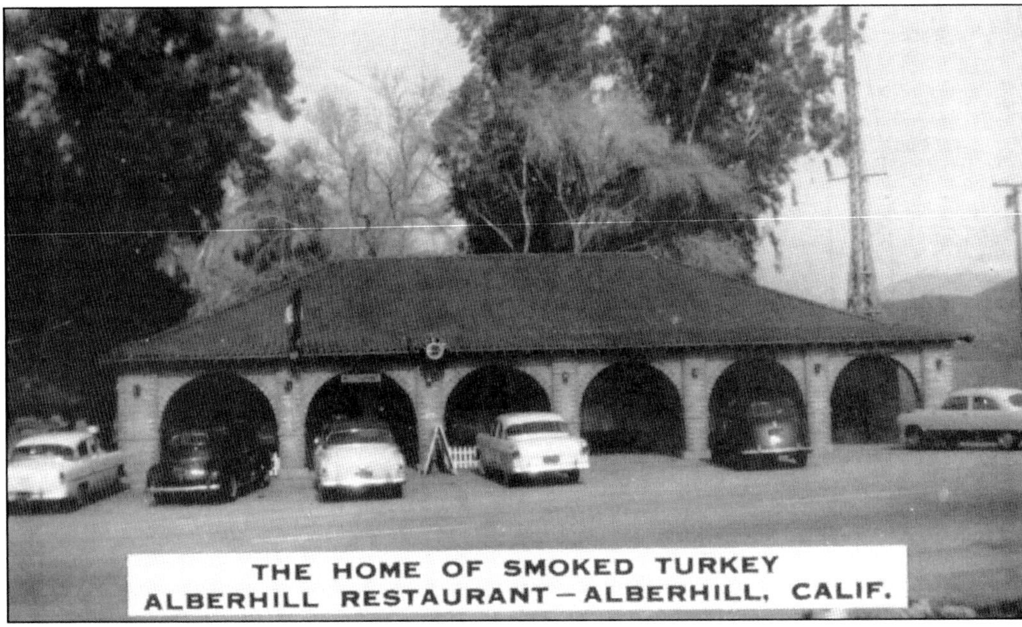


Alberhill Restaurant, the home of smoked turkey, was located on the Corona-Elsinore Highway in Alberhill. Many people remember the restaurant and continue to rave about its smoked turkey and turkey jerky. This postcard was mailed on November 28, 1956, with the message "Hi Mom, Thought you'd get a bang out of where we are." By then, the rate had been raised to 3¢ for postcards. (PCKB.)

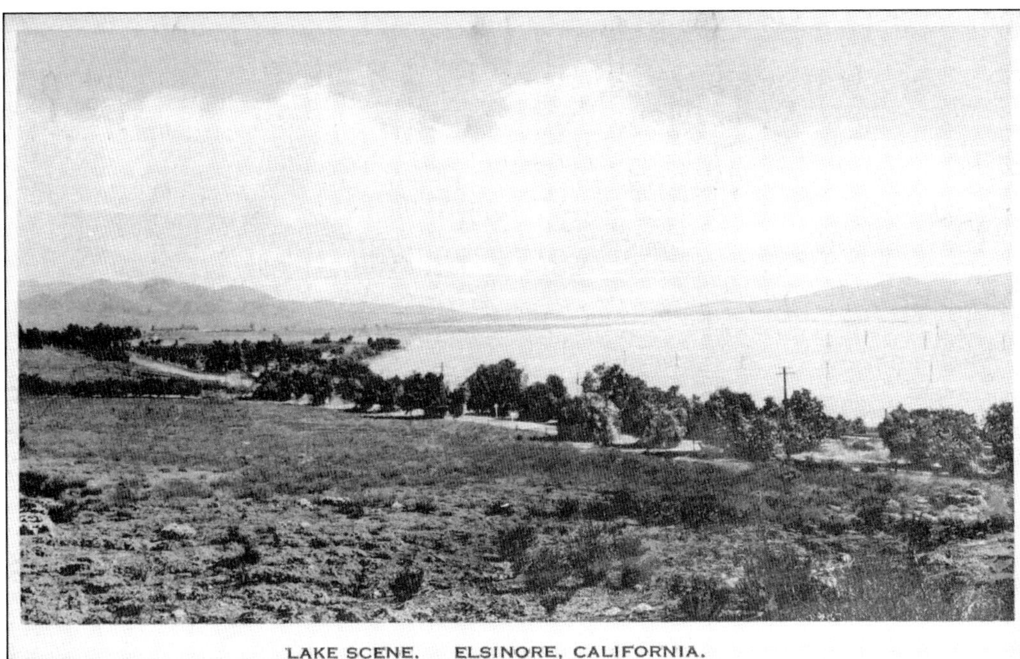


This lake view looks east over some crops in the foreground. The street at the edge of Lake Elsinore is Riverside Drive as it curves into Grand Avenue. The height of the trees suggests a date in the 1930s. The mountains on the left are home to Country Club Heights. (AC.)

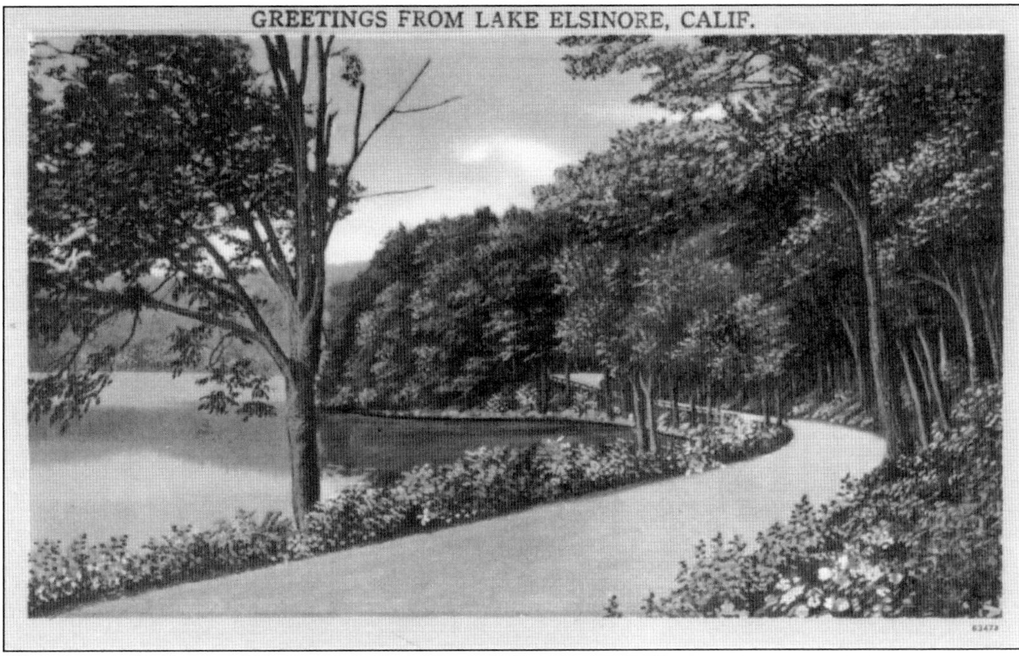


Here an artist has rendered the drive around the lake. This postcard was mailed from Elsinore in August 1950 with a 1¢ stamp and bears the message "It's still pretty wonderful—May go to Arrowhead tomorrow." It was received by a friend in San Diego with an address of "Foot of Texas St & El Camino Real." (TB.)

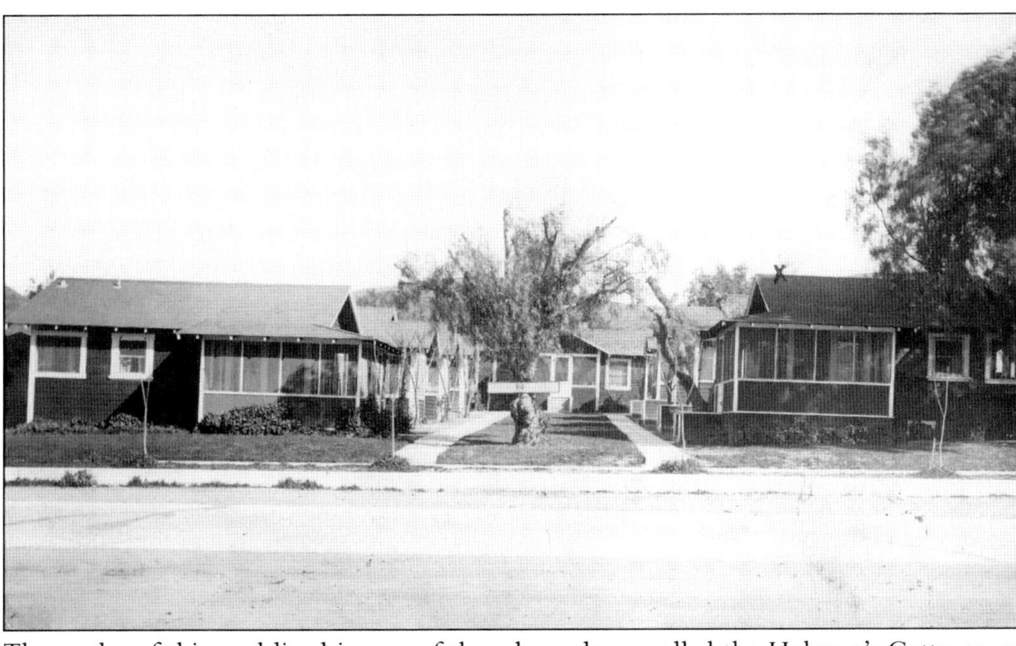

The sender of this card lived in one of these bungalows, called the Hohman's Cottages, on Grand Avenue. She stated that she had lovely neighbors and that the community was having "a social to-nite [*sic*]." Cottages such as these were named for their owners. (CG.)

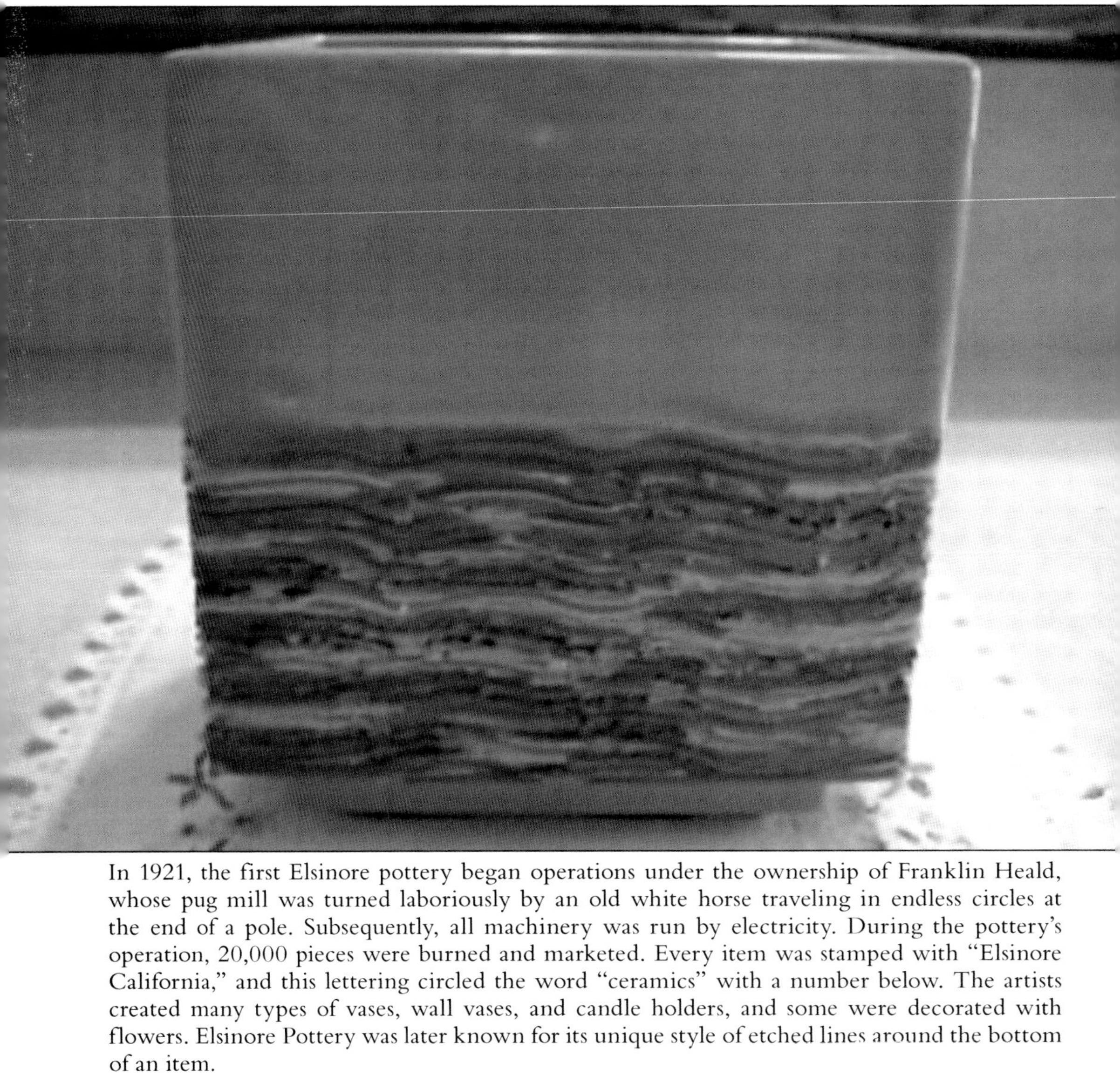

In 1921, the first Elsinore pottery began operations under the ownership of Franklin Heald, whose pug mill was turned laboriously by an old white horse traveling in endless circles at the end of a pole. Subsequently, all machinery was run by electricity. During the pottery's operation, 20,000 pieces were burned and marketed. Every item was stamped with "Elsinore California," and this lettering circled the word "ceramics" with a number below. The artists created many types of vases, wall vases, and candle holders, and some were decorated with flowers. Elsinore Pottery was later known for its unique style of etched lines around the bottom of an item.

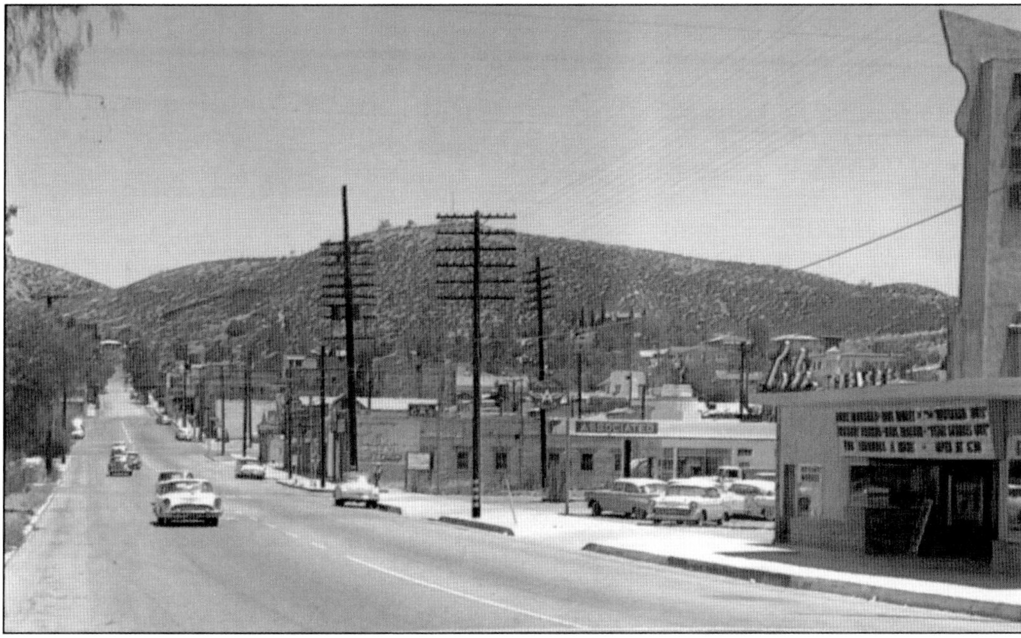

The Lake Theatre was built at the corner of Graham Avenue and Langstaff Street and opened to the public in August 1950 under the ownership of Nellie Jackson, her daughter Florence Lynch, and Mr. and Mrs. Clay Scott. Today the building is owned by the City of Lake Elsinore. It is occupied by the Lake Elsinore Recreation Department, which runs many recreation programs for the community. (JC.)

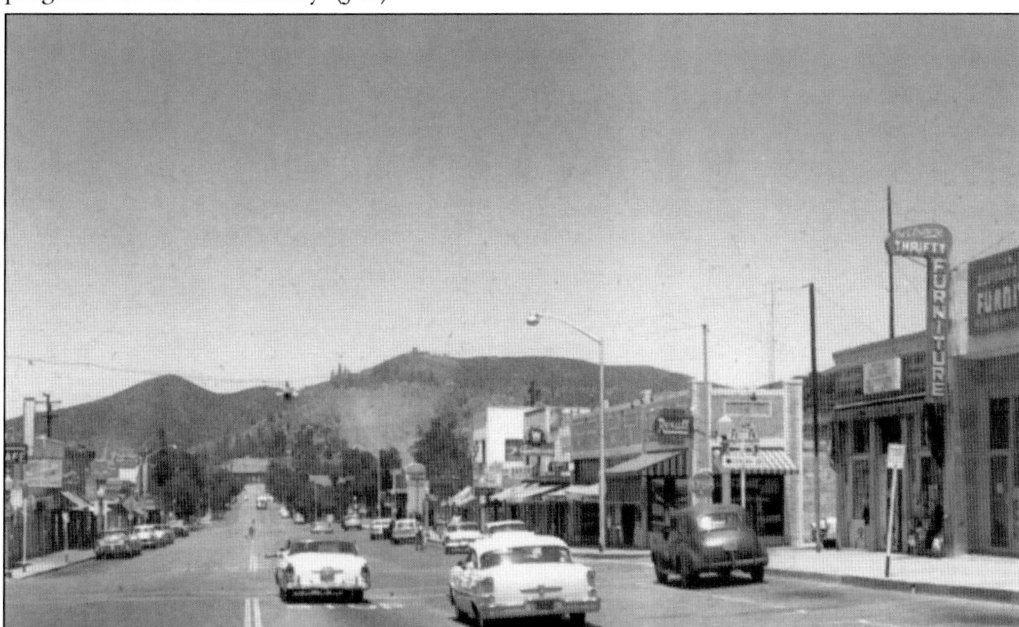


Main Street remains heavily traveled, though many of the businesses have changed. The intersection of Main Street and Graham Avenue still has it four-way stop sign, but the flashing red light is gone. In the 1990s, Main was given a face lift that included street-level lights at all of the corners, adding to today's charm. (JC.)

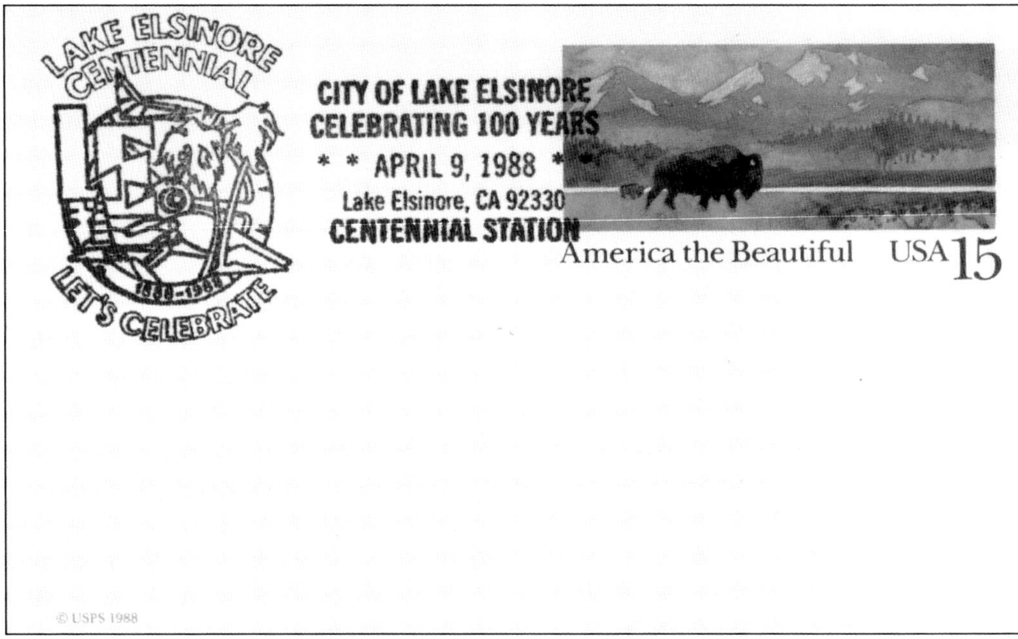


Created for Lake Elsinore's centennial, this postcard reads, "City of Lake Elsinore celebrating 100 years ⋆ April 9, 1988 ⋆ Lake Elsinore CA 92330—Centennial Station." The cost to mail the card was 15¢, with the "America the Beautiful" stamp showing buffaloes grazing near the lake. (USPS/ JG.)

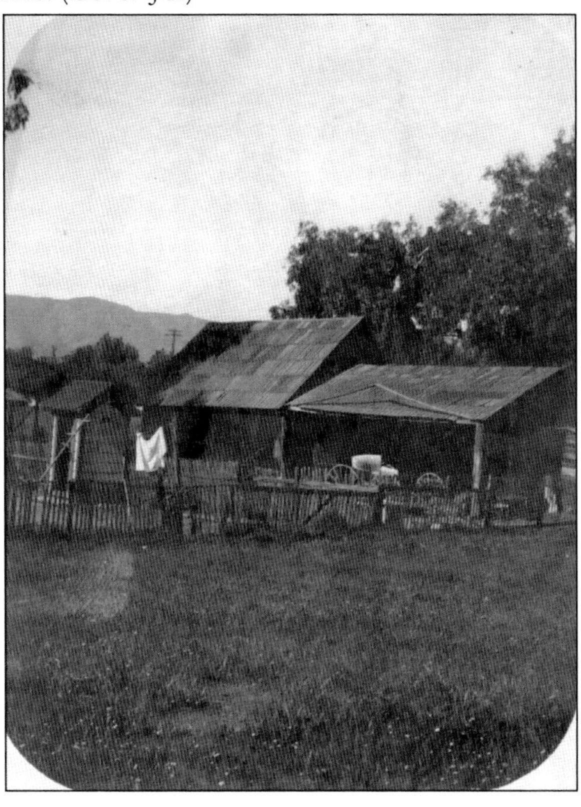

This Isaac B. Dutton Barn postcard is dated April 1888. Another photograph indicates that the barn was built in back of the family's house on Poe Street and that the house was built in 1887. Mrs. Roy Dutton, the wife of Isaac's son, planted a pepper tree seed, and the tree that grew from it was still living in April 1953.

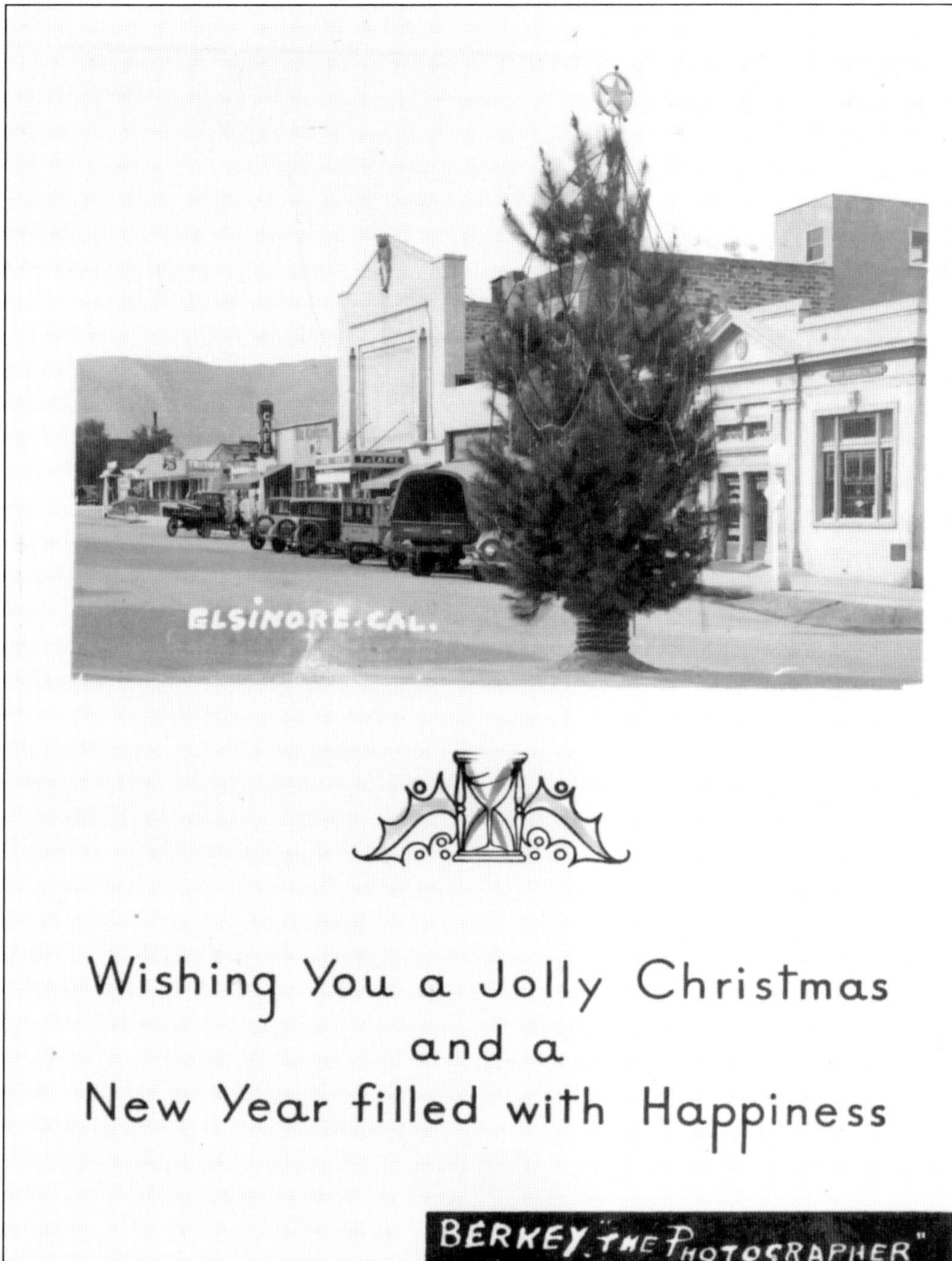


This Christmas card, signed by Berkey the photographer, bears a Main Street view looking south from the intersection with Graham Avenue. A large Christmas tree stands in the middle of Main Street. The building to the left of the tree is the theater. The card was addressed to "Tom Boyle, Fire Chief, City," and mailed in December 1934.

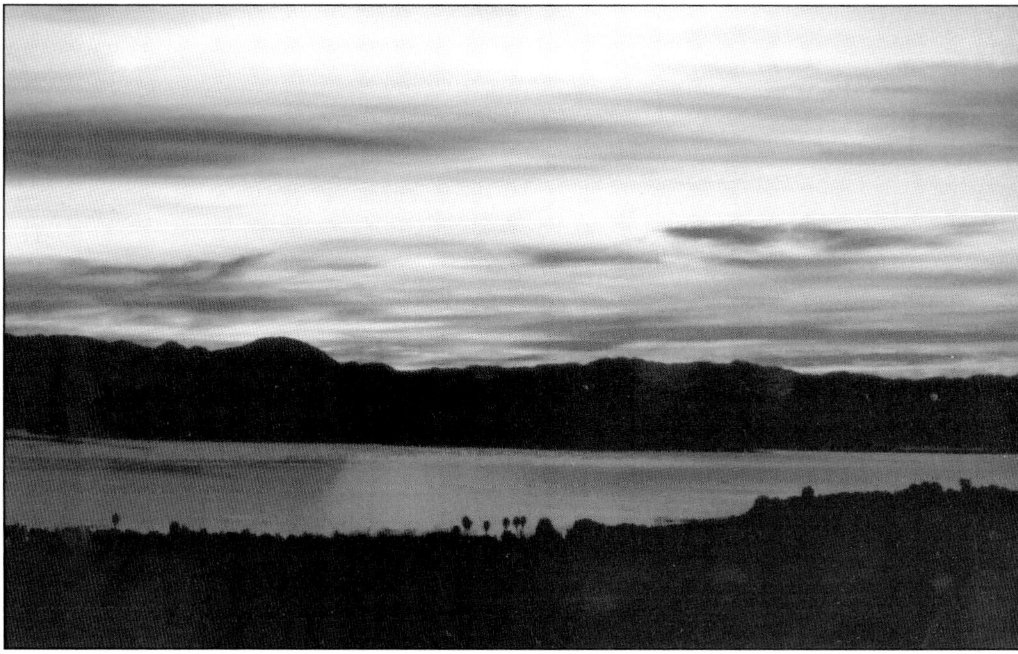

This view was taken from the eastern hills of Lake Elsinore looking west over the lake and captures the Elsinore Mountains and the spectacular colors of the sun setting behind the mountains. As in the Christmas poem by Clement Moore, "Not a creature was stirring/ not even a mouse."

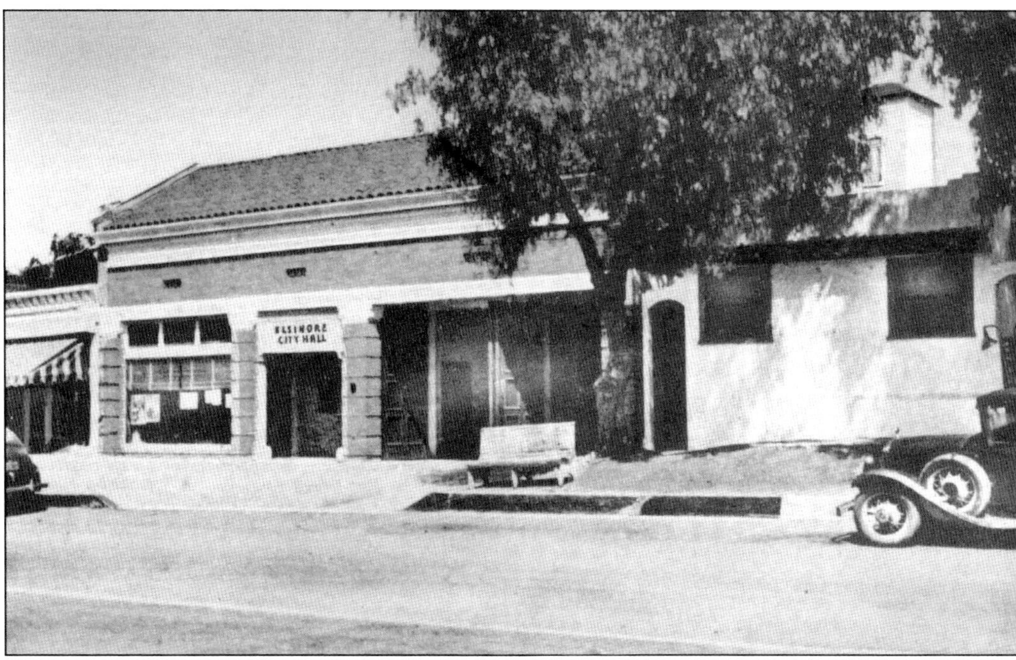


The new Elsinore City Hall at 130 South Main Street was dedicated on July 7, 1934. Meetings were originally held on the second floor of the Consolidated Bank building. The second location was a storeroom at the corner of Main Street and Graham Avenue. The third was a small building purchased by the city on the site of the present city hall. (EP.)

# *Two*

# Transportation and Agriculture

In 1883, the Old Laguna Station was situated about two miles from Elsinore on the California Southern Railroad. Santa Fe Railway established the Elsinore Station at its present site in April 1896. The first agent, O. F. Smith, arrived the next year. The new depot was an ornament to Elsinore, and its location at the corner of Spring Street and Graham Avenue could not have been better in the interests of the town. The building was more complete in accommodations than other depots, featuring three rooms besides the summer waiting room. The telegraph instrument was located in the office. The freight platform was fitted with chutes on both sides for unloading freight and baggage.

Agriculture was a major industry in the area. Important crops grown were alfalfa, hay, grain, walnuts, pecans, almonds, citrus fruits, grapes, apricots, pears, peaches, watermelons, tomatoes, and olives. Crops were extremely prolific. For example, in 1913, six carloads of apricots were sold at $200 a ton for a total of $30,000; in 1927, the walnut crop was estimated at 150 tons, selling at 17¢ per pound for a value of $5.65 million; and with the 1936–1937 rains, 500,000 pounds of watermelons were harvested. By the end of 1938, a $750 million value was placed on the crops in the valley.

Historian Altha Merrifield Cauch writes about the "Hamilton Double residence on the road to Alberhill." She notes that he was "raising Belgian hares, hens and turkeys as well as a fine vegetable garden. We noticed potatoes, onions, cabbages, etc., also strawberries, and the orange trees in bloom gave the air of a delicious fragrance. Mr. Double has a fine apricot orchard. The olive trees are in bloom and it seems the land is excellent for that fruit."

The *Lake Elsinore Valley Sun* newspaper reported that the watermelon yield in 1966 was more than 6,000 tons. In fact, one farmer's field produced 125 tons of melons in a single day.

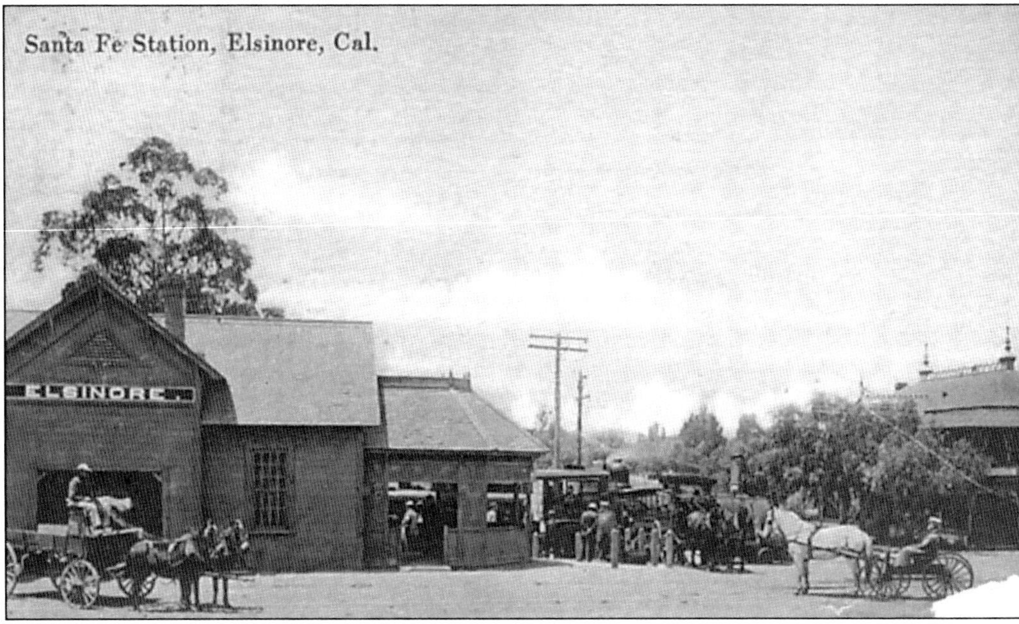


The Elsinore Station (above), formerly known as the Laguna Station, was built in 1896 by the Santa Fe Railway Company and closed in 1968. It replaced the old Elsinore Junction Station, which had been in operation since the 1880s and was located approximately at Railroad Canyon Road and the Highway 15 Freeway. The station was heavily used for passenger transit as well as for shipments of agricultural products to market and new livestock to ranchers. When the livestock was grown, the ranchers shipped the mature animals to market to be sold. In the image below, note the Crescent Bath House with its covered swimming pool in the background.

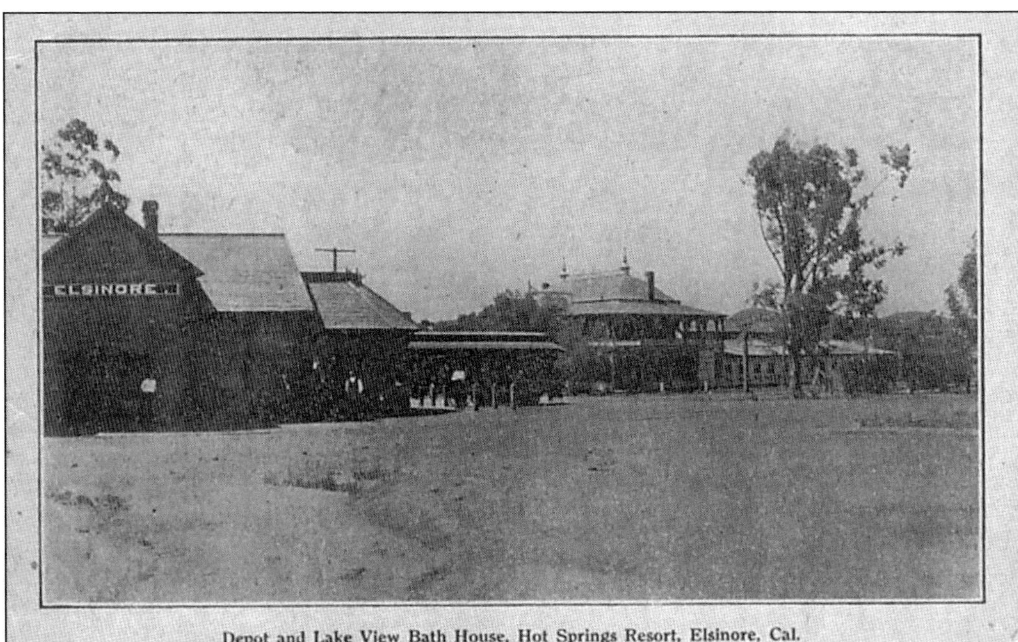


Depot and Lake View Bath House, Hot Springs Resort, Elsinore, Cal.

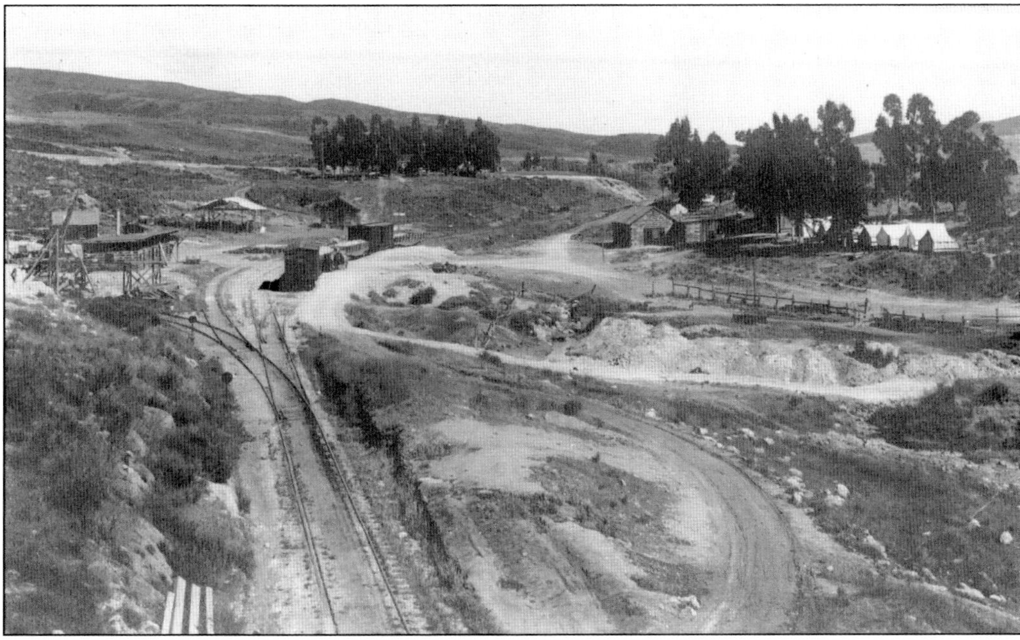

This image shows clay mining in progress at Alberhill in the early 1900s. Note the railroad in the foreground; it was a spur from the Santa Fe Depot in Elsinore. A great variety of fine-quality clay deposits was located here, where the Los Angeles Brick Company, the Gladding-McBean Company, and the Alberhill Coal and Clay Company employed many men.

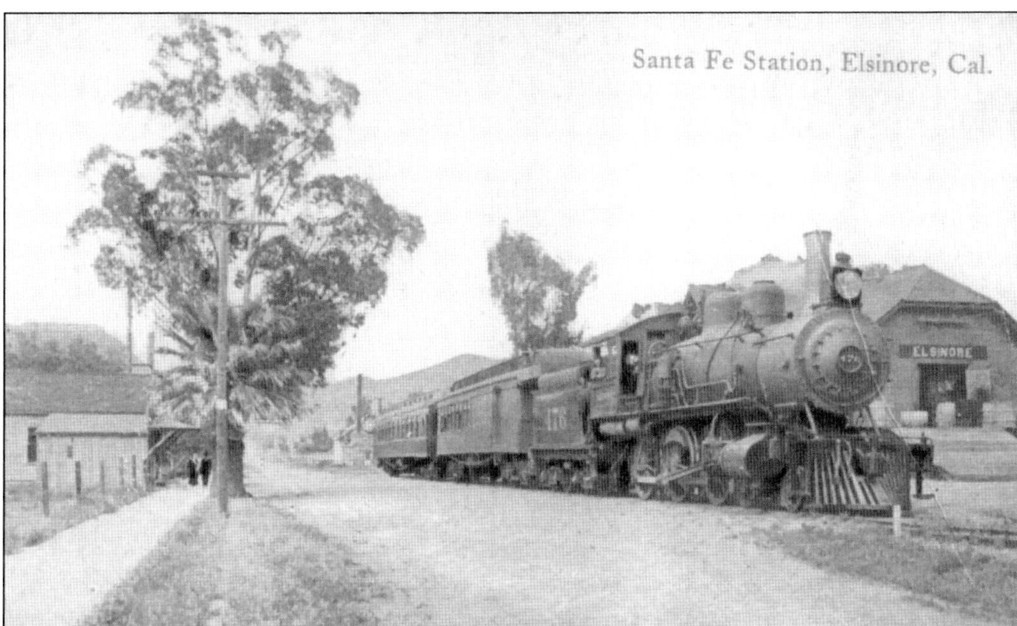


The Santa Fe train, sitting at the station at Graham Avenue and Spring Street, had an attachment of two cars, indicating that it would take on mostly passengers. This *c.* 1910 image depicts an Elsinore of unpaved streets. In the background, note the mountains north of the city. (MSL.)

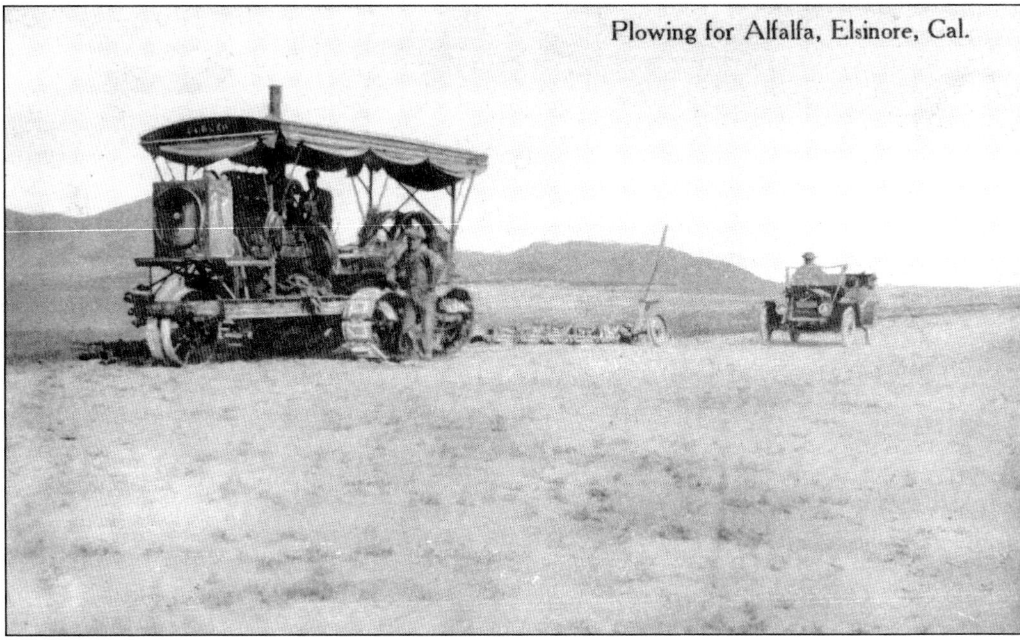


The newest thing in the early 1900s, the tractor for plowing alfalfa made the farmer's life much simpler. While a team of horses was suitable for some jobs, a tractor accomplished the plowing, harrowing, harvesting, and hauling of heavier loads in a shorter length of time. (MSL/ CyG.)

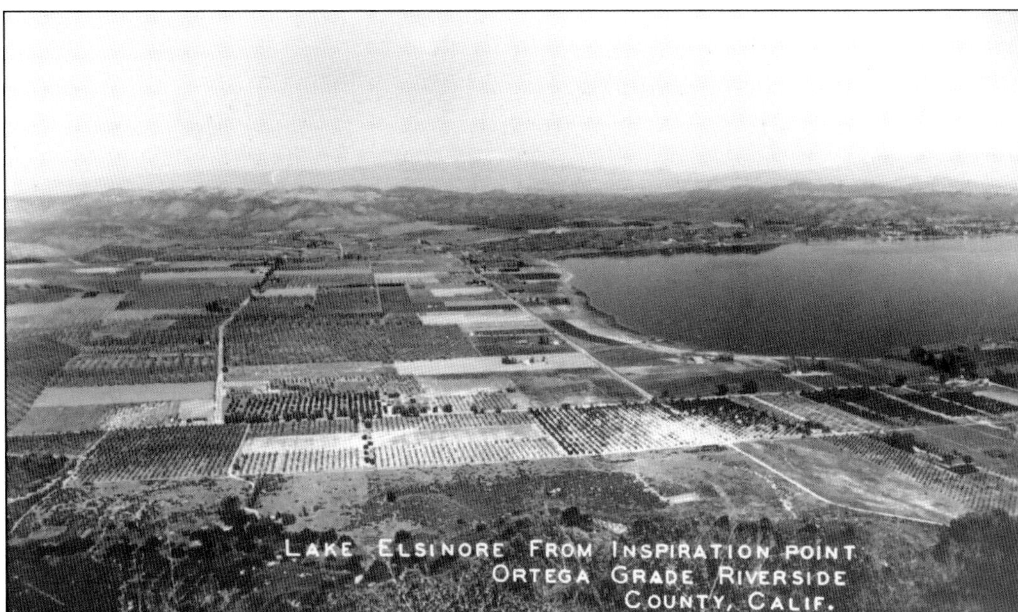


The farmland of the Lake Elsinore Valley, as viewed from Inspiration Point on the Ortega Grade, provides a spectacular image. On the north side of the lake, the Country Club Heights development is visible above the shoreline. On the horizon are the mountains near Palm Springs.

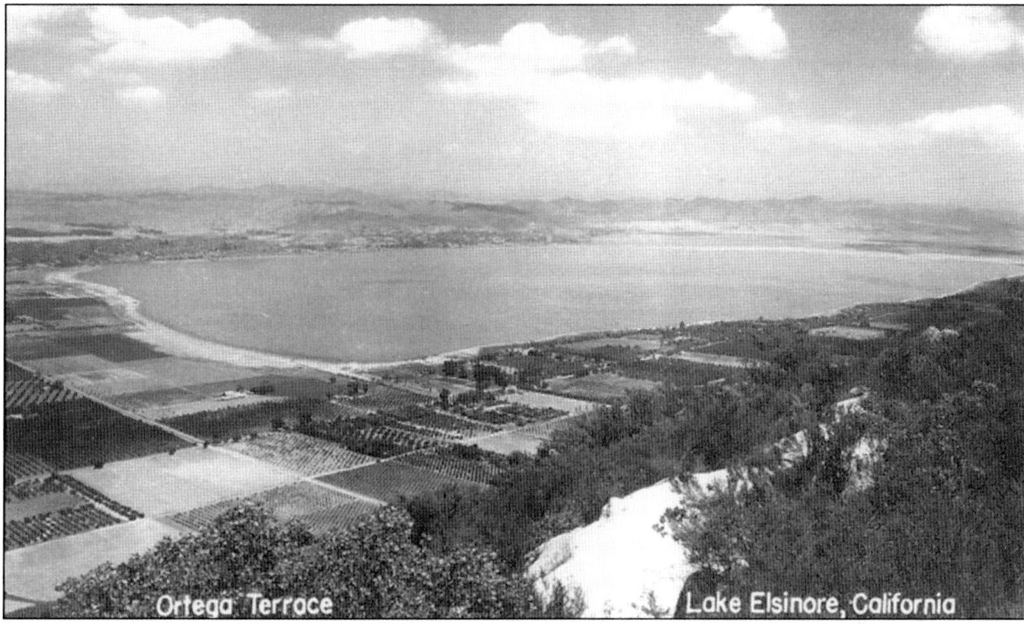


This view from the Elsinore Mountains captures the southern shore of Lake Elsinore, showing all of the lake's 2,900 acres. One of the largest and finest olive farms was located along this area of the lake. C. K. Albers of Alberhill fame named his brand of olives Albers Folly.

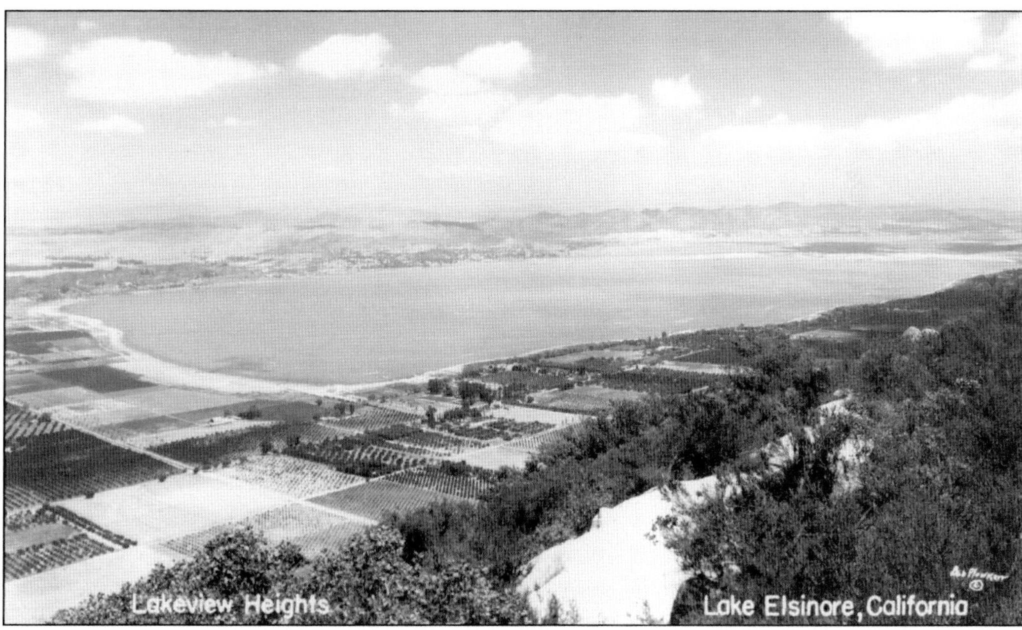


While the farmers were planting their crops, the developers were starting small tracts for the new residents coming to Elsinore. These people did not farm but rather performed other kinds of work. Vista del Lago was one such development located in the area. Today there is no evidence the little tract existed. (CG.)

No. 1] [Sep. 16th, 1858.

# OVERLAND MAIL COMPANY.

THROUGH TIME SCHEDULE BETWEEN

## ST. LOUIS, MO., MEMPHIS, TENN. } & SAN FRANCISCO, CAL.

GOING WEST.

| LEAVE. | DAYS. | Hour. | Distance, Place to Place. | Time allowed. | Av'ge Miles per Hour. |
|---|---|---|---|---|---|
| St. Louis, Mo., & Memphis, Tenn. } | Every Monday & Thursday, | 8.00 A.M | Miles. | No. Hours | |
| P. R. R. Terminus, " | " Monday & Thursday, | 6.00 P.M | 160 | 10 | 16 |
| Springfield, " | " Wednesday & Saturday | 7.45 A.M | 143 | 37¾ | 3¾ |
| Fayetteville, " | " Thursday & Sunday, | 10.15 A.M | 100 | 26½ | 3¾ |
| Fort Smith, Ark. | " Friday & Monday, | 3.30 A.M | 65 | 17¼ | 3¾ |
| Sherman, Texas | " Sunday & Wednesday, | 12.30 A.M | 205 | 45 | 4½ |
| Fort Belknap, " | " Monday & Thursday, | 9.00 A.M | 146½ | 32½ | 4½ |
| Fort Chadbourn, " | " Tuesday & Friday, | 3.15 P.M | 136 | 30¼ | 4½ |
| Pecos River, (Em. Crossing.) | " Thursday & Sunday, | 3.45 A.M | 165 | 36½ | 4½ |
| El Paso, | " Saturday & Tuesday, | 11.00 A.M | 248½ | 55¼ | 4½ |
| Soldier's Farewell | " Sunday & Wednesday, | 8.30 P.M | 150 | 33½ | 4½ |
| Tucson, Arizona | " Tuesday & Friday, | 1.30 P.M | 184½ | 41 | 4½ |
| Gila River,* " | " Wednesday & Saturday | 9.00 P.M | 141 | 31½ | 4½ |
| Fort Yuma, Cal. | " Friday & Monday, | 3.00 A.M | 135 | 30 | 4½ |
| San Bernardino " | " Saturday & Tuesday, | 11.00 P.M | 200 | 44 | 4½ |
| Ft. Tejon, (Via Los Angeles) | " Monday & Thursday, | 7.30 A.M | 150 | 32½ | 4½ |
| Visalia, " | " Tuesday & Friday, | 11.30 A.M | 127 | 28 | 4½ |
| Firebaugh's Ferry, " | " Wednesday & Saturday | 5.30 A.M | 82 | 18 | 4½ |
| (Arrive) San Francisco, | " Thursday & Sunday, | 8.30 A.M | 163 | 27 | 6 |

GOING EAST.

| LEAVE. | DAYS. | Hour. | Distance, Place to Place. | Time allowed. | Av'ge Miles per Hour. |
|---|---|---|---|---|---|
| | | | Miles. | No. Hours | |
| San Francisco, Cal. | Every Monday & Thursday, | 8.00 A.M | 163 | 27 | 6 |
| Firebaugh's Ferry, " | " Tuesday & Friday, | 11.00 A.M | 82 | 18 | 4½ |
| Visalia, " | " Wednesday & Saturday, | 5.00 A.M | 127 | 28 | 4½ |
| Ft. Tejon, (Via Los Angeles) | " Thursday & Sunday, | 9.00 A.M | 150 | 32½ | 4½ |
| San Bernardino, " | " Friday & Monday, | 5.30 P.M | 200 | 44 | 4½ |
| Fort Yuma, " | " Sunday & Wednesday, | 1.30 P.M | 135 | 30 | 4½ |
| Gila River,* Arizona | " Monday & Thursday, | 7.30 P.M | 141 | 31½ | 4½ |
| Tucson, " | " Wednesday & Saturday | 3.00 A.M | 184½ | 41 | 4½ |
| Soldier's Farewell, | " Thursday & Sunday, | 8.00 P.M | 150 | 33½ | 4½ |
| El Paso, Tex. | " Saturday & Tuesday, | 5.30 A.M | 248½ | 55¼ | 4½ |
| Pecos River, (Em. Crossing.) | " Monday & Thursday | 12.45 P.M | 165 | 36½ | 4½ |
| Fort Chadbourn, " | " Wednesday & Saturday | 1.15 A.M | 136 | 30¼ | 4½ |
| Fort Belknap, " | " Thursday & Sunday, | 7.30 A.M | 146½ | 32½ | 4½ |
| Sherman, " | " Friday & Monday, | 4.00 P.M | 205 | 45 | 4½ |
| Fort Smith, Ark. | " Sunday & Wednesday, | 1.00 P.M | 65 | 17¼ | 3¾ |
| Fayetteville, Mo. | " Monday, & Thursday, | 6.15 A.M | 100 | 26½ | 3¾ |
| Springfield, " | " Tuesday & Friday, | 8.45 A.M | 143 | 37¾ | 3¾ |
| P. R. R. Terminus, " | " Wednesday & Saturday | 10.30 P.M | 160 | 10 | 16 |
| (Arrive) St. Louis, Mo., & Memphis, Tenn. } | " Thursday & Sunday, | | | | |

This Schedule may not be exact.—Superintendents, Agents, Station-men, Conductors, Drivers and all employees are particularly directed to use every possible exertion to get the Stages through in quic

This Overland Mail Company schedule, between St. Louis/Memphis and San Francisco, shows the times "going west" and "going east." It details the city from which the train leaves, the departure day, hour, number of miles traveled, time allowed, and average miles per hour. The notes state that the schedule may not be exact.

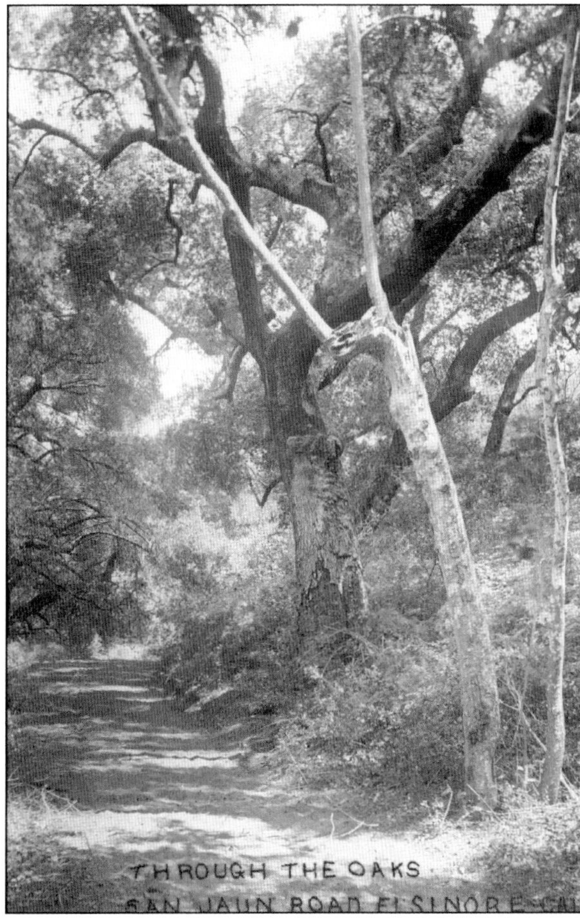


The beautiful drive pictured at right led travelers through the oaks on San Juan Road over the Elsinore Mountains to Orange County in the days before the Ortega Highway, seen below, was completed. In some of the valleys, there are areas along the road where one can find bucolic places to stop and relax or picnic. (CyG.)

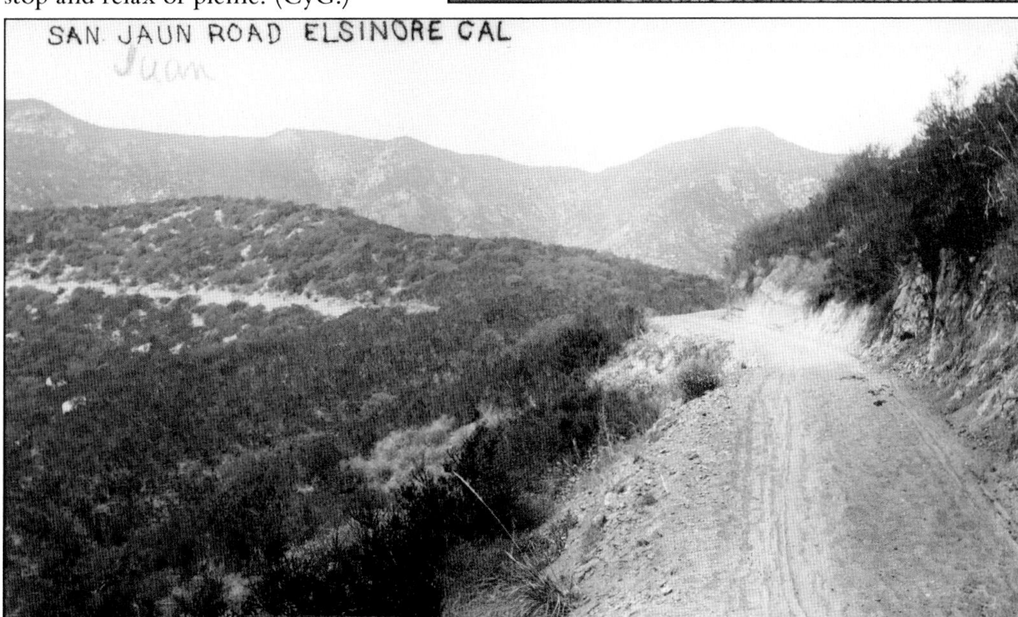

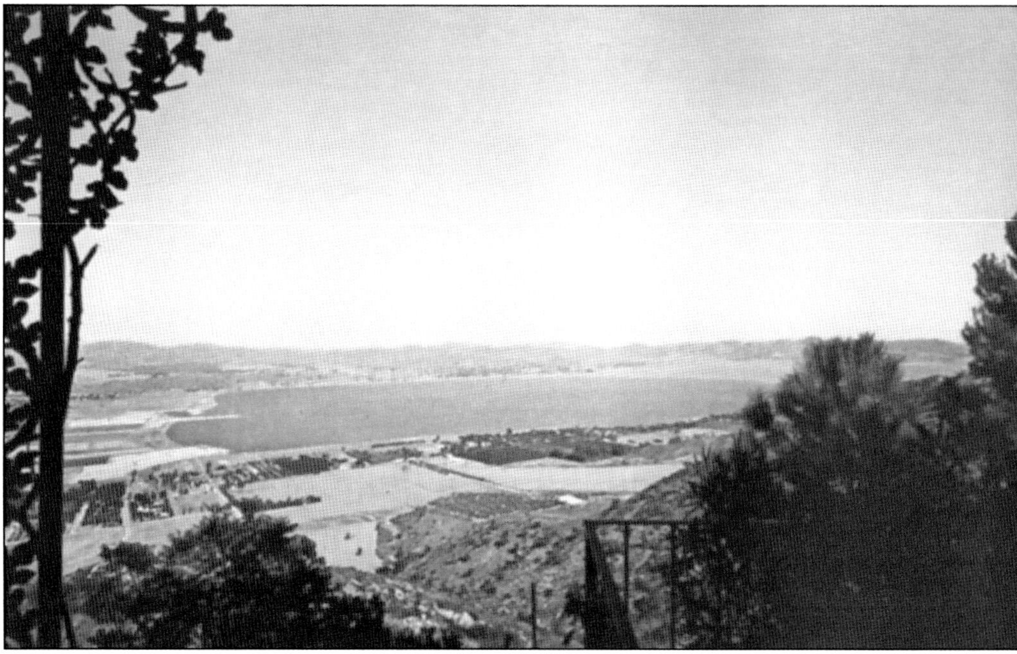

Taken from the southwest corner of the lake up in the Elsinore Mountains, this postcard shows farms extending almost to the water's edge. In the years of sufficient rain, these farms produced bumper crops. Today the fields of crops are things of the past, and the area is instead filled with houses as far as the eye can see.

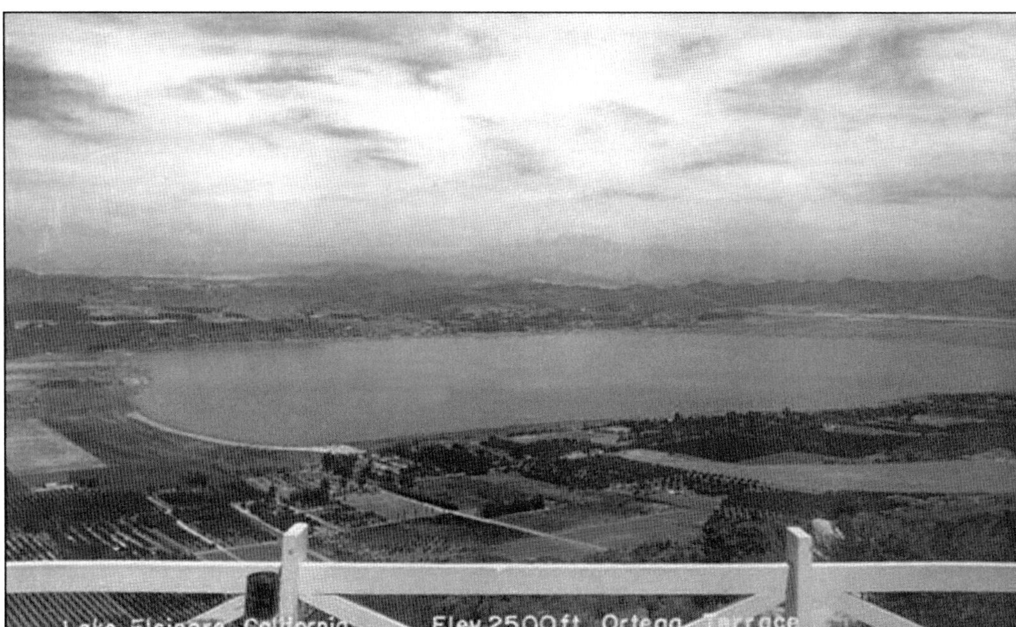


This panoramic view from the Ortega Highway reveals the lake, fields, and mountains in the distance. Garden produce, such as lettuce, tomatoes, and onions, was grown here very profitably, as were nuts, citrus, barley, olives, and grapes.

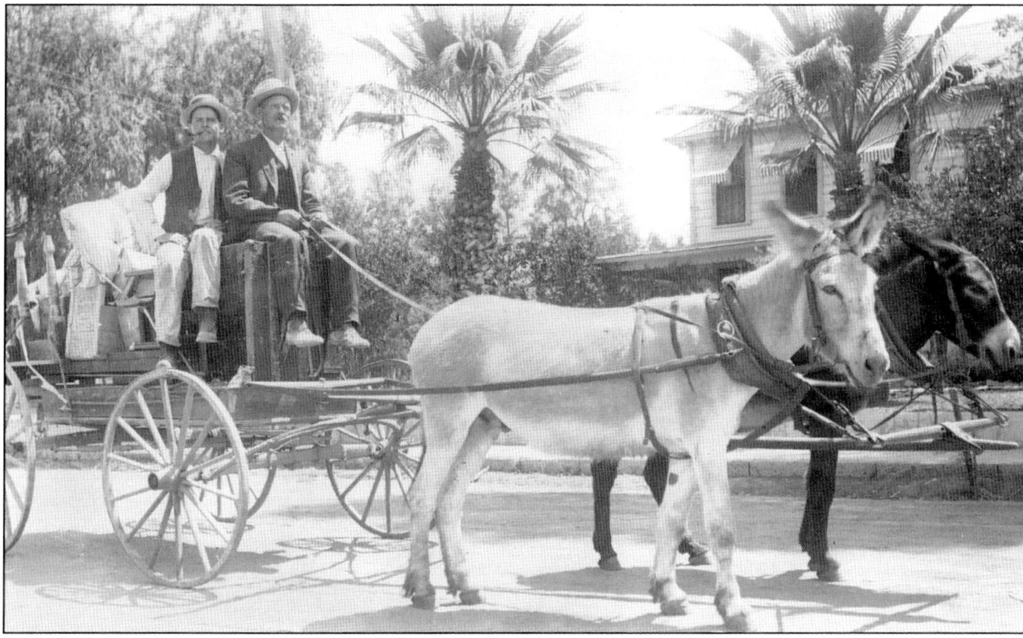

Not seen in the previous postcards is the new mode of transportation introduced in the early 1900s, before the streets were paved. The well-dressed driver and his passenger appear to be making deliveries to local businesses. Little has been written about mules and donkeys being used in town. (CyG.)

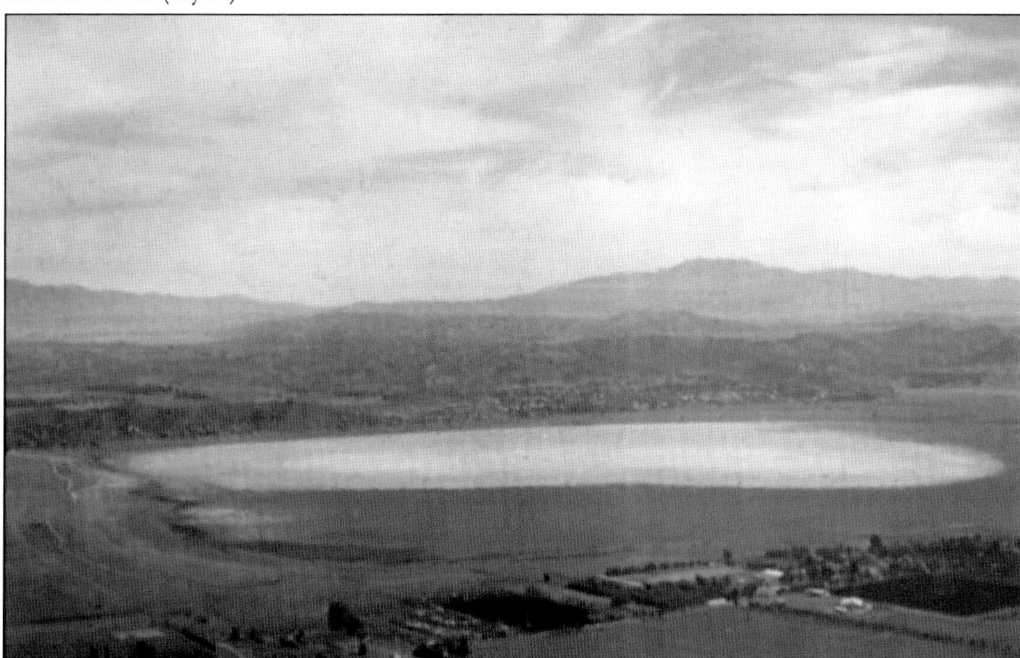

This is a panoramic view overlooking Lake Elsinore, Perris, Romoland, and the Hemet-San Jacinto Valley. Mount San Gorgonio can be seen in the distance. The postcard dates to the early 1900s since there are no crops on the west side of the lake. The fields display a mix of low-growing crops, such as alfalfa, oats, and garden produce.

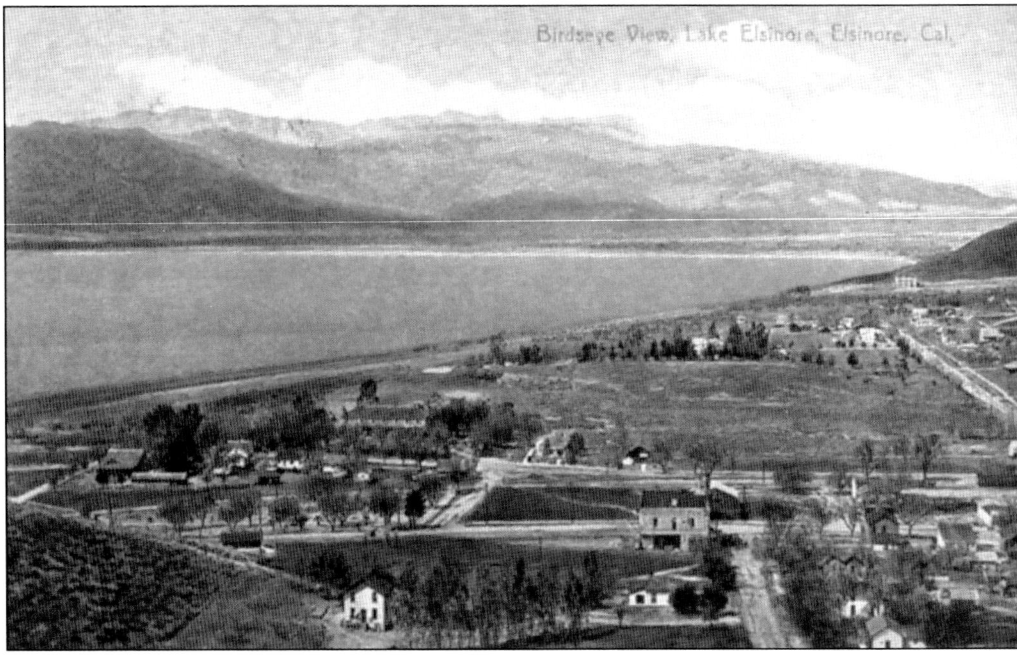


This is a postcard postmarked in Elsinore on July 7, 1914, from Uncle Duncan to Maggie, and mailed with a one-cent stamp. The message reads: "I am up here in the mountains for a few days. This lake is 1315 ft. above sea level and is six mile long & 3 miles wide and 75 miles from Los Angeles. Suppose you have your vacation now." The postcard is titled, "Birdseye View, Lake Elsinore, Elsinore, Cal.," and is one of the more scenic views.

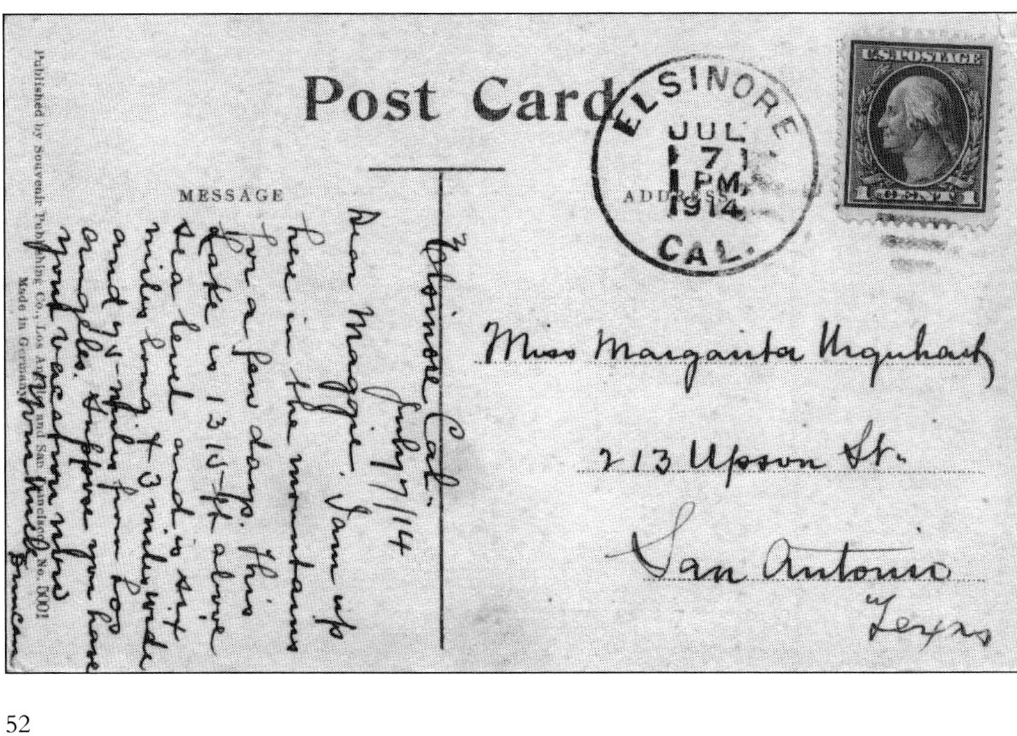

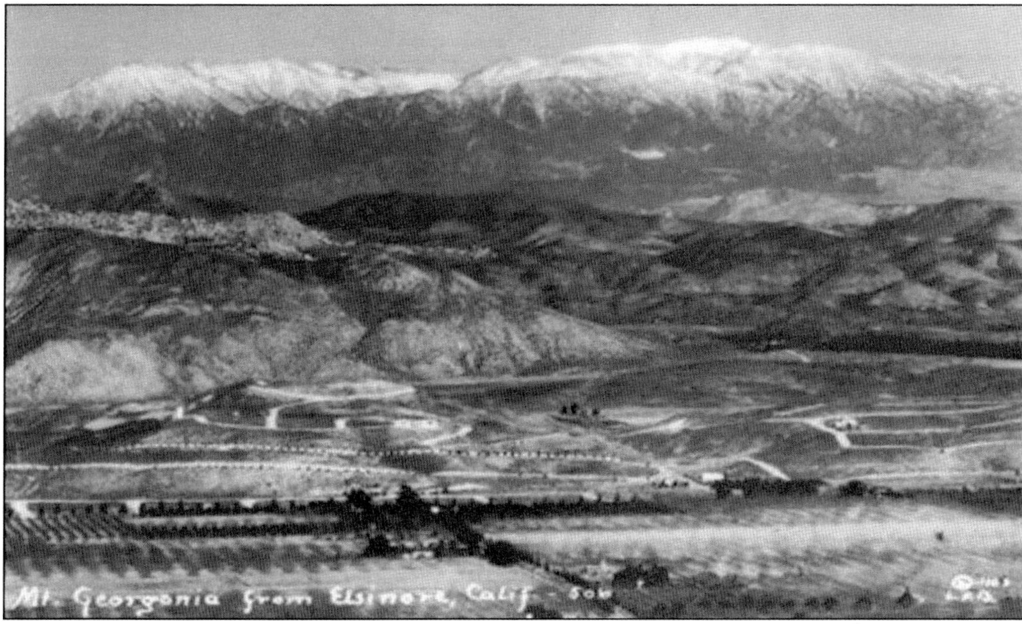


Lake Elsinore is a natural bowl surrounded by mountains. These views look to the north, with the San Gorgonio and San Jacinto Mountains in the background. In the wintertime, when the mountains are covered with snow, they sparkle beautifully.

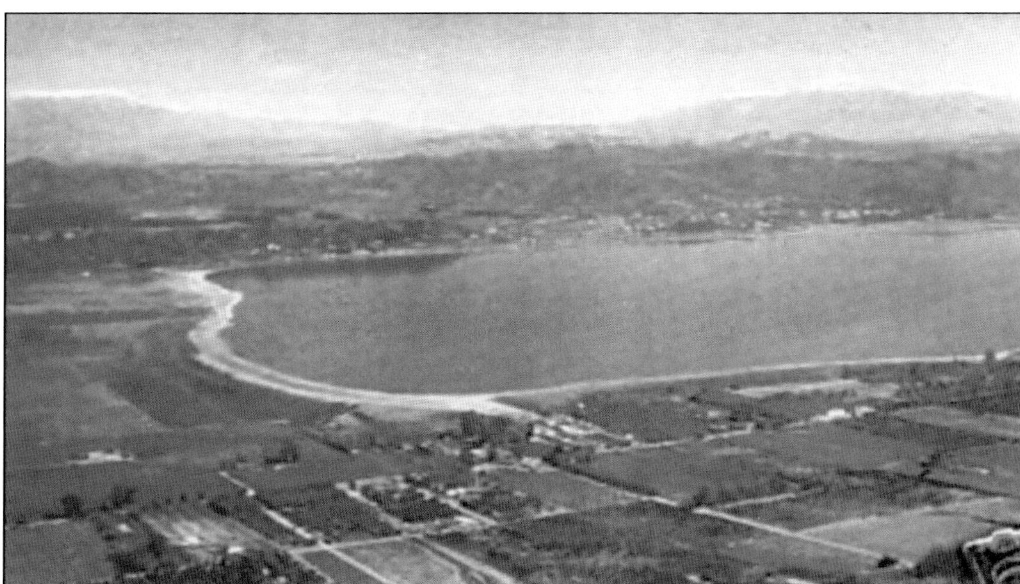

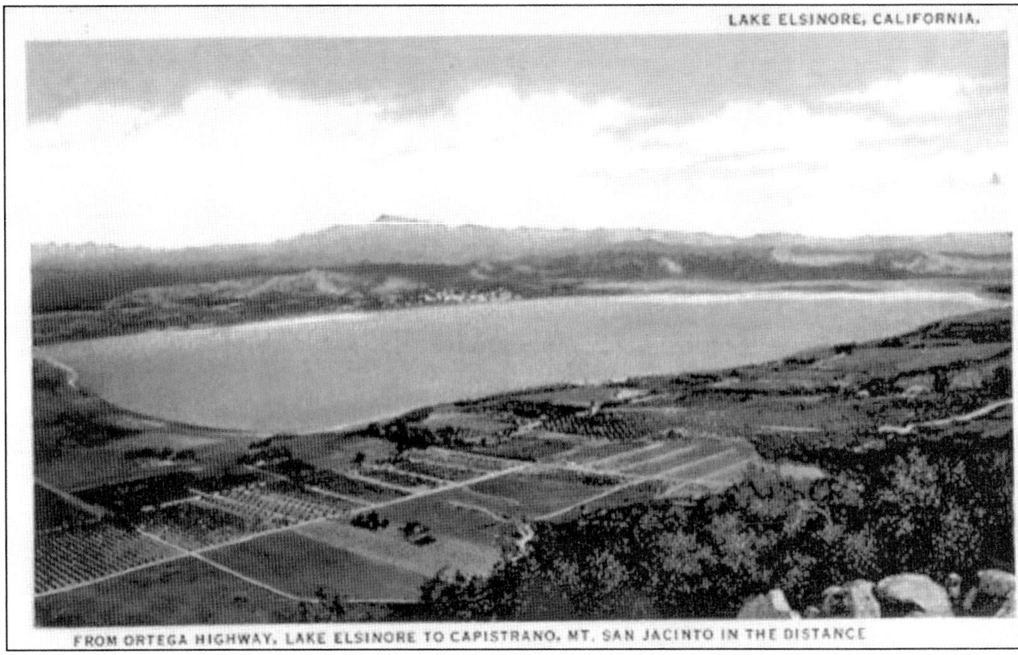


This view from the Ortega Highway forms almost a complete image of the 2,900-acre Lake Elsinore, the only natural lake in Southern California. As such, it is dependent on the rain received each year. The lake lies 1,240 feet above sea level and, with normal amounts of precipitation, is about 20 feet deep.

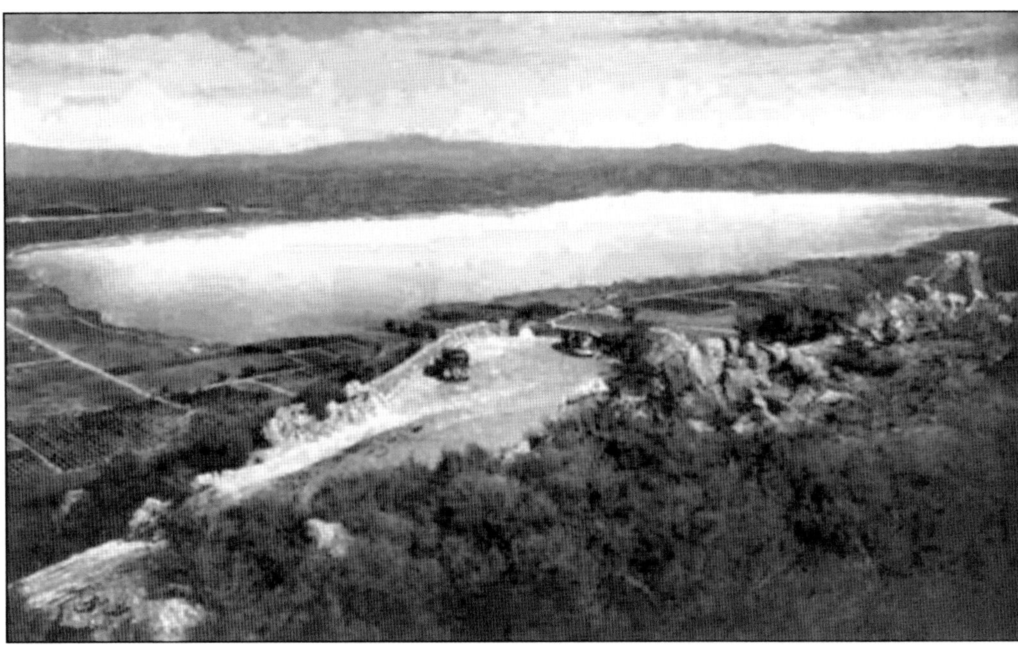

Beautiful views of the lake can also be gained at the Lookout, which was built to allow people enjoyment of the scenery. Today the spot includes a restaurant and has become a weekend favorite for visitors traveling via cars and motorcycles.

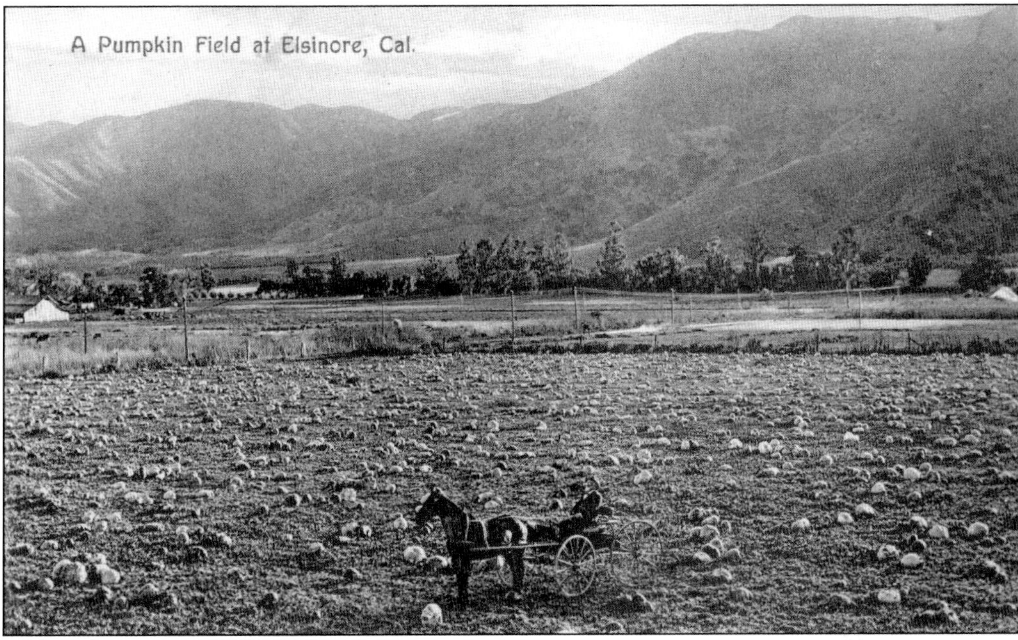


Shown here is a rare postcard mailed from Elsinore in May 1909 with a 1¢ stamp. Pumpkin Field, located northwest of the lake, is revealed in this view toward the Elsinore Mountains. The area is now filled with houses and the new, modern Lakeside High School, where classes began in September 2005. The original field was part of the Torn Ranch property. (NPC.)

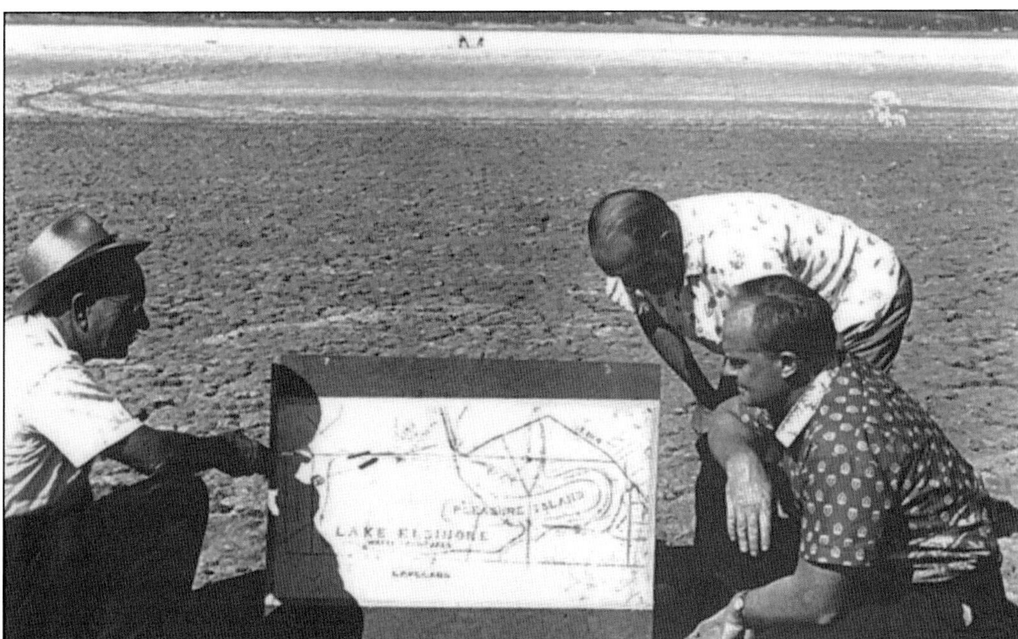

Three gentlemen try to solve the problem of Lake Elsinore being dry. People were known to drive across the lake when there was little or no water in it. Another story tells of a local schoolteacher who taught some of his students to drive on the lake bed. The last time the lake was dry was from 1951 to April 1964.

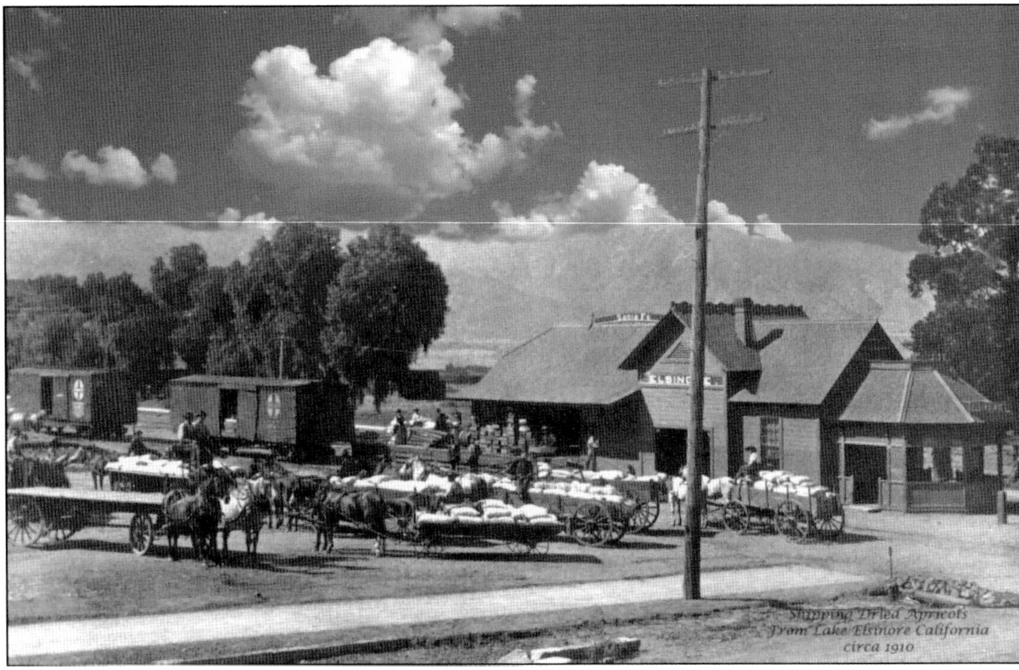


Farmers have brought their wagons, pulled by horses, to the Santa Fe Station to ship their apricots to market. The crops in 1913 were extremely prolific: six carloads of apricots sold for $200 a ton for a total of $30,000 of added income to the valley. (OPC.)

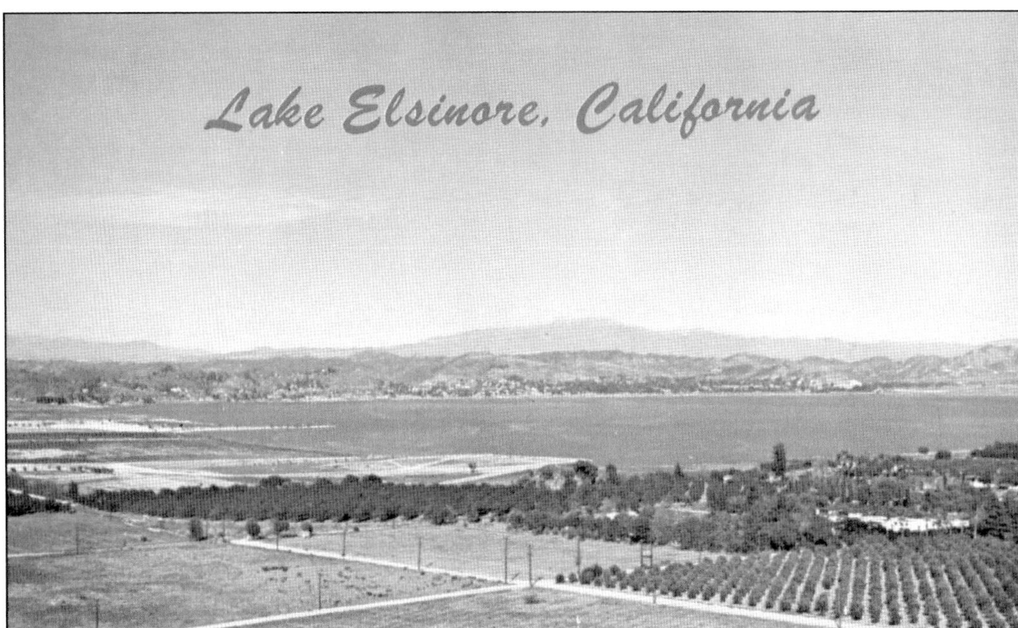


The view looks south across Lake Elsinore toward the city. The new marina at the state park, jutting out prominently on the middle left side, is rapidly becoming a favorite playground area. Farmland was still prevalent in the 1950s. (CWI.)

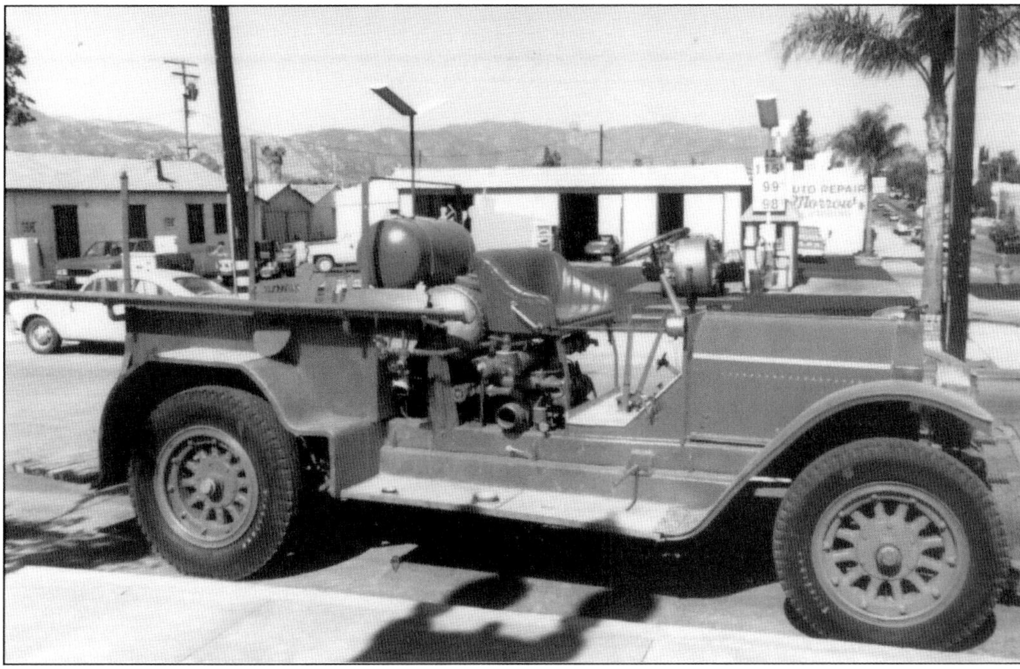

Above is the 1925 American LaFrance that was Elsinore's first fire engine. The city could not afford to buy it, so residents raised $3,000, and the city paid the remainder of the $8,500 in lease payments. When the fire engine had been paid in full, there was a ceremony at which the contract was burned. Today Elsinore's Fire Engine No. 1, pictured below, has been restored to its original grandeur. A copy of the original equipment list showing every nut and bolt used in its assembly was provided to the men who performed the restoration.

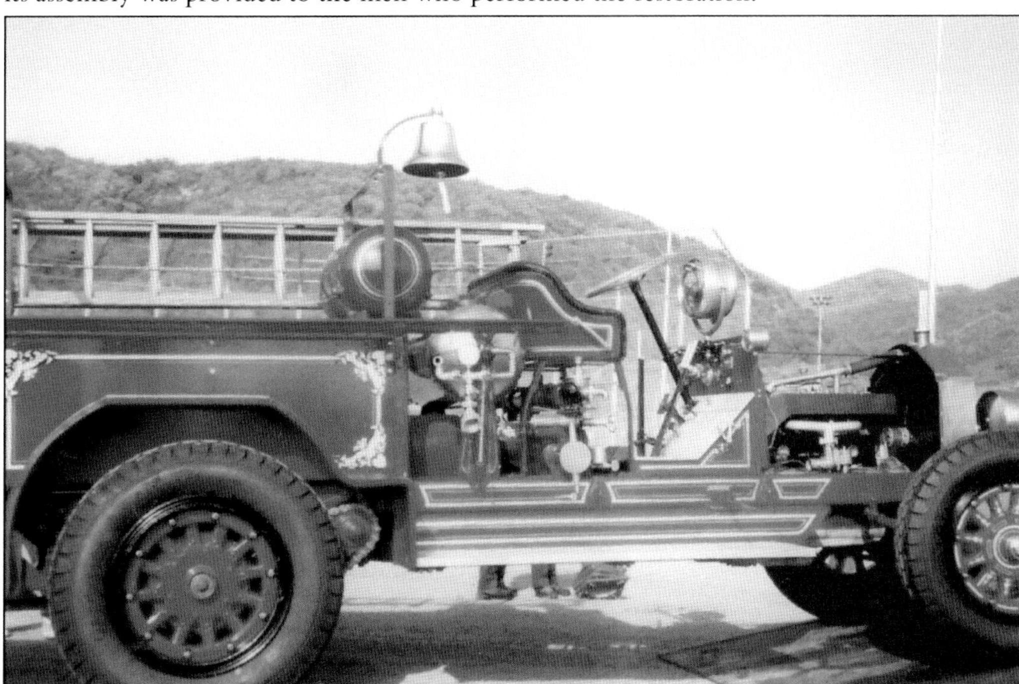

## A SOUVENIR LETTER FROM ELSINORE, CAL.

THE SCENIC

Health Resort of Southern California located midway between Los Angeles and San Diego on the Mission Inland Route. Broad Concrete Highways lead into this famous

HEALTH

Retreat, where the hot spring waters have relieved thousands who now advertise its wonderful curative qualities. Not only the Baths, but the Lake and Mountains make it the most beautiful and restful

RESORT

that can be found anywhere. Fishing and Hunting with a swim or a sail on the Lake add to the pleasure of the health seeker.

EVERY ONE KNOWS

that the most beautiful home sites in the state are situated in Elsinore Valley over-looking its beautiful lake and enjoying a delightful view of Southern California's most famous snow capped Mountains.

ELSINORE VALLEY

contains a large area of fertile soil, large portions of which are lately being put under irrigation offering splendid opportunities to home seekers at attractive prices.

WHERE EVERYTHING GROWS

From Alfalfa grown for dairy purposes or seed, to the finest quality of Navel Oranges, Lemons and Grape Fruit. Every kind of Orchard may be found here, such as Olives, Peaches, Apricots, Walnuts, Almonds and also every variety of garden truck, including both summer and winter vegetables, conditions being especially favorable for winter truck farming. Market facilities for these products were increased lately by the building of a $50,000.00 Cannery and the establishment of excellent motor truck service to larger markets.

*Communications sent to the Chamber of Commerce, Elsinore, Calif. will receive prompt attention.*

This interesting souvenir letter was written by the chamber of commerce in Elsinore. The stated facts agree with what has been recorded by local residents regarding their successes with crops planted and the return received when the products were sold at market. This was probably written in the early 1950s.

# *Three*

# Aimee Semple McPherson

Aimee Elizabeth Kennedy was born on October 9, 1890, on a small farm near Ingersoll, Ontario, Canada. Her mother, a Salvation Army soldier, consecrated her to God before she was born. Despite her mother's actions, she was said to have been a scamp in school.

Aimee married Robert Semple in 1907, and the two served as missionaries to China, where Robert was stricken with fever and died. Aimee's first child, Roberta Star Semple, was born in Hong Kong in 1909, soon after her husband's death. Her marriage to Harold McPherson lasted until 1921, when the couple was divorced. Of this union, a son, Rolf, was born.

The most famous evangelist of her day, Aimee came to California in 1917, settled in Los Angeles in 1922, founded the International Church of the Foursquare Gospel, and built Angelus Temple, which was of Hollywood dimensions, in downtown Los Angeles. It opened officially on January 1, 1923, and is still in use today.

Aimee then wed Dave Hutton on September 13, 1931, but the union was short lived. Immediately a woman named Hazel St. Pierre sued him for breach of promise to marry; she wanted $2,000. Hutton lost the case, costing him $5,000. After an accidental fall, Aimee vacationed in Europe alone. She took her time, and the separation became permanent.

Some speculate Aimee committed suicide in a San Francisco hotel on September 27, 1944. Further research shows that she was in San Francisco and was very excited about the sermon she was to deliver the next day. After taking a new medication, she died before a doctor could reach her. Like many deaths, no one can say with true certainty what really happened.

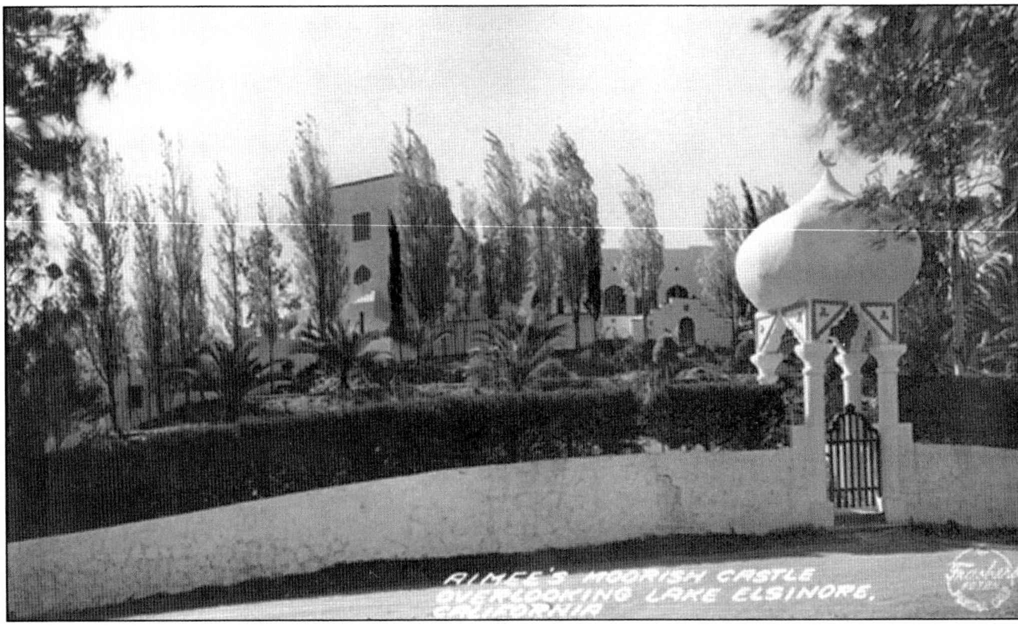


Aimee Semple McPherson's home in Lake Elsinore is pictured in these two views. Aimee traveled the world; however, these travels were not well-known. She took numerous trips to the Holy Land, as reflected in the turrets and other Moorish architecture of her home. These rare photographs show the extensive terracing and landscaping down the hill on the property. The castle, built at a cost of $229,000, featured 14 rooms with real gold and imported marble from Europe in a decor of conspicuous consumption. The closets in the bedrooms were very small for one reason: this was a "vacation home," and guests were not expected to bring many clothes with them. (Below, CyG.)

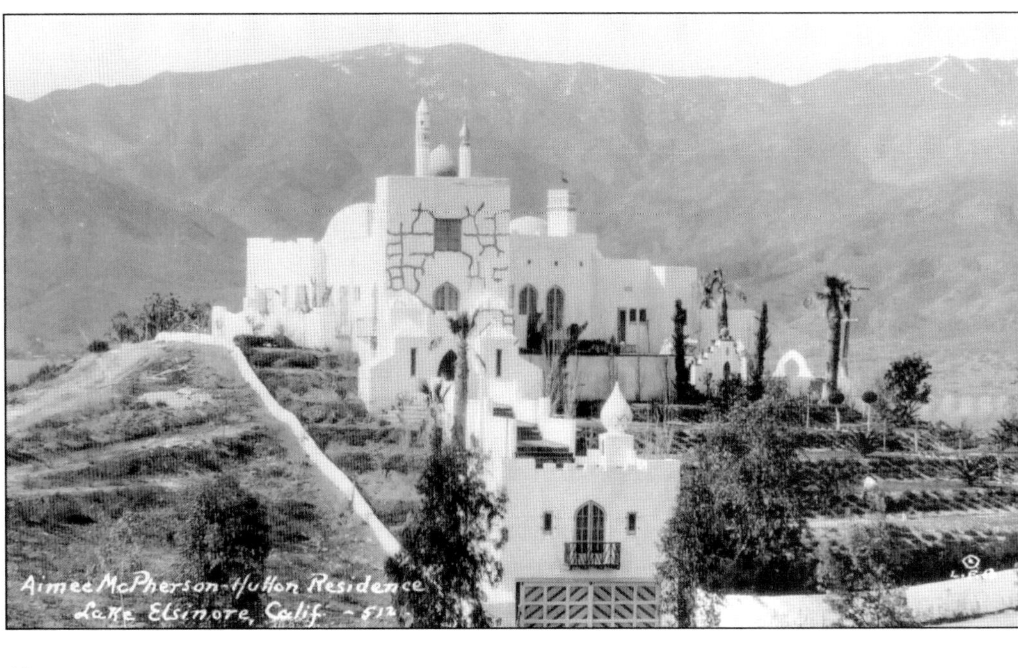

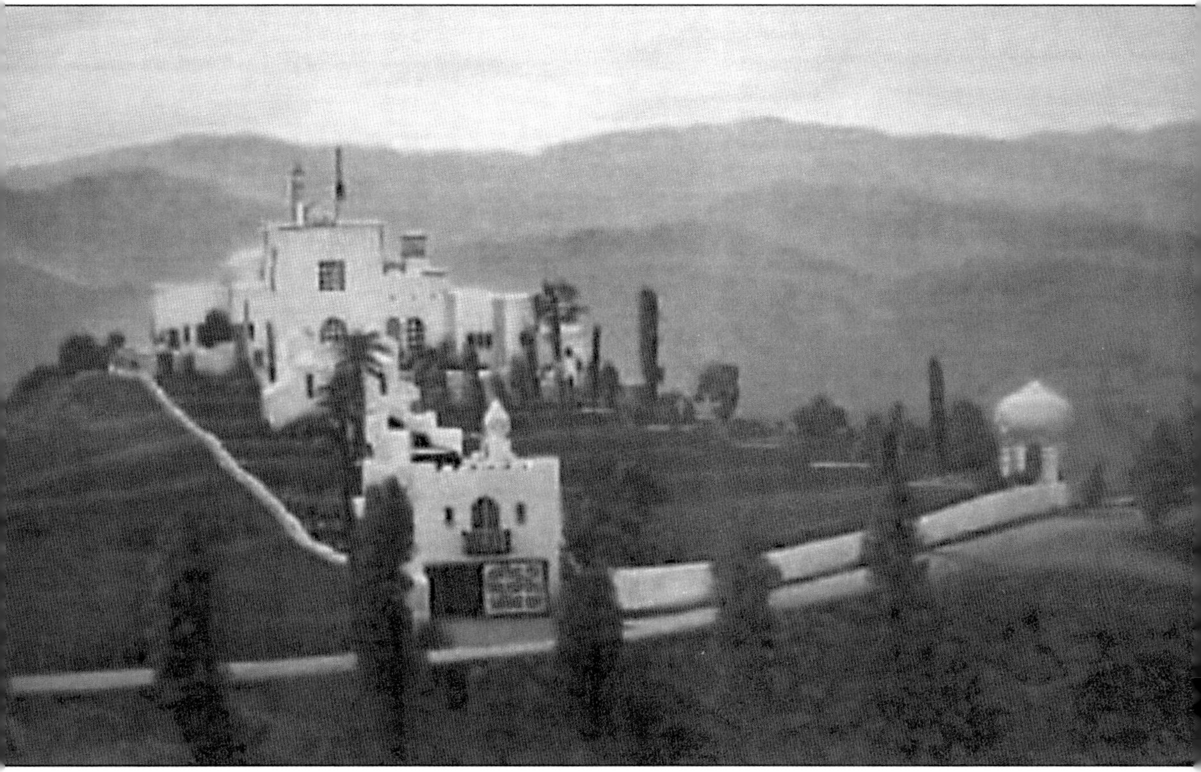

The hilltop home has a 360-degree view of the Lake Elsinore Valley. To the north are the San Jacinto and San Gorgonio Mountains; to the south, the lake and its many activities; and in the background, the Elsinore Mountains. In the wintertime, one can occasionally see snow glistening on the higher levels of the Elsinore Mountains. On a clear day, one can even watch the cars drive over the Ortega Highway, the connection between Lake Elsinore and Orange County cities. Not shown in this postcard view is the swimming pool outside the salon.

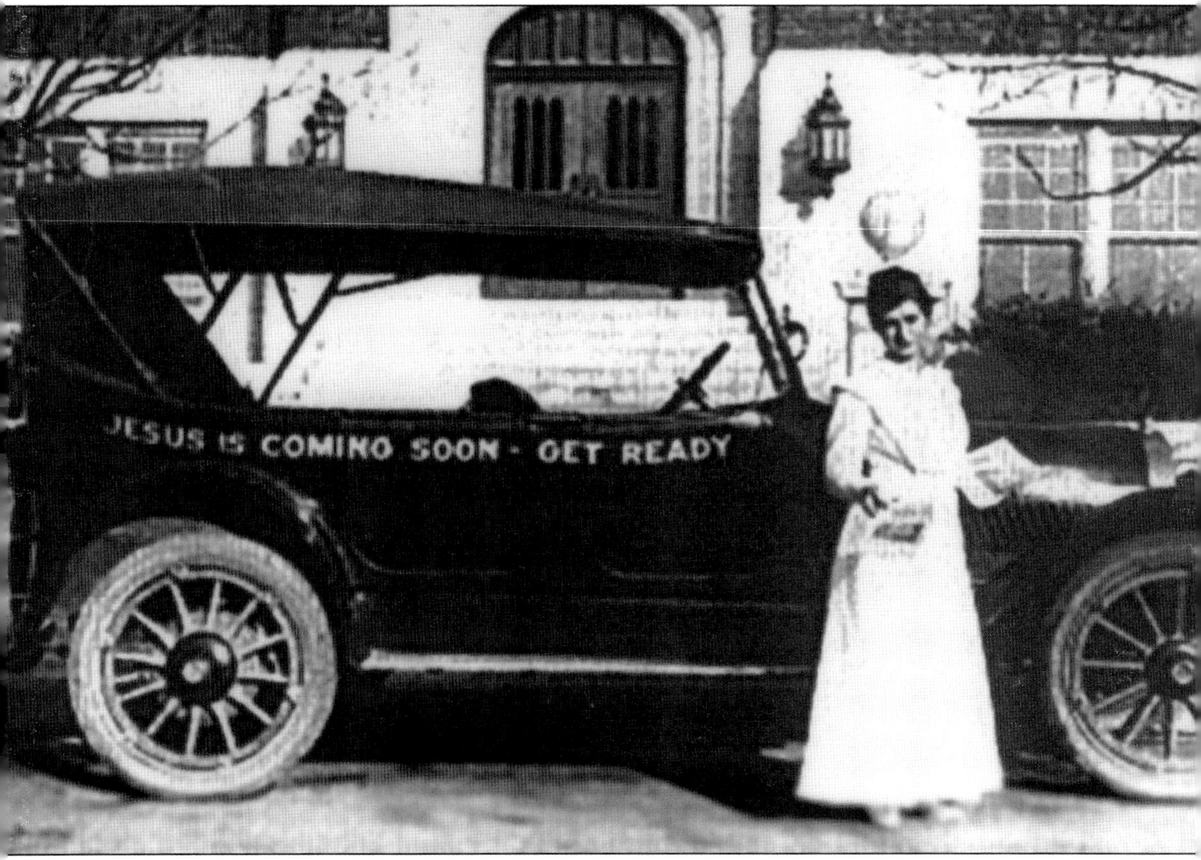


Aimee Semple McPherson was very flamboyant during her evangelistic services. Sometimes she was sponsored by an organization in a specific city, and other times she felt "called" to go to certain locales to preach the gospel and heal the sick. Aimee and her mother, along with her children, traveled from coast to coast without the aid of a man. If a tire became flat, the women fixed it. Aimee's Sunday evening services at the Angelus Temple in Los Angeles often attracted 5,000 attendees. Charlie Chaplin advised her on the sets, and Anthony Quinn played saxophone in the pit.

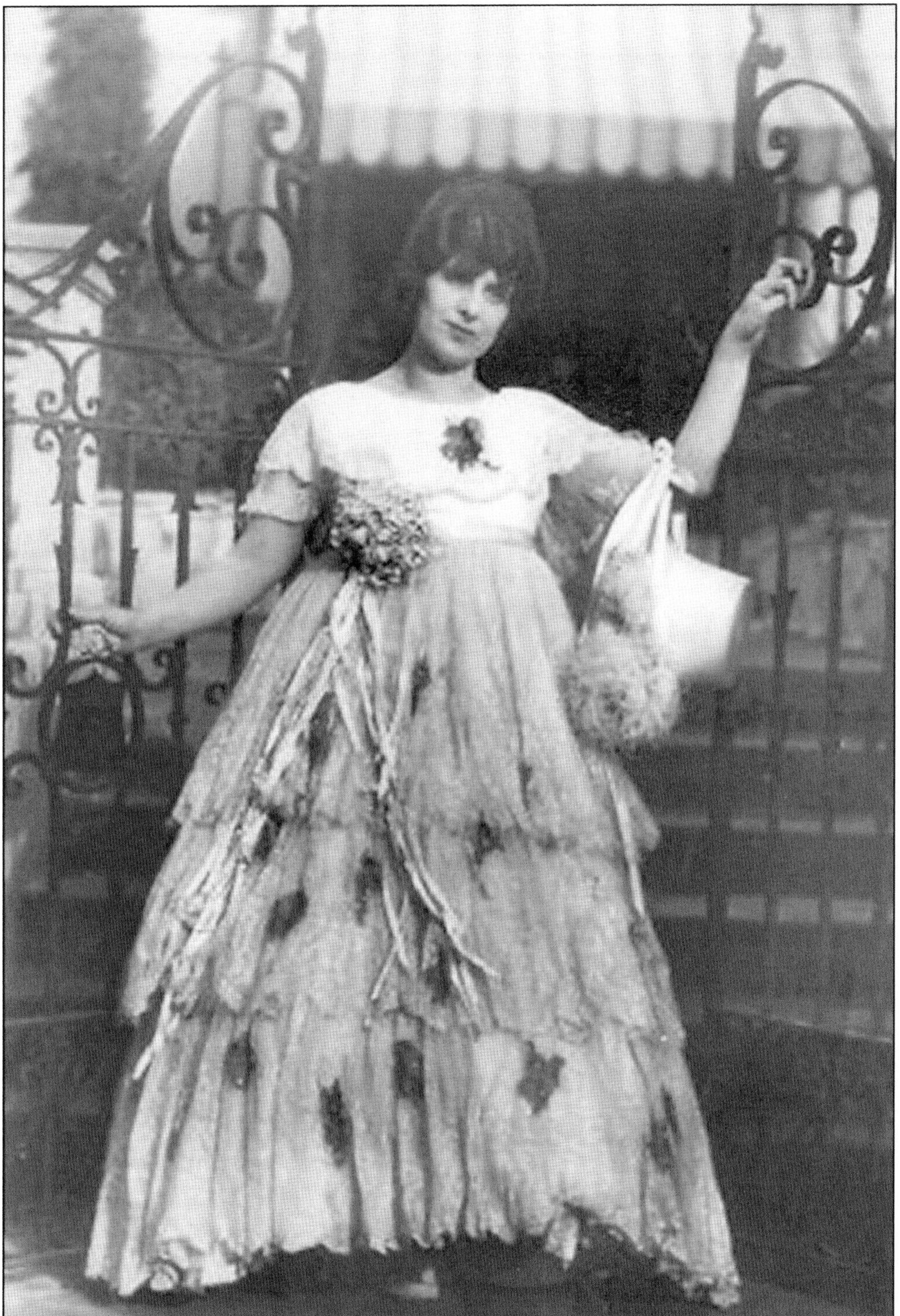

On July 3, 1928, Aimee conducted services in the hall at the now-defunct Brenneke Park. More than 500 people were seated in the hall, and 500 more stood inside and outside the building. The developers of Country Club Heights gave her five city lots and built her a palatial home. Their desire was to attract buyers to their project. In October 1928, construction began on the palatial home, dubbed "Aimee's Castle" by local residents. In the coming months she visited Elsinore many times to note the progress. Aimee is pictured here outside the home.

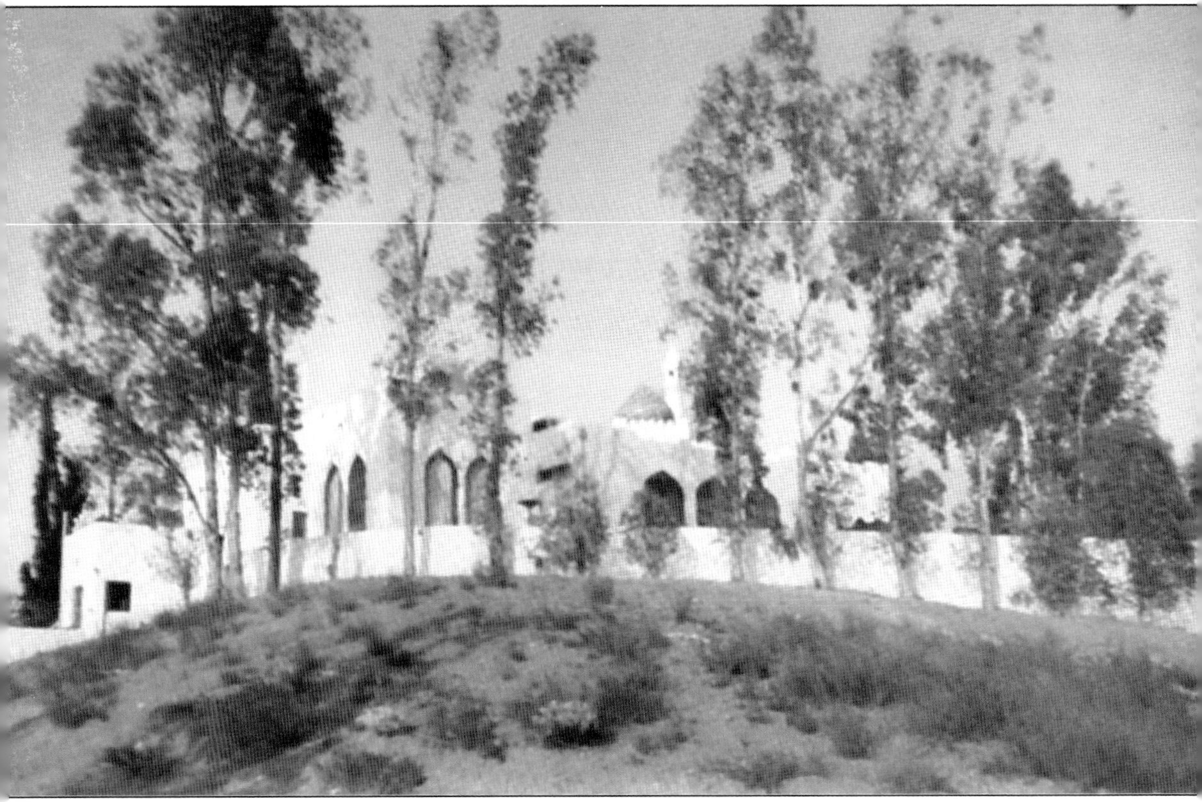

Pictured is a postcard of evangelist Aimee Semple McPherson's former home in Elsinore, California. The date of the card is approximately 10 years ago, during which time her home was owned and occupied by Violet McFarland, a world traveler and journalist. Today the home is owned by the International Church of the Foursquare Gospel, and it has been completely restored to the way it looked when Aimee lived there. The home will be a retreat for their pastors and a private facility.

# *Four*

# Schools and More

Education was important to the three town founders, all college graduates themselves. On July 1, 1884, a petition was granted by the San Diego supervisors for the Elsinore School District. Elsinore Elementary, originally called Elsinore Grammar, was the first school opened, in 1884. Its curriculum served students in the first through eighth grades. When the time arrived to begin a high school in the 1890s, a petition was sent by 100 leading citizens to Sacramento requesting the establishment of just such an institution. California legislature decreed that a high school union could consist of Elsinore, Lucerne, Lake, and Grand Schools' student bodies.

In 1988, a unification vote was approved to combine the Elsinore Elementary District (kindergarten to eighth grade) and the Elsinore Union High School District into one with a single governance body.

In 1991, the new Temescal Canyon High School opened to serve students from the valley, including those from the recently formed city of Canyon Lake. The newly opened state-of-the-art Lakeside High on the northwest side of the lake began serving students in September 2005 and will have its first graduating class in the 2008 centennial year. At the start of the 21st century, each comprehensive high school was graduating more than 500 yearly.

Today the Lake Elsinore Unified School District has one continuation and three comprehensive high schools. Lakeside, the newest, opened in September 2005, and will have its first graduating class in June 2008. Elsinore and Temescal Canyon were both named Distinguished High Schools for 2006–2007 and are the only two in the state to be in the same district. Ortega Continuation is an alternative school, the first ever constructed in the state to serve students who cannot function in regular classroom settings. Additionally, the district includes 5 middle schools and 15 elementary schools.

In 2007, these educational institutions, along with Tri-Valley Community Day, Gordon Kiefer Independent, and home-schooling programs, served close to 22,065 students aged 5 to 18. The school district employs more than 3,000 adults, who are involved in operations ranging from teaching to building and maintenance.

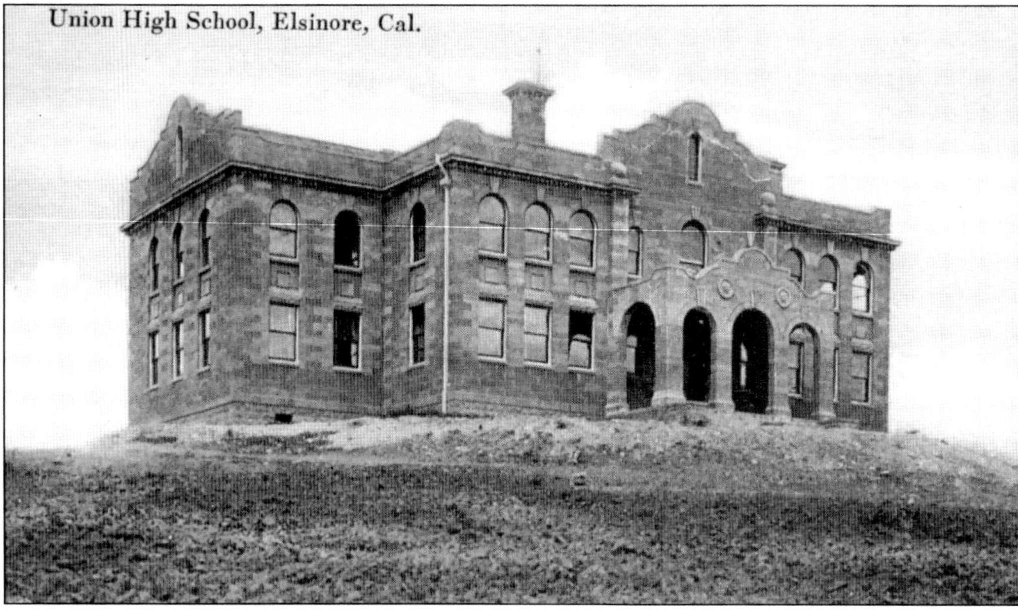


The Elsinore Union High School District (not to be confused with the elementary schools) was created by an act of the California legislature in 1891. In September of that year, the first group of 17 students met in the second-story rooms of Elsinore Grammar School, located on Sumner, Heald, and Lindsay Streets. The group pledged that they would always have 10 students daily to keep the high school open. Those students who kept the pledge were dubbed "the Immortal Ten." They selected the original school motto, *Semper paratus* ("Always ready") and gained perfect attendance.

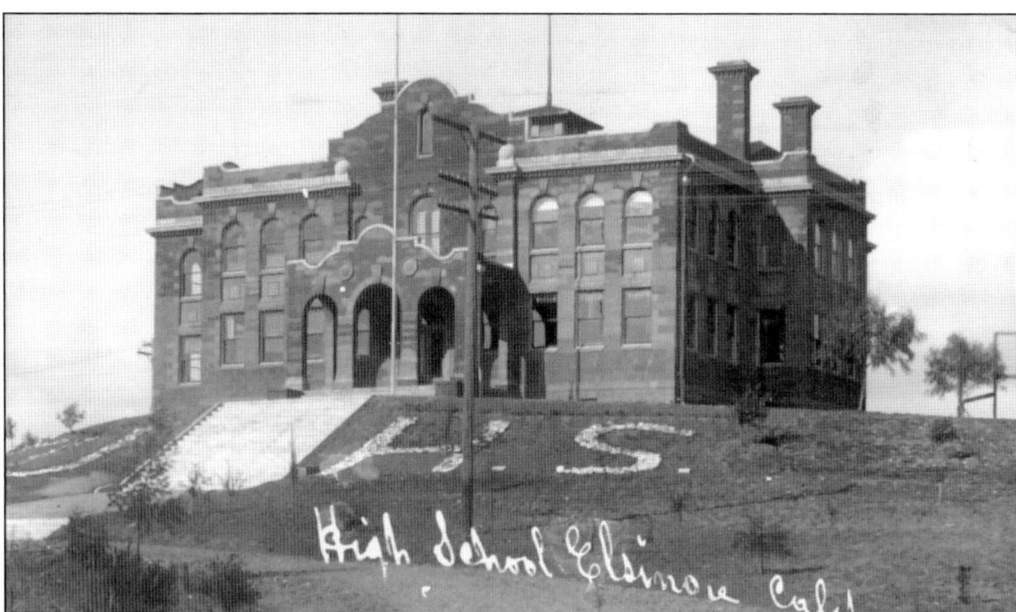

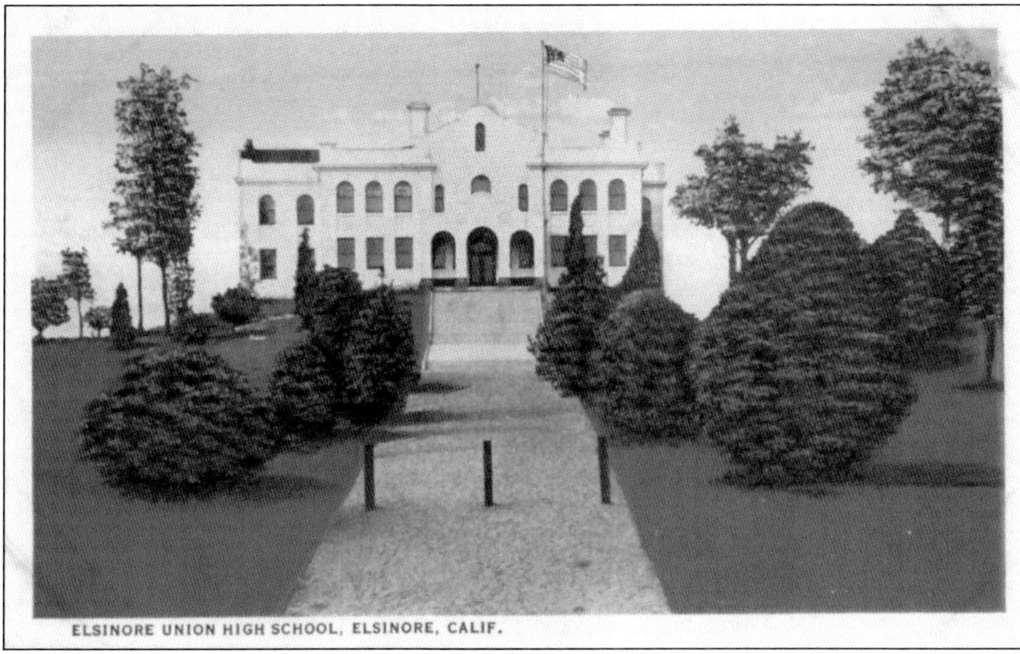


Elsinore High School was started in 1891 with classes held at the Elsinore Grammar School. Classes were moved to the second floor of the Consolidated Bank building in 1898 for two years before returning to Elsinore Grammar. In 1907, the high school moved to the Grand Army of the Republic Building at Main and Franklin. The first building specifically serving the high school was constructed in 1911 on West Graham Avenue. Students from Temecula, Murrieta, and Wildomar, a few from Meadowbrook, and more from the entire valley came to Elsinore to attend high school. In 1968, a new structure was built in Secdo Hills on Canyon Drive. (Above, EP; below, AC.)

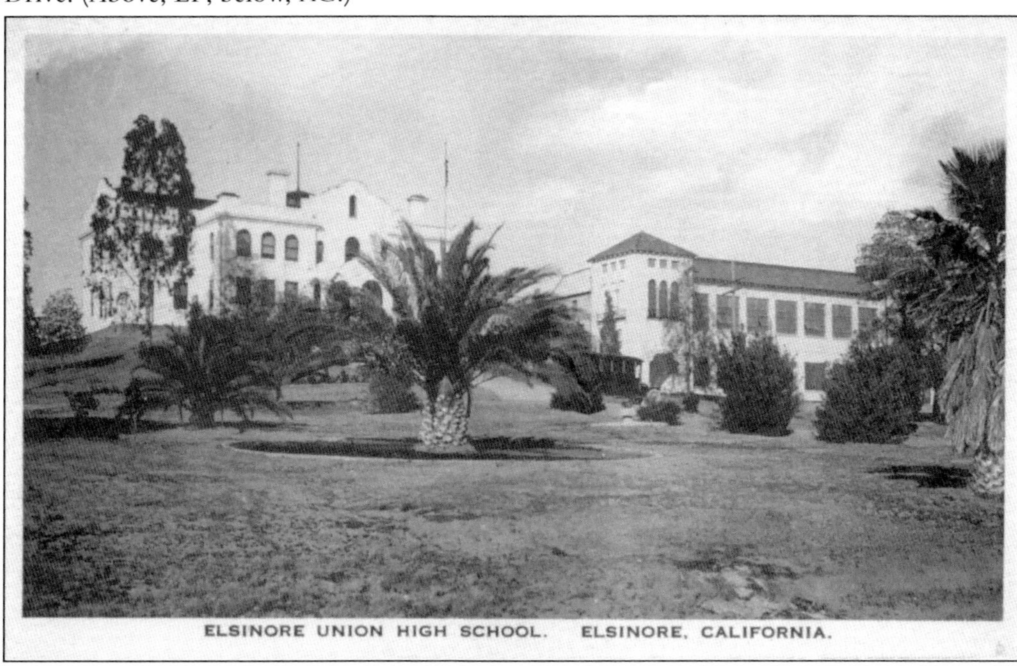

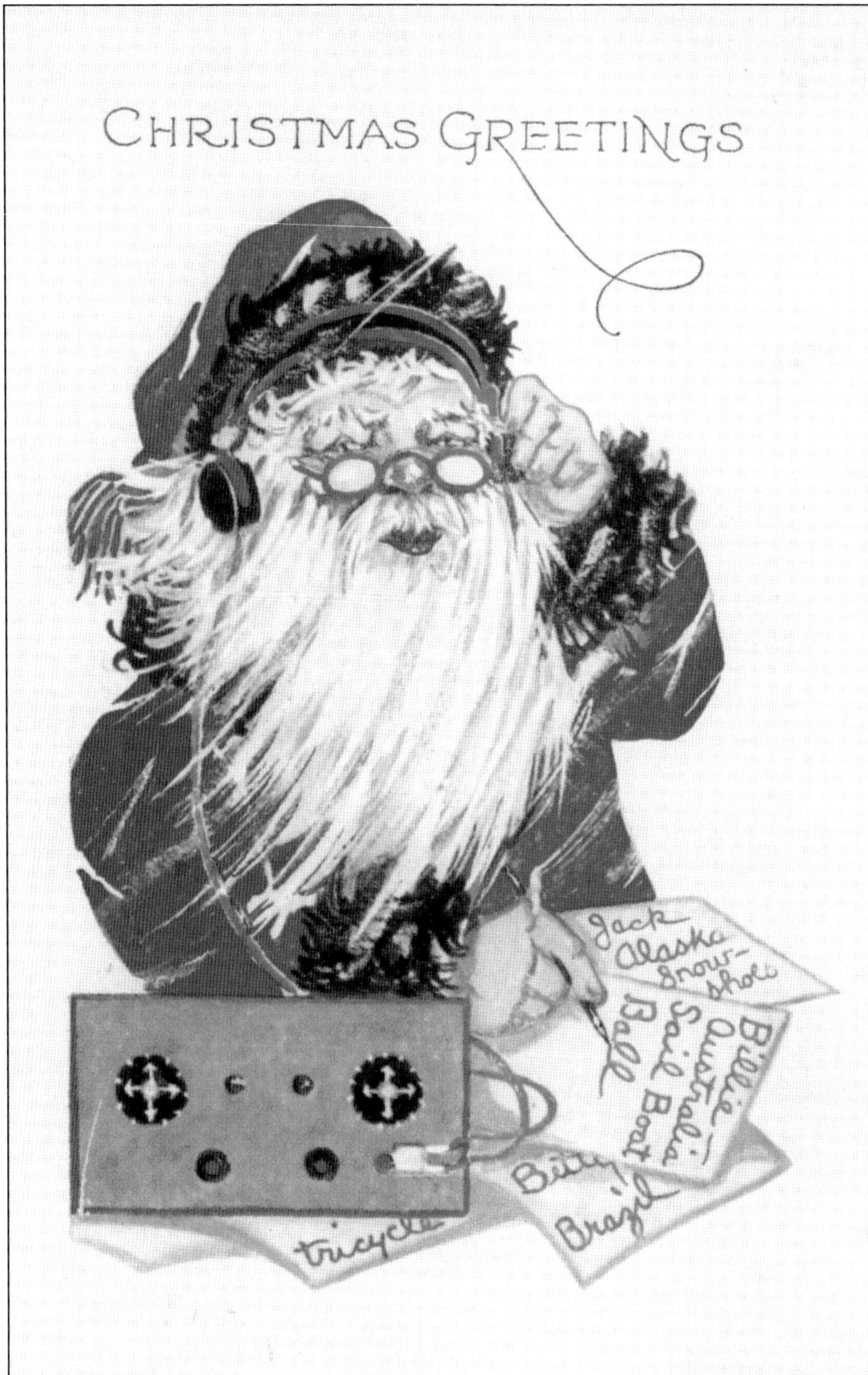


This 1925 Christmas card was sent to Maxine LaBrier, an active student and a graduate of Elsinore High School. All of her memorabilia has been donated to the Lake Elsinore Historical Society. She saved her class programs, photographs of her friends, and items from her graduating class. (AC.)

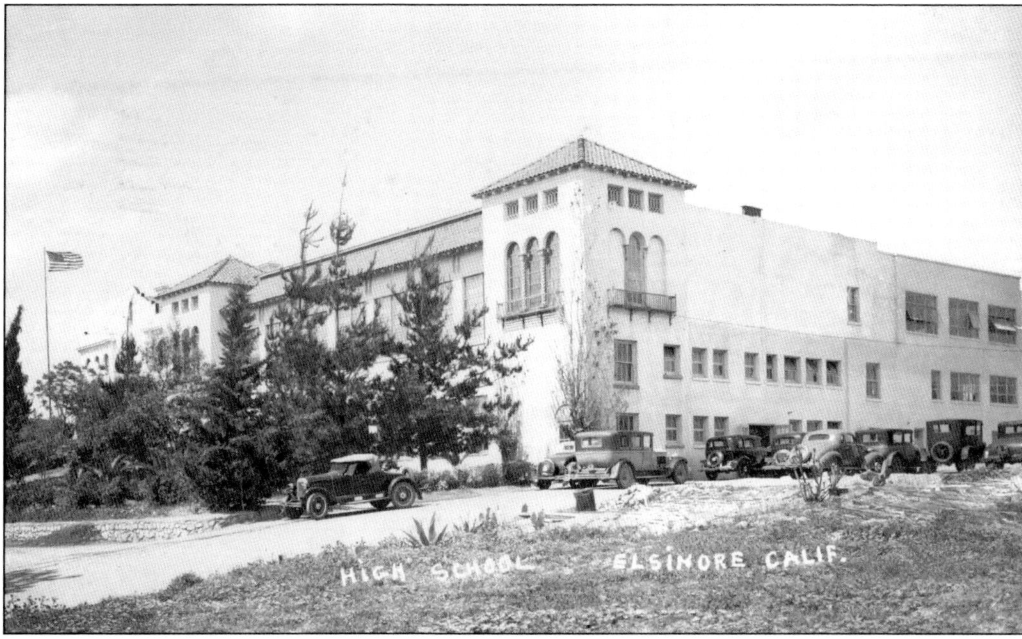


John N. Sumners served as the high school's first principal. By 1895, twenty students were attending, and those who did not reside within "union boundaries" paid $12 tuition. The first graduation ceremony took place in June 1894 with five graduates. The second graduation occurred on June 4, 1897, in the Consolidated Bank hall, where classes were held at that time. In June 1909, bonds were approved to build an actual school site at an initial cost of $12,000; work began in 1910. The structure, a two-story Mission-style building, opened its doors in September 1911 to 35 students. In 1968, the school was relocated to Sedco Hills, where it was accessible to students from Murrieta and Temecula, as well as those from Elsinore, Alberhill, Meadowbrook, the Grove, and Wildomar. (Both AC/ JC.)

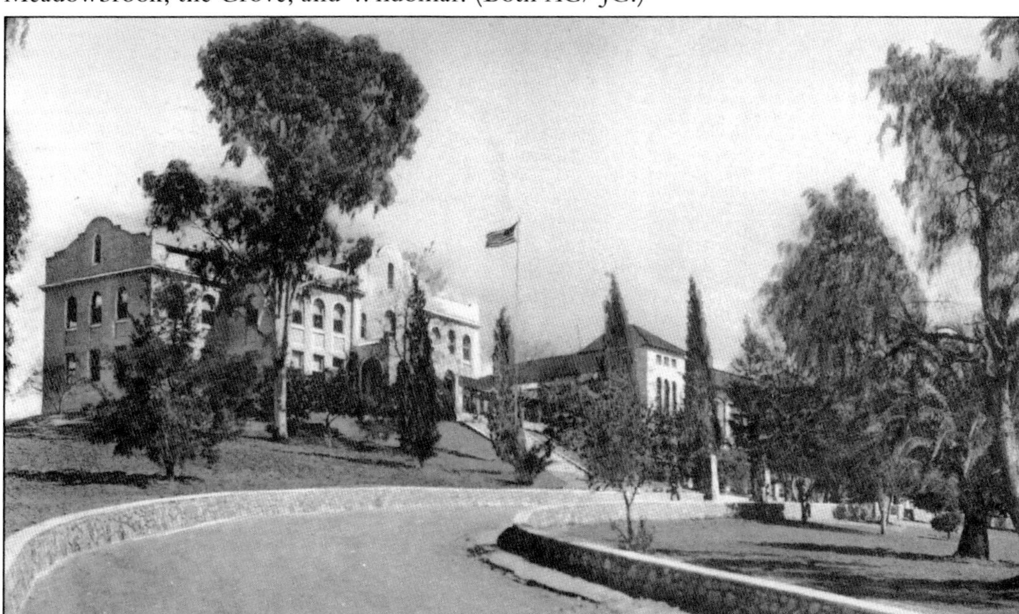

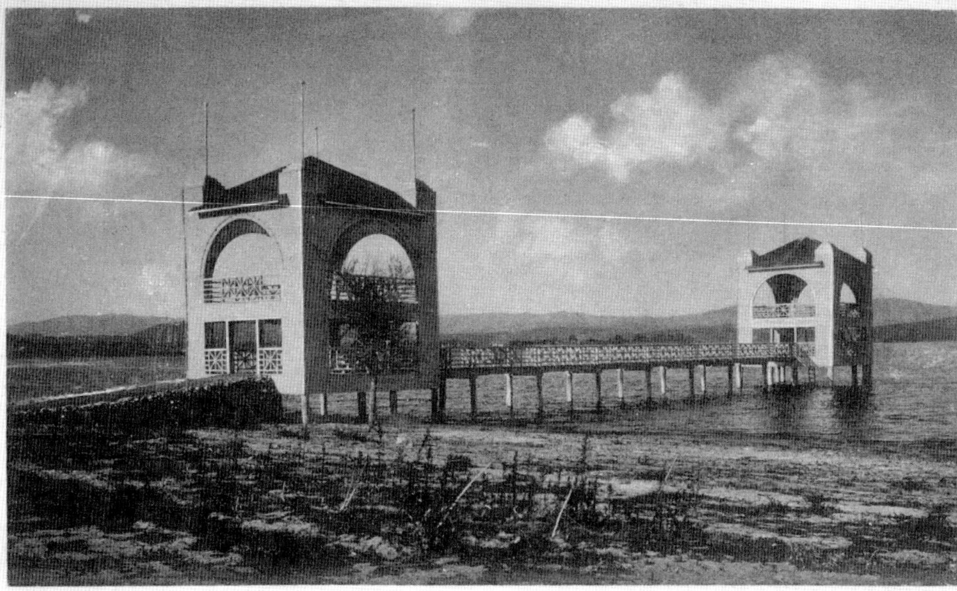

Pier, Southern California Athletic and Country Club

This photograph provides a rare view of the Southern California Athletic and Country Club pier, which was built at the country club. By 1925, the Los Angeles financiers sponsoring the construction of the country club had encountered monetary difficulties, and the newly completed clubhouse would never be used for its original purpose.

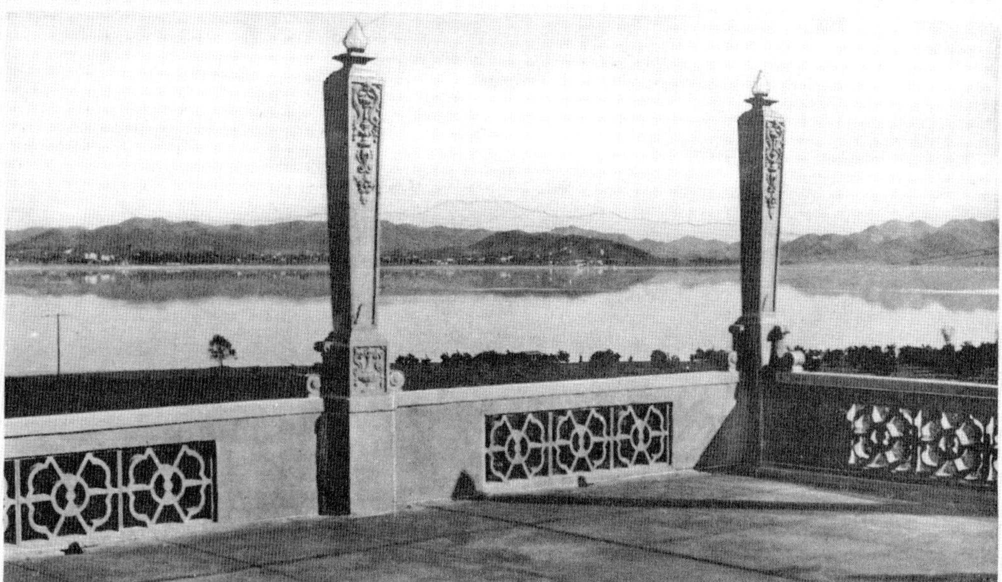

BEAUTIFUL LAKE ELSINORE ELSINORE, CALIFORNIA

Taken from the swimming pool of the Elsinore Naval and Military Academy on Grand Avenue, this view looks over Lake Elsinore and toward Country Club Heights, above Lakeshore Drive. The San Gorgonio Mountains appear in the distance. The property beyond the pool is part of the academy. (AC.)

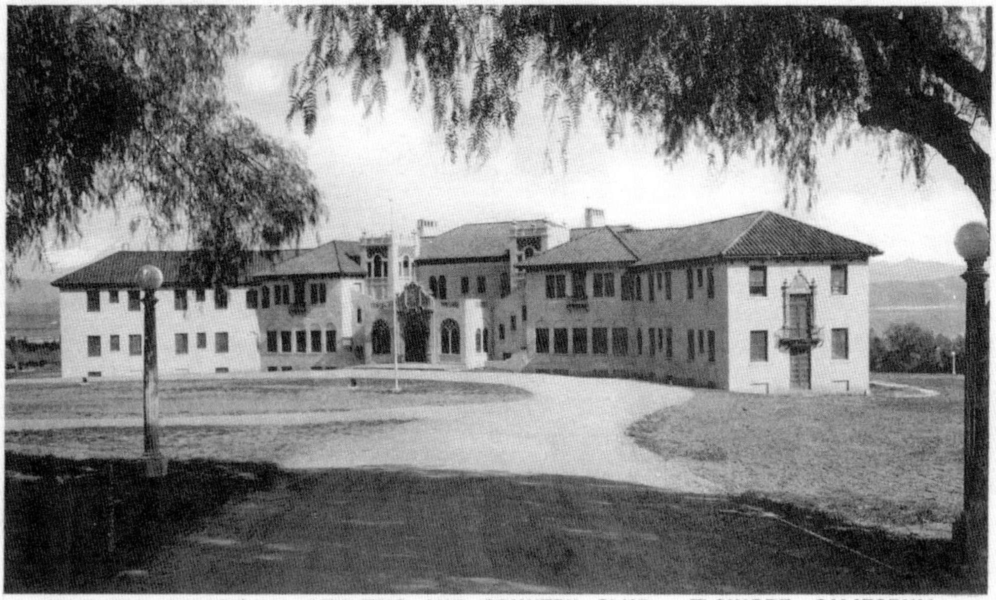

SOUTHERN CALIFORNIA ATHLETIC AND COUNTRY CLUB. ELSINORE, CALIFORNIA.

The headline of the *Press* on January 5, 1923, was "The Greatest Country Club in America!," referring to the Mount Elsinore Country Club. Originally, it was to have 300 sleeping rooms; however, the number was reduced to 40 with the finest appointments money could buy. After a name change to the Southern California Athletic and Country Club, construction began on the project, which was underwritten by a group of Los Angeles financiers. Along with the country club, a golf course was constructed near Grand Avenue and Corydon Street. The golf course did open, but it is uncertain for how long. (Both AC.)

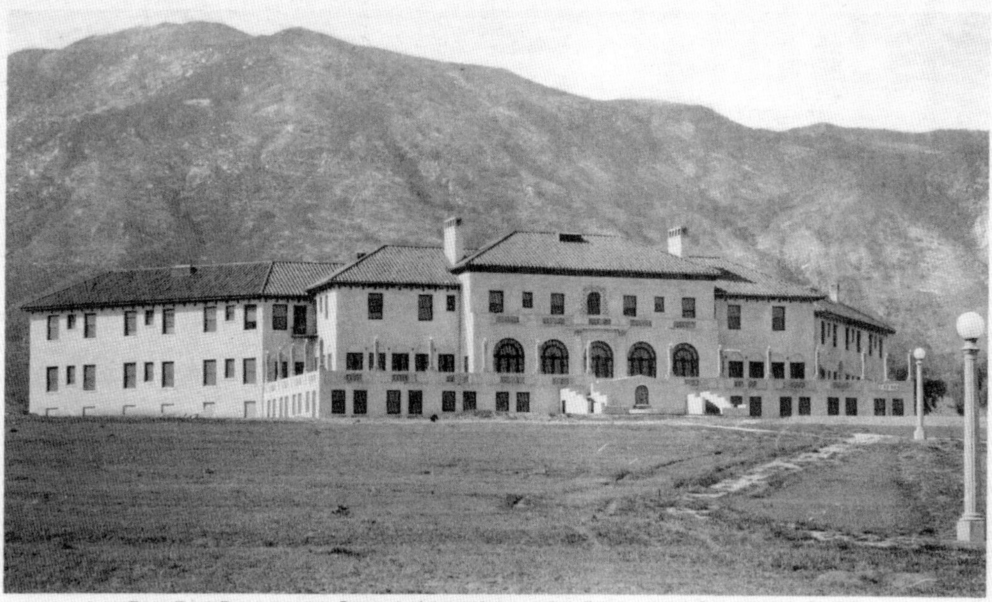

LAKESIDE VIEW. SOUTHERN CALIFORNIA ATHLETIC AND COUNTRY CLUB. ELSINORE, CALIFORNIA.

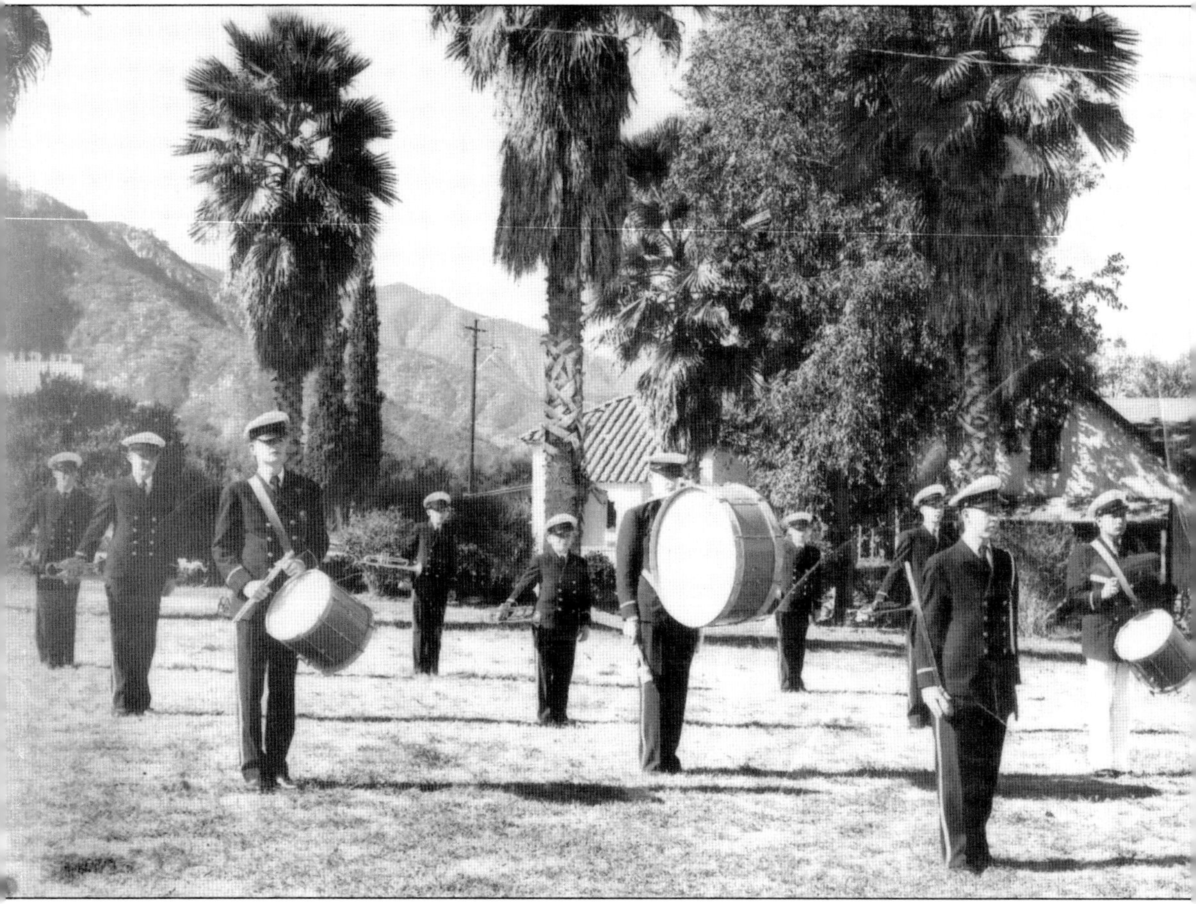

The Elsinore Naval and Military Academy Band practices on the lawn in this *c.* 1950 view with the Elsinore Mountains in the background. The group included bandleader Joe Henry Vaught, snare drummer P. Somerset, and trumpeters John E. Gurley Jr., Billy C. Ambrose, Ed Bitler, and Dave Slater. This photograph was taken by the Russell Gates Studio.

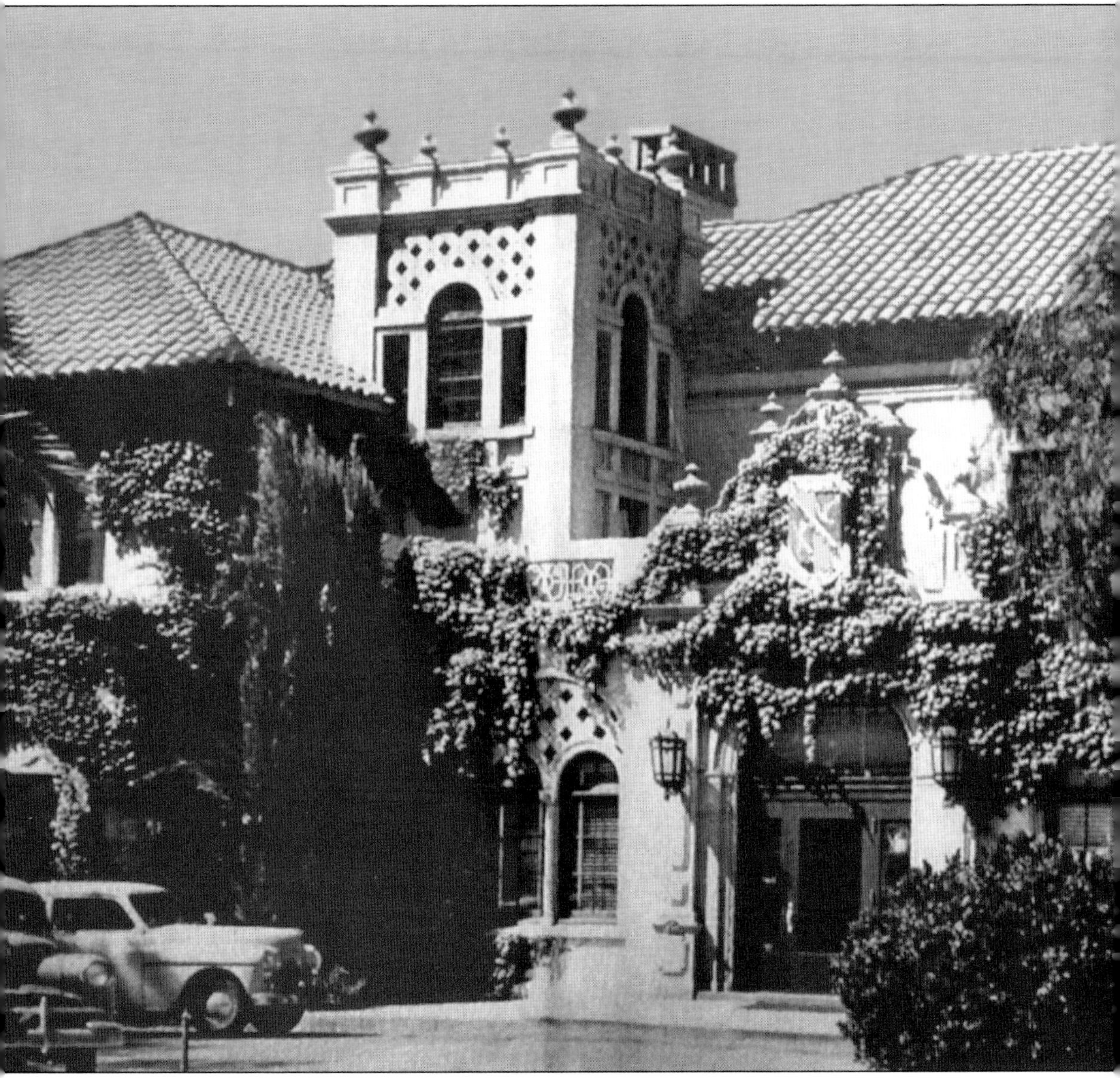

In 1933, the Southern California Athletic and Country Club clubhouse was purchased by Maj. Glen Conklin and Capt. P. A. Jones, who had brought a group of cadets from the Pacific Military Academy in Los Angeles for the summer session. In July of that year, the Elsinore Naval and Military School was established and settled in the clubhouse. Conklin operated the school for boys, which served grades 1 through 12, for 43 years until his death in 1976. Afterward, the school assumed the name G. R. Conklin Academy and moved to Redondo Beach. The Conklin Corporation sold the property to the Garrett Group in May 2004.

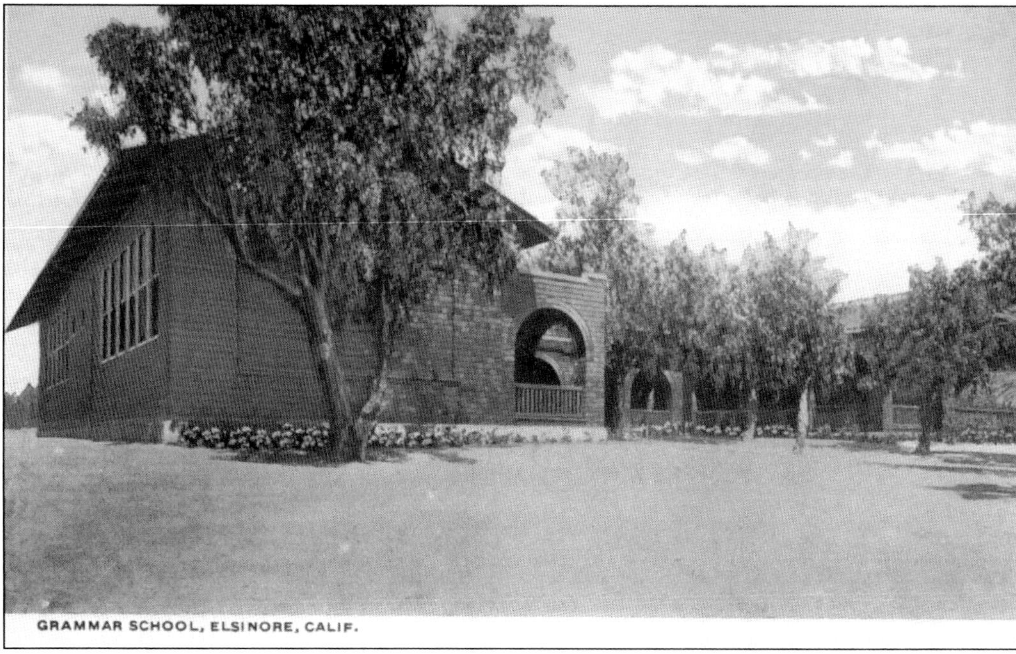


The Elsinore Grammar School started in November 1884 on Langstaff Street. While the school has always been at this location, two or three different facilities have occupied the Elsinore Elementary property. The brick building pictured here was condemned, left unused after 1962, and eventually torn down. The classrooms had been built in the 1940s and 1950s. A new office building was constructed in a different location on the property facing Sumner Street in 1964. Four generations of the Merrifield family have attended this school, beginning with Leslie and continuing with Leslie's son John, John's daughter Lori Snider, and Lori's children. John Merrifield also taught at the school. (Above, EP.)

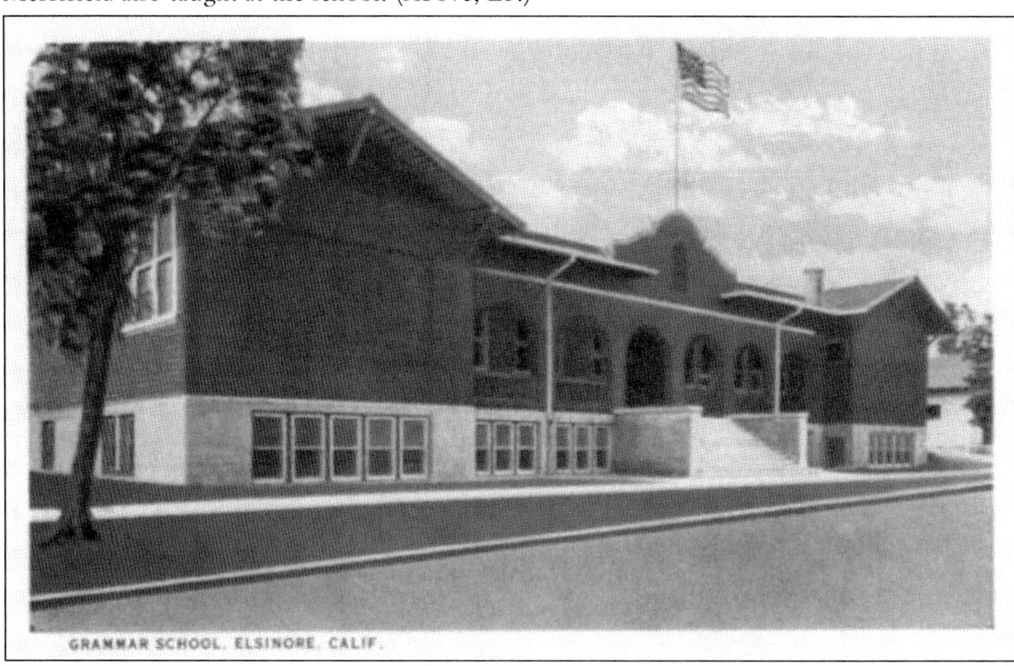

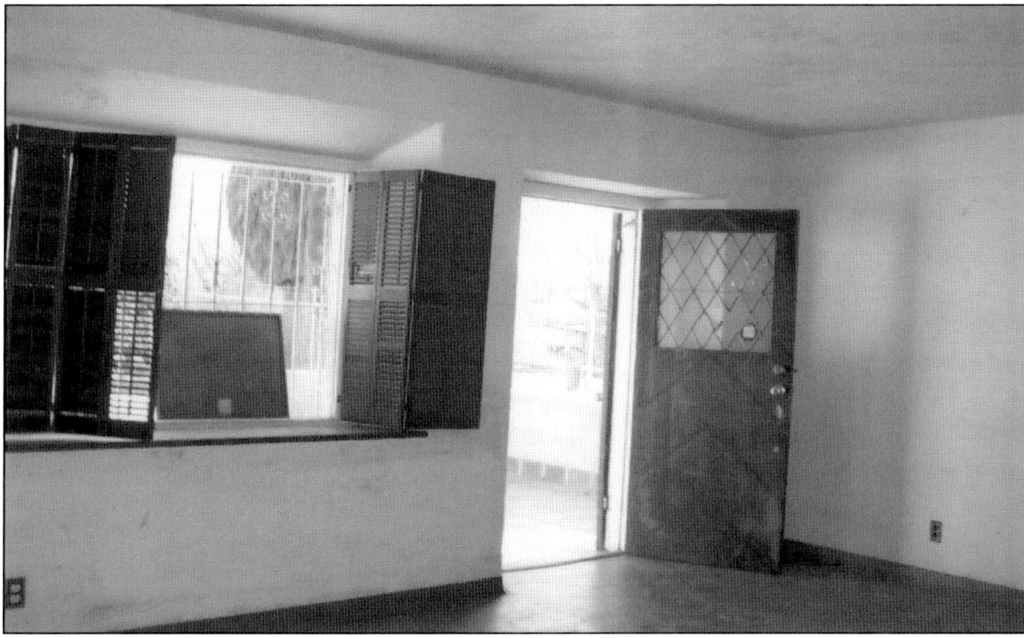

Built in 1858, the Machado Adobe is the oldest building standing in Lake Elsinore. It is located on Grand Avenue just beyond the curve where Grand joins Riverside Drive. As the years have passed, a house has been built around the adobe. In the near future, the site will be restored as a historic spot for Lake Elsinore residents.

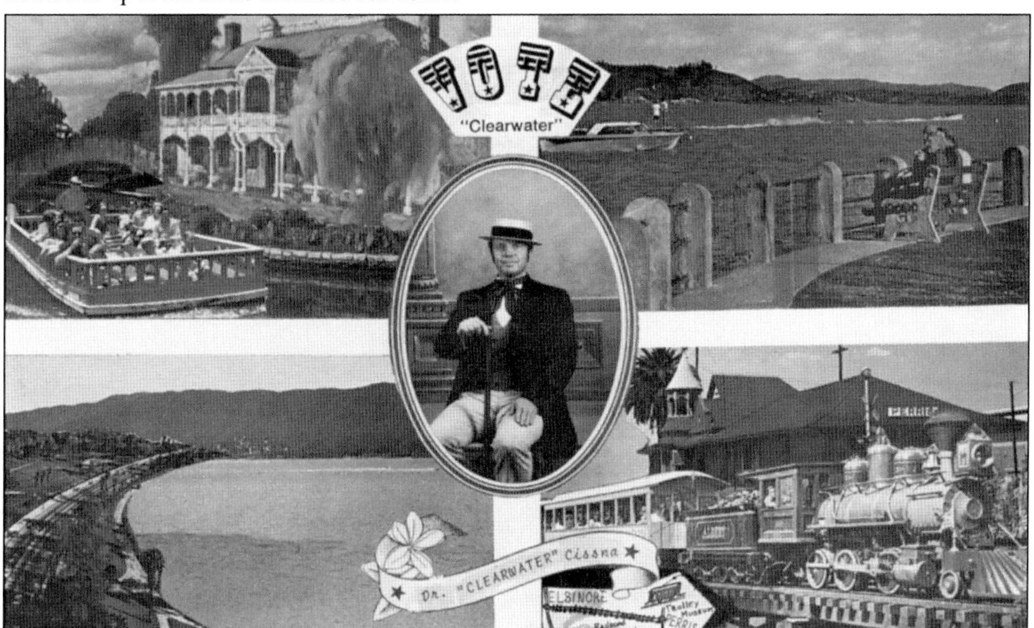


"Vote Clearwater" was a promotional campaign postcard by Bob Cissna. The advertisement depicts, clockwise, the *Elsinore Dream* launch on Grand Canal by the visitors' center; the lake promenade passing palatial homes, resorts, and parks; the *Clearwater Express* bound for Elsinore; and Dike's Boulevard from downtown to Lakeland. "Dr. Cissna has already been instrumental in progress toward establishing the visitors' center and $500,000 for the dike," it states.

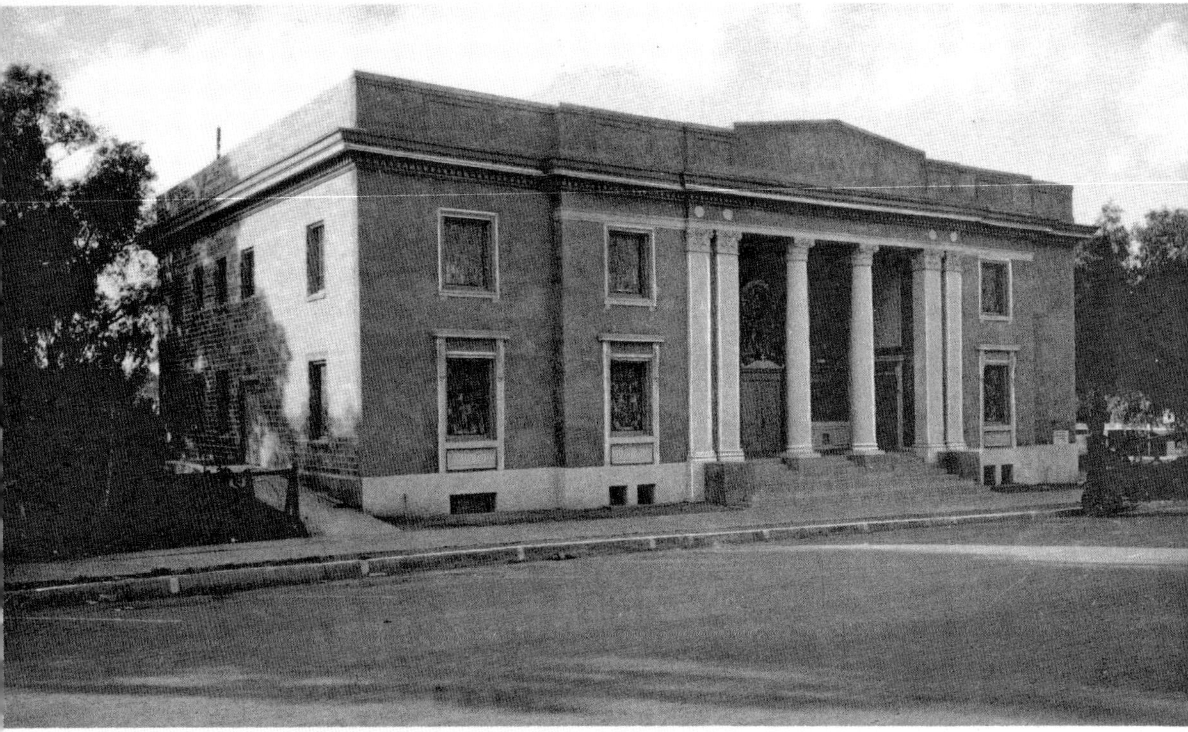

METHODIST CHURCH. ELSINORE, CALIFORNIA.

Elsinore had hardly begun its transition from rancho to village when the first church was formed. The Methodist church was established in 1883, followed by the Presbyterian church in 1886, the Catholic church in 1887, the Episcopal church in 1902, and the Christian church in 1923. The synagogue was built on Limited Street in 1943 and was destroyed by fire in March 1978. The Methodist church was established in Elsinore in a small frame building at the corner of Heald Avenue and Poe Street but was destroyed by a windstorm in September 1888. The Methodists built a new structure at the corner of Heald Avenue and Main Street. The cornerstone reads, "Methodist Episcopal Church, A.D. 1923." This facility was used until the early 1990s, when the congregation merged with another. The church attempted to sell the building but was not successful. The City of Lake Elsinore then purchased it, renovating it into the City of Lake Elsinore Cultural Center, where all of the city's official meetings are held.

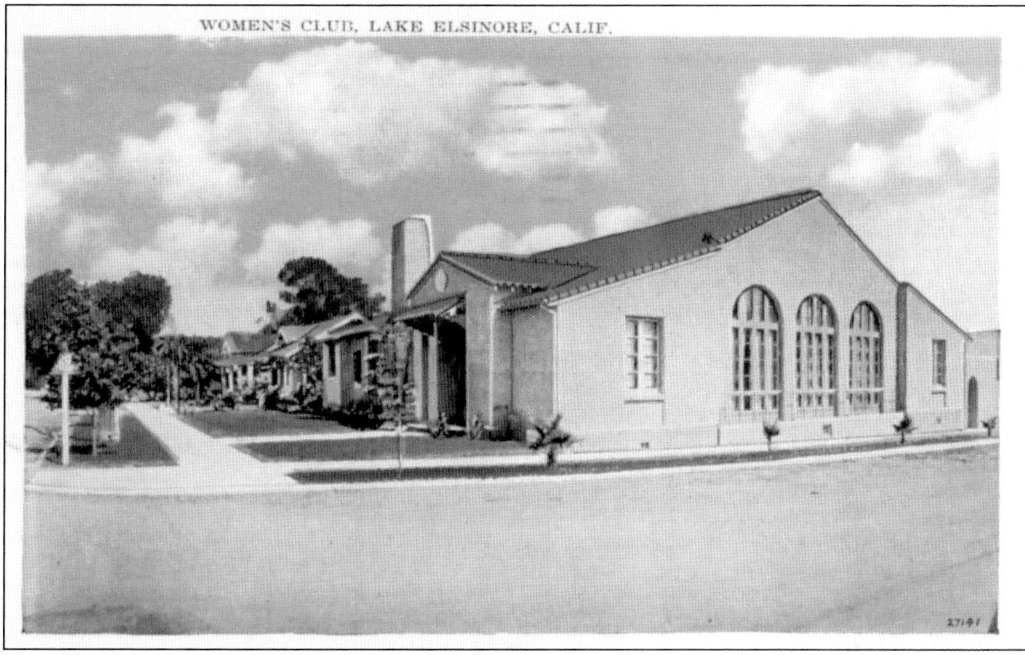


This lot, located at the corner of Graham Avenue and Lowell Street, was donated to the Elsinore Woman's Club by Isabella Norris. The cornerstone for the $15,000 clubhouse was laid on July 1925, and the building held its festive opening on December 5. Registered as a California Historic Point of Interest, the structure still accommodates group functions. (MK.)

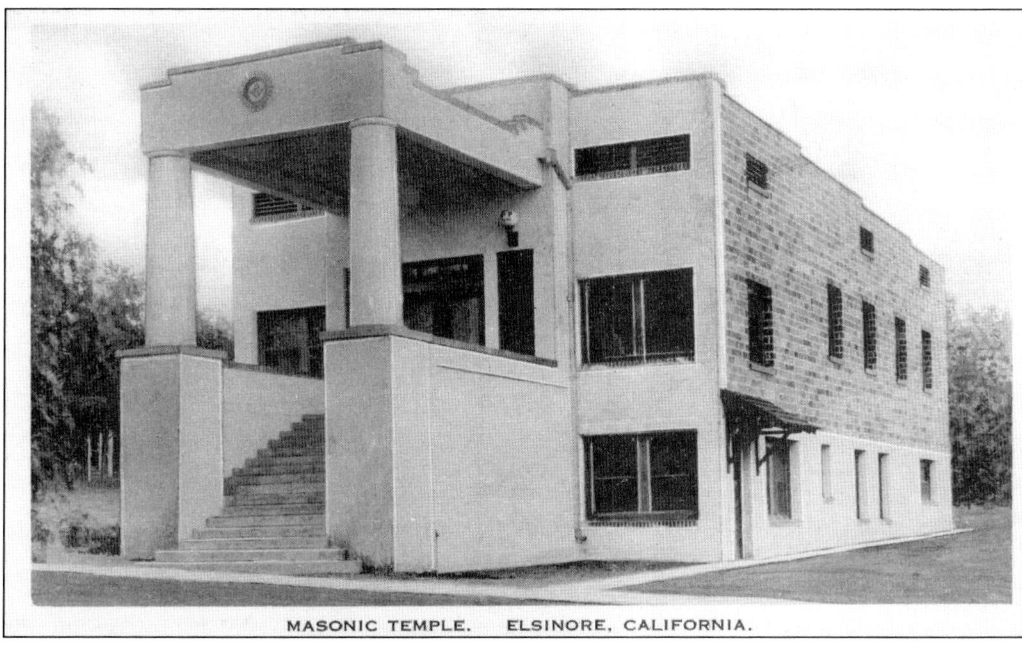


The Masonic Temple was built on East Graham Avenue at a cost of $25,000 and dedicated in May 1923. The ceiling of the ballroom is covered with gold leaf, and the tin ceiling is embossed with a pretty design. The Lake Elsinore group has since combined with the Masonic Temple in Sun City; thus, the building was put on the market in 2007. (AC.)

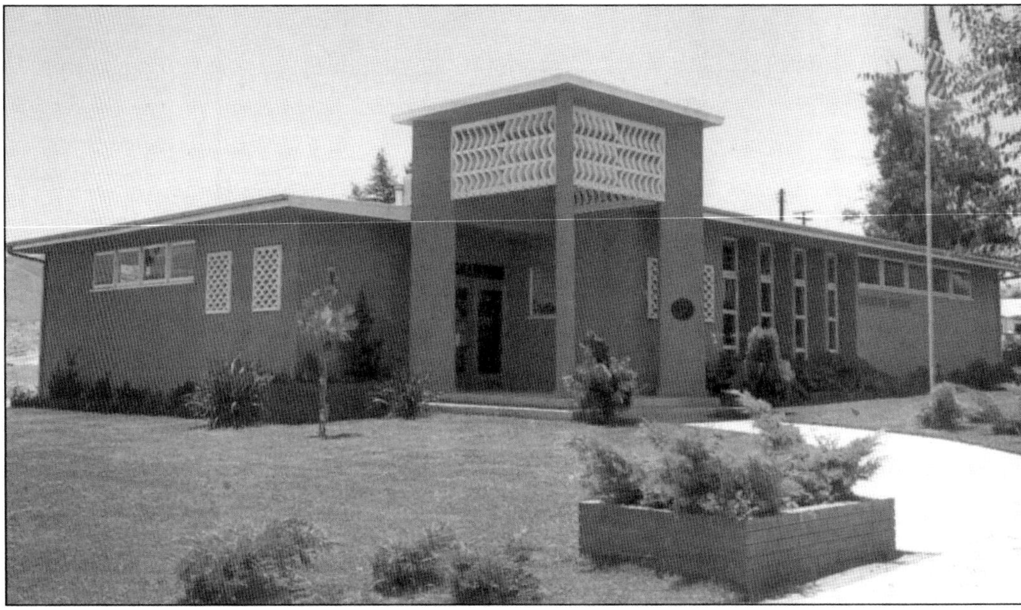

The first library was just a few shelves in Altha Merrifield's father's store on Main Street. Plans were adopted for a building on Graham Avenue in 1949, and the new Elsinore Public Library was opened to the public in February 1955. This structure served as its home until the late 1990s, when the library moved to the Laguna Savings and Loan building two blocks away on Graham Avenue. (JC.)

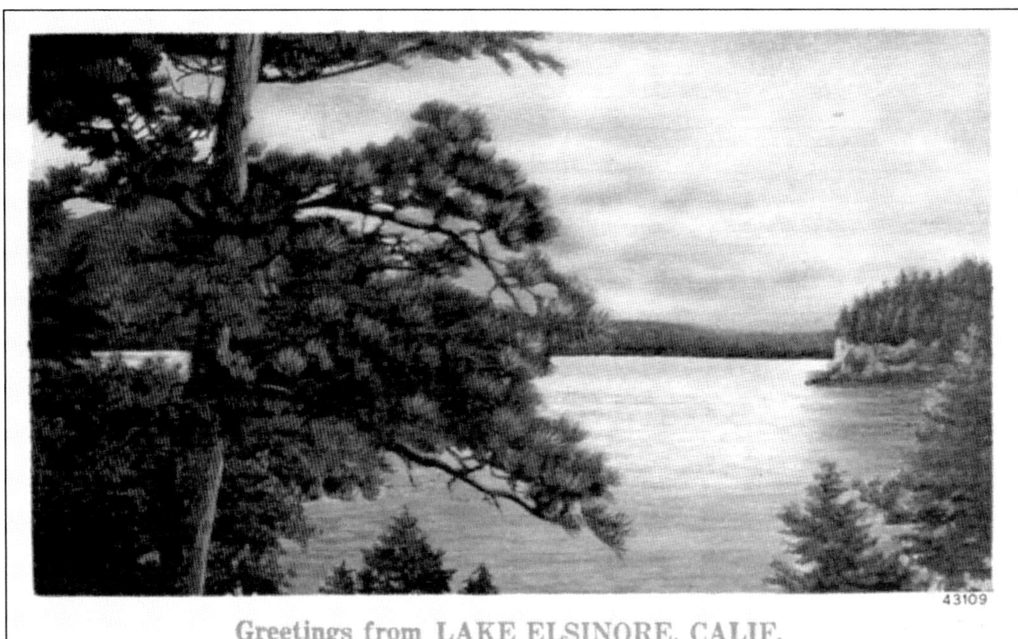


"Greetings from Lake Elsinore" postcards are great for recalling highlights of weekends or vacations. Lake Elsinore is a recreational favorite of sport enthusiasts. While this picture suggests quiet time on the lake, the area on weekends is filled with people boating, waterskiing, fishing, picnicking, and relaxing in the sun.

# *Six*

# Hotels of Elsinore

Franklin Heald saw only beauty the first time he gazed upon the Big Lagoon, as it had become known, despite the fact that it was almost dry. After his transactions to acquire Rancho Laguna with Graham and Collier, he wrote letters to his family in Iowa, and soon people started to come to California to see the colony Heald had described.

Immediately upon the arrival of new residents to Elsinore, housing was needed. Since this was a virgin area with no homes, the new citizens had to have some place to live until their homes were fit to be occupied. Some people lived in tents on a temporary basis, and others stayed in hotels.

The first bathhouse stood at the corner of Spring Street and Graham Avenue, and plans for a hotel were prepared. Early residents besides Franklin Heald were H. C. Kellogg, Allen Poe, Madison and Esther Chaney, P. W. Minthorn, D. S. Buterbaugh, and John Leach and his family. Heald hired professional builder Frank Ferris to construct the Crescent Bath House at an estimated cost of $10,000.

The ready sale of lots and acreage in the valley made possible the rapid construction of substantial buildings. A number were started in the late 1880s, including the Lake Dale Hotel and the Consolidated Bank building, which would be known as the Ambassador Hotel. Other hotels built during this period were the French, the Jones, and the Bundy.

ANALYSES OF WATER FROM

# Lake View Inn Hot Springs

ELSINORE, CAL.

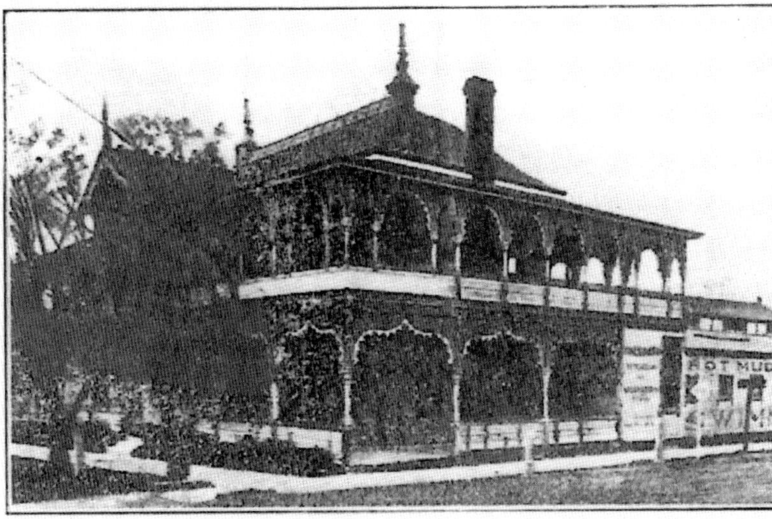


LAKE VIEW INN HOT SPRINGS BATH HOUSE

UNIVERSITY OF CALIFORNIA

COLLEGE OF AGRICULTURE

BERKELEY, CALIFORNIA

LAKE VIEW INN HOT SPRINGS,
Elsinore, Cal.

Dear Sir:

The result of the analyses of the Lake View Inn Hot Springs are as follows:

| | Original Hot Springs Gr. per Gal. | White Sulphur Springs Grs. per Gal. |
|---|---|---|
| **Total Residue by evaporation** | **19.82** | **19.40** |
| Soluble in water after evaporation | 13.12 | 11.83 |
| Insoluble in water after evaporation | 3.79 | 5.24 |
| Organ c matter and chemically combined water | 2.91 | 2.33 |
| **The soluble parts consist of** | | |
| Sodium and Potasium Sulph's | 7.07 | 4.09 |
| Sodium chloride (common salt) | 3.38 | 5.07 |
| Sodium carbonate [sal soda] | 2.67 | 2.67 |
| **The insoluble parts consist of** | | |
| Calcium and magnesium carbonates } Calcium sulphate [Gypsum[ } | 1.92 | |
| Calcium and magnesium carbonates | | 2.33 |
| Silica | 1.87 | 2.91 |

During the era of mineral springs, the facilities in the area printed cards showing the analysis of their water. This card from the Lake View Inn Hot Springs indicates water analyzed by the University of California at Berkeley. The building was constructed in 1887 by Franklin Heald as the Crescent Bath House for the use of guests at the Lakeview Hotel, one block away. For years, it has been occupied by the Chimes antiques store, a favorite of many customers.

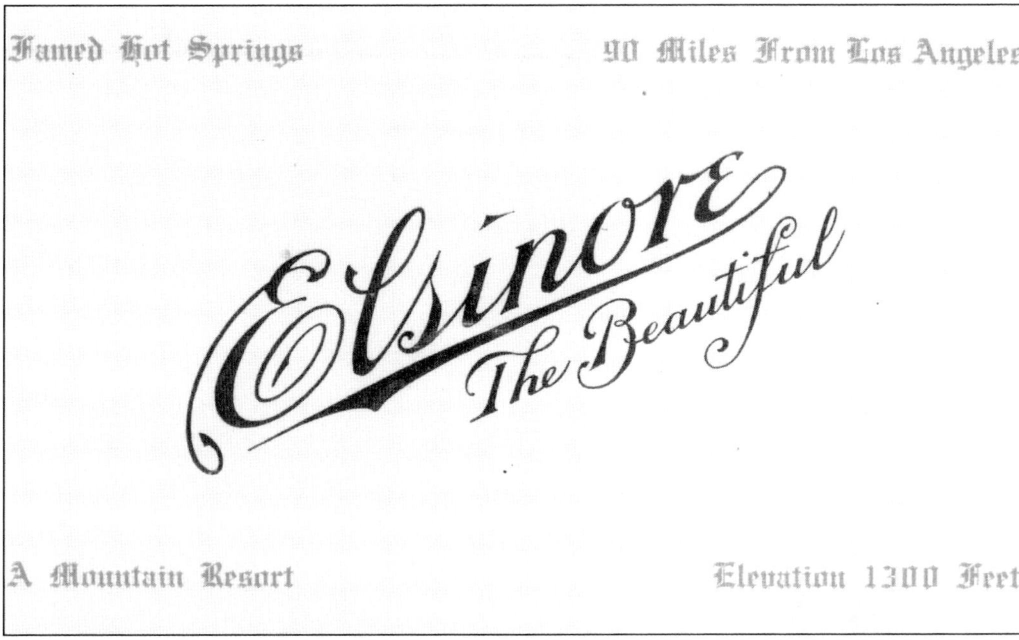


"Elsinore the Beautiful," an advertisement for the area, promoted Elsinore to people interested in the wonderful growth of this ideal resort for health and recreation. "At the present time, it is a beautiful little city, with a high-thinking, prosperous population with schools, churches and religious environments," the back of the card reads.

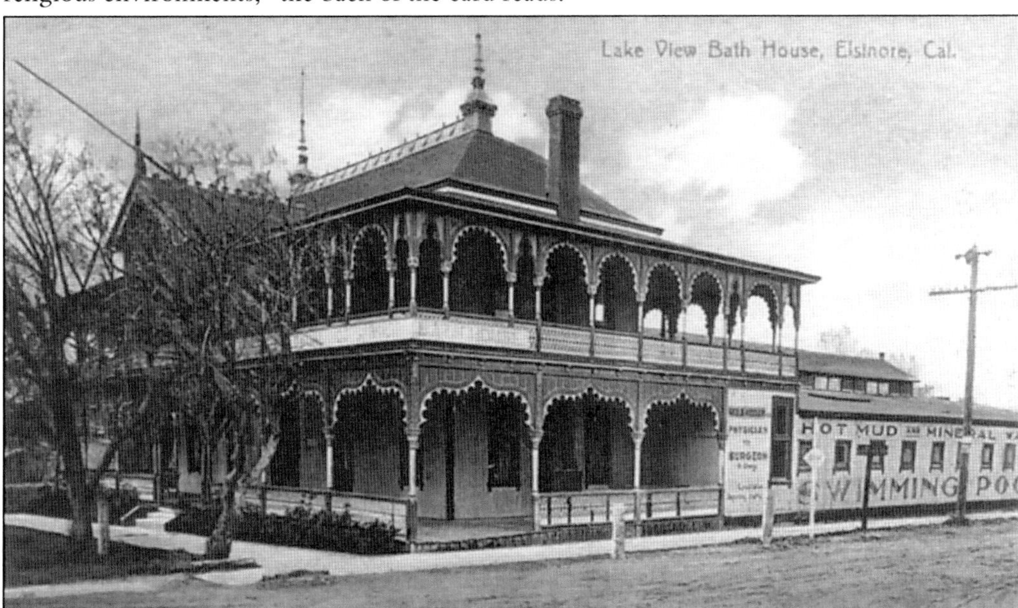


This ornate building, identified as the Lake View Bath House, was known as the Crescent Bath House for many years. Franklin Heald hired professional builder Frank Ferris to construct the Moorish-style facility, popular in the Victorian era. The covered swimming pool was removed after a boy drowned in 1935. The building has been maintained and remains in excellent condition today.

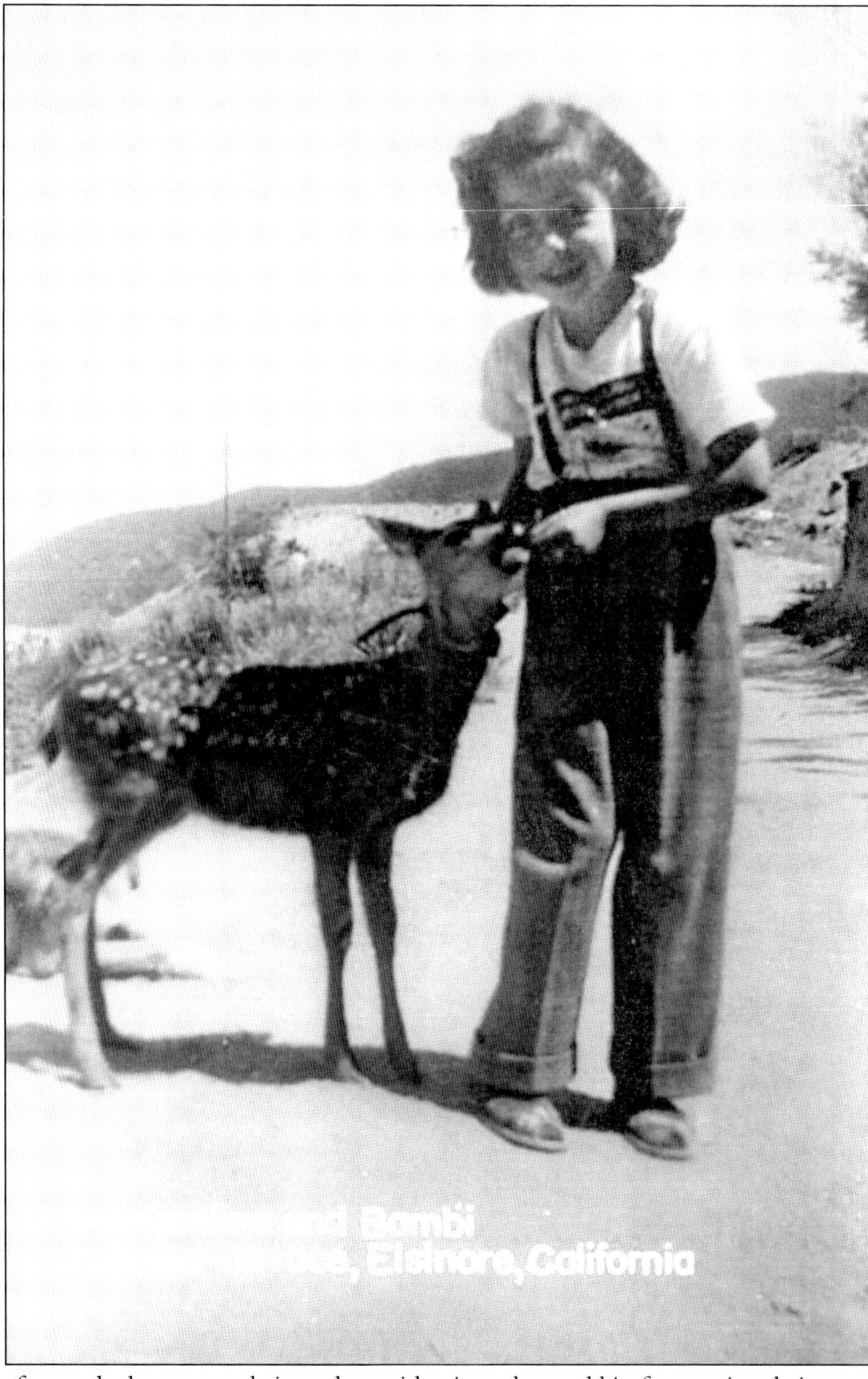


Some farmers had to protect their gardens with wire to keep rabbits from eating their vegetables. Years ago, hunters came to the area, but Elsinore is no longer known for hunting. Today plenty of deer still inhabit the Elsinore Mountains; however, as more homes are constructed, one does not hear the howl of coyotes at night any longer.

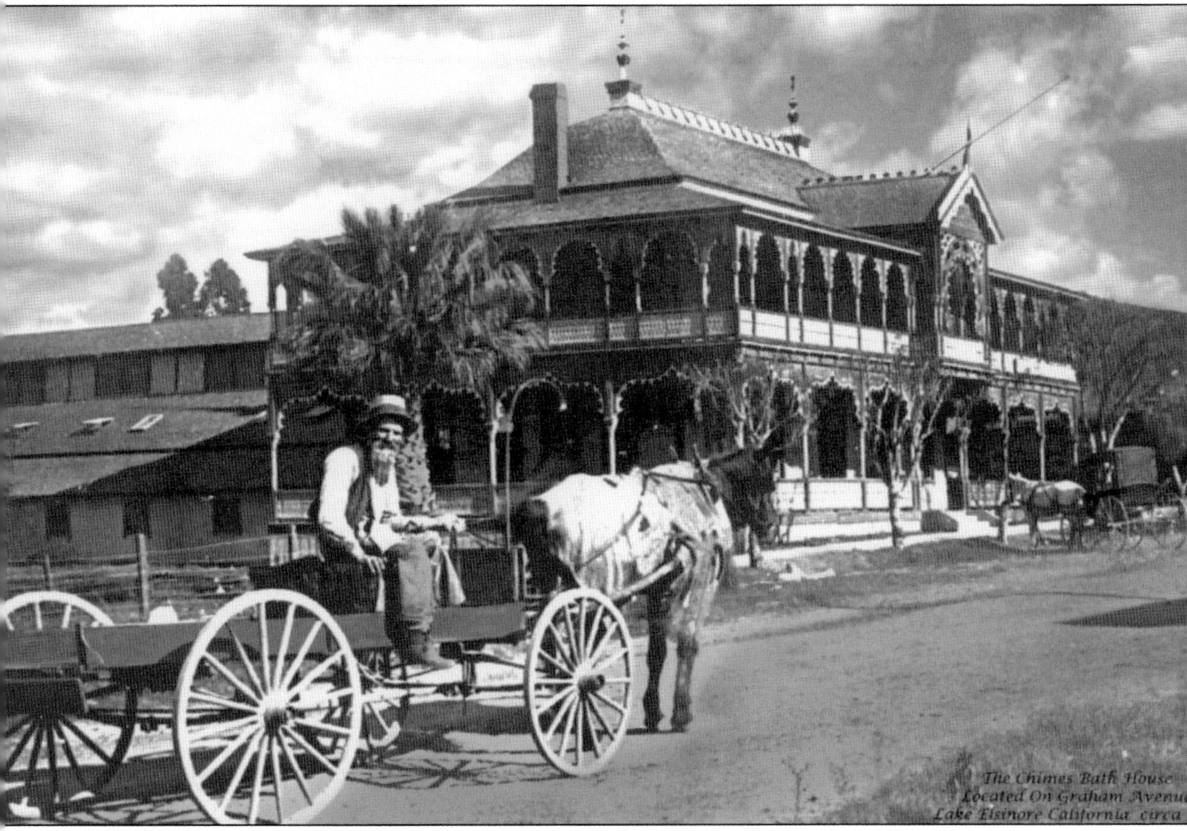


The developers of 1883 advertised in Los Angeles, Pasadena, and Eastern newspapers the availability of mineral water coming from the ground at 110 degrees. Hot water bubbled up out of the ground, and it was said one could not stay in the water more than 15 minutes. Baths were taken, the water was drunk, and in a short time the bather felt much better. The Crescent Bath House, built in 1887, was designed after the Moorish style of architecture of the Victorian era. It is doubtful if the Moors ever had a bathhouse half as handsome. The bathhouse utilized the hot sulphur water that came to the surface at a temperature of 132 degrees and offered a choice of plunge, sweat, mud, or porcelain tub baths. The baths proved an effective remedy for rheumatism, kidney troubles, rickets, arthritis, and many other kinds of diseases. (OPC.)

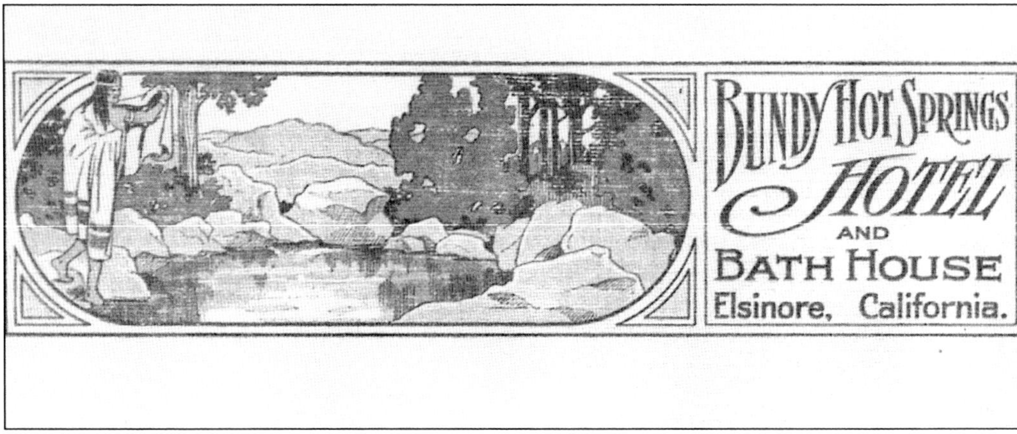


This advertisement tells of country comforts and city conveniences offered at the Bundy Hotel and Hot Springs Bath House. Elsinore is a city that has the advantage of being situated on the shore of the only large lake in Southern California and is modern, refined, and comfortable. The Bundy Hotel was a scientific adjunct to the natural attractions of the location.

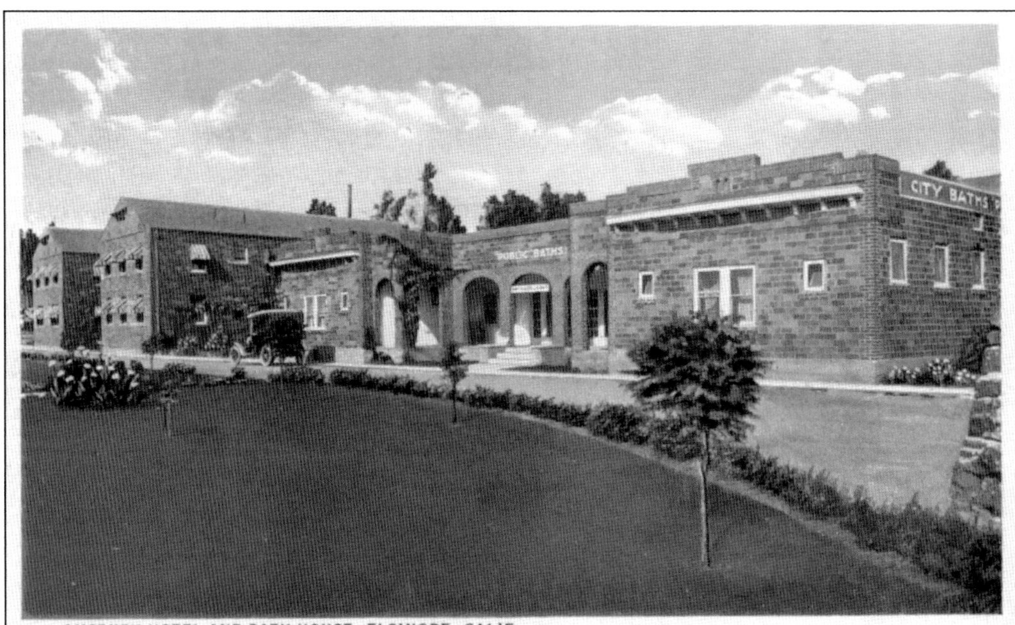


Owned by O. W. and F. A. Amsbury, this hotel combined a main office building, which contained the parlors, music room, large dining room, and writing room; eight cottages, some of which had raised sides to admit air and sunshine; two bathhouses where men and women could bathe separately and receive treatment; and a newly built annex where steam heat tempered the evening air. (EP.)

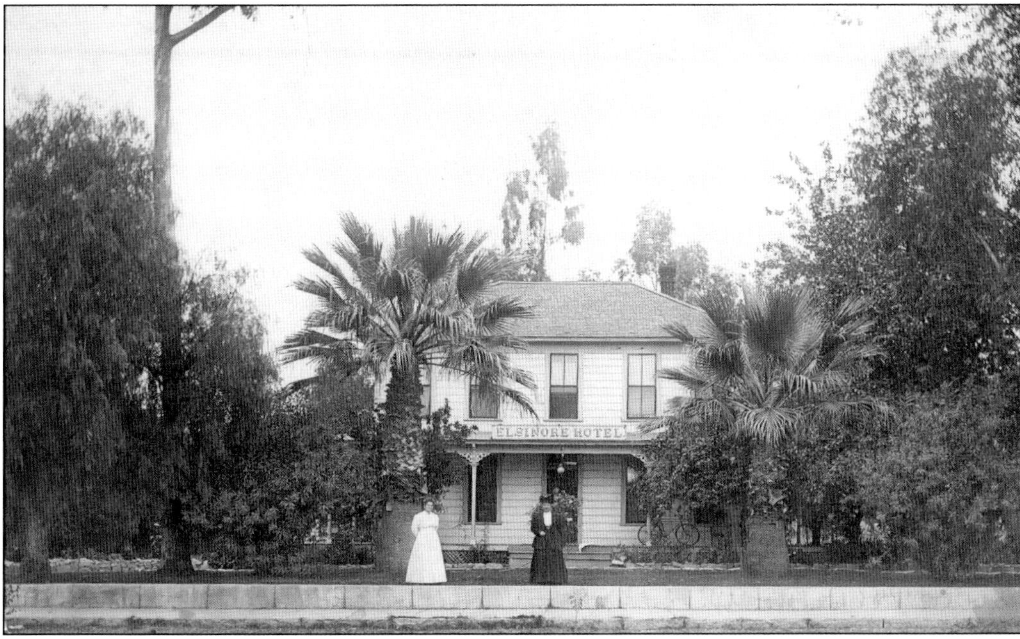


The Hotel Elsinore was another name for the facility formerly known as the Bundy Hotel and Bath House, the Amsbury Hotel and Bath House, and the Wreden Hot Springs Hotel. The most common complaints treated in the pioneer days were rheumatism, sciatica, lumbago, and neuralgia. The scientific administration of the healing waters and mud attracted thousands who suffered from other maladies or who merely needed rest. In those days, one saw miracles performed by the waters. Occasionally a patient unable to aid himself, with hope gone and a life of only pain, was carried to Elsinore on a cot. In a month, step firm, eyes bright, head erect, he walked to the station and left completely restored to health. Such cases as these became frequent, making popular this resort. (Both EbP.)

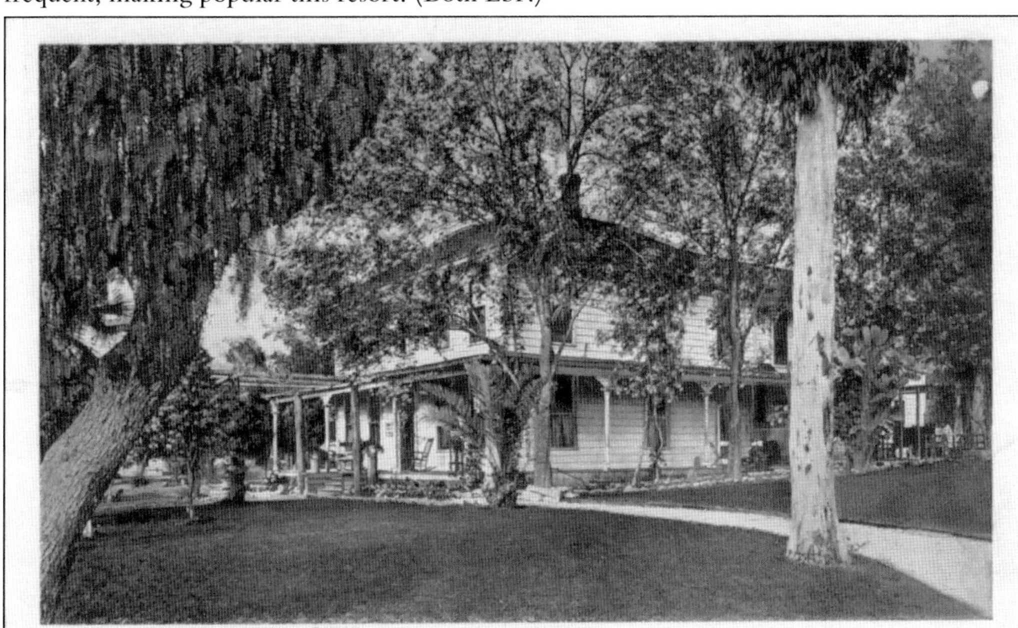

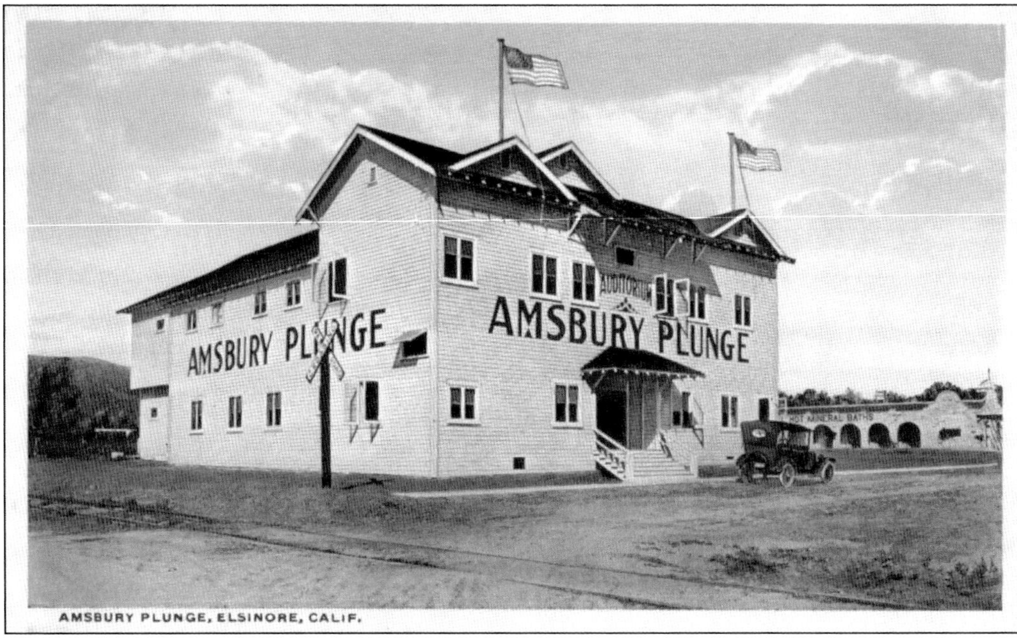


The Amsbury Plunge was erected over several of the largest springs. It contained four large plunges and two smaller baths, through which hot sulphur water, at 104 degrees, flowed uninterruptedly 72,000 gallons each 24 hours. The water was strongly impregnated with sulphur, iron, magnesia, and other ingredients. Its health-giving qualities were thoroughly tested by thousands. (EP.)

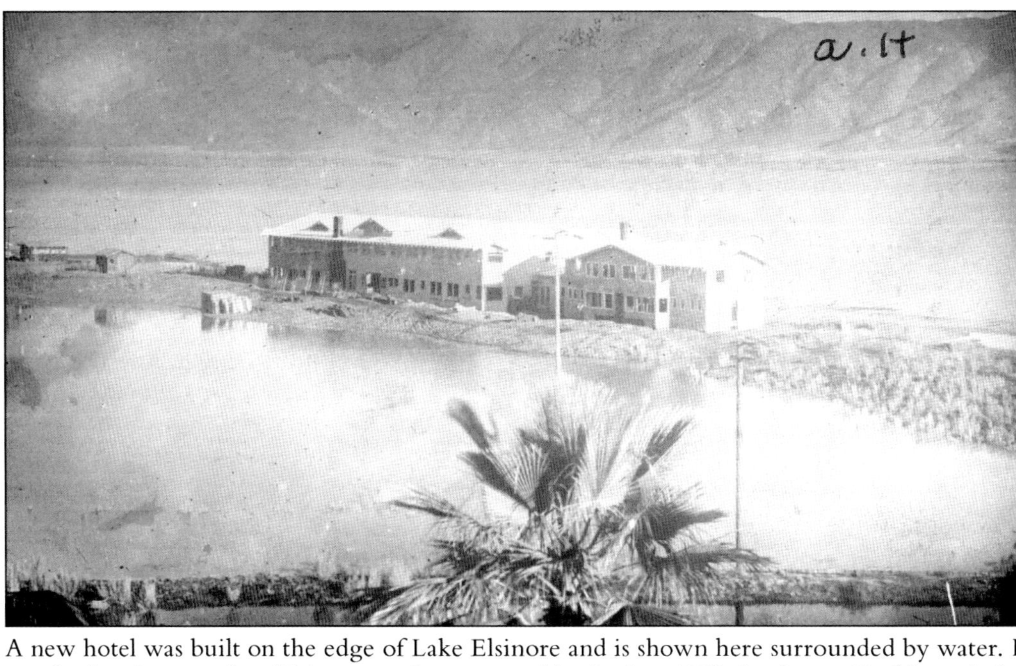


A new hotel was built on the edge of Lake Elsinore and is shown here surrounded by water. It caught fire the next day. This postcard was owned in the late 1880s by Agnes Heald, a relative of Franklin Heald. According to cemetery records, she may have been his daughter-in-law.

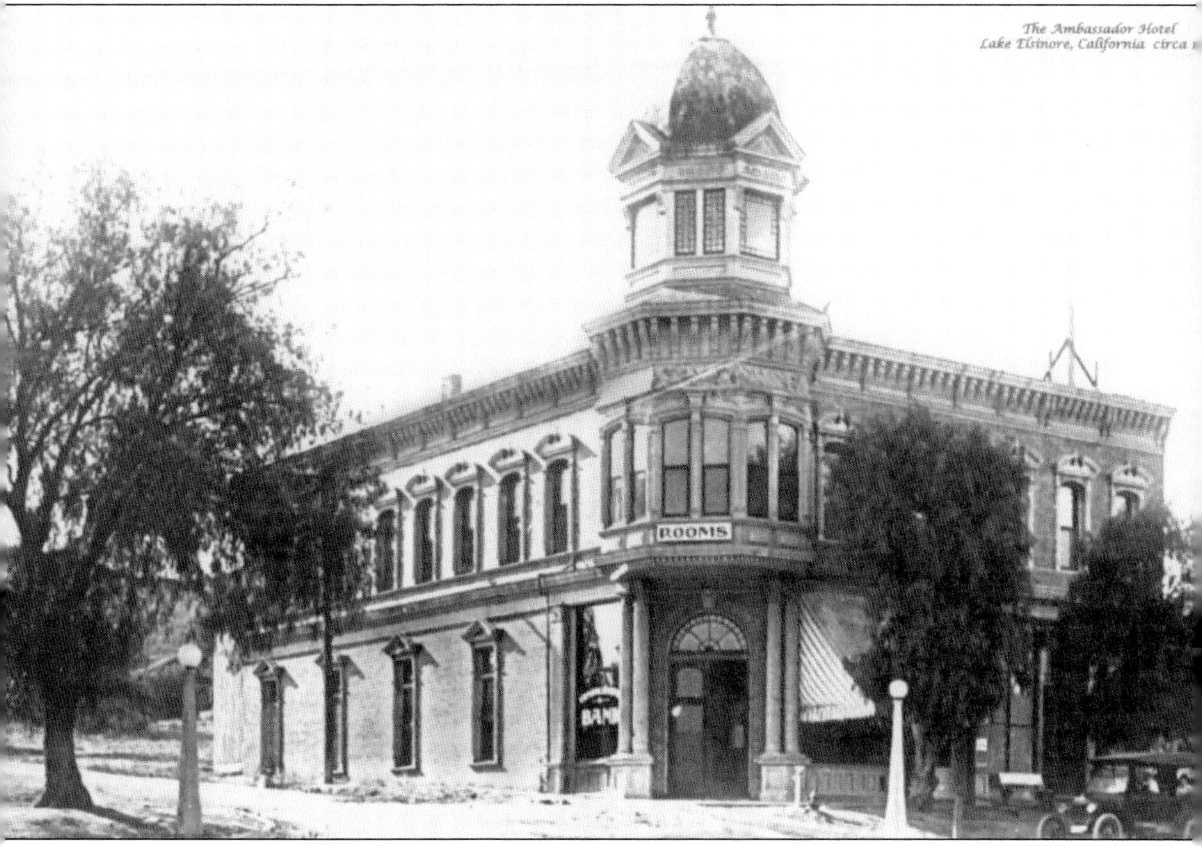


In 1887, this building was constructed at Main and Prospect Streets as the home of the Consolidated Bank. The second floor provided space for Elsinore High School classes from 1898 to around 1900. The residents voted in 1912 to issue $20,000 in bonds to finance a sewer system for Elsinore, and the Consolidated Bank bought the entire issue. In 1916, the structure was remodeled and renamed the Pitt Hotel. After World War II, two more floors were added, making this the tallest building in Elsinore and the only one to have an elevator. It later became the Ambassador Hotel and then served as a retirement home for many years. The building has been vacant for the past 15 years. (OPC.)

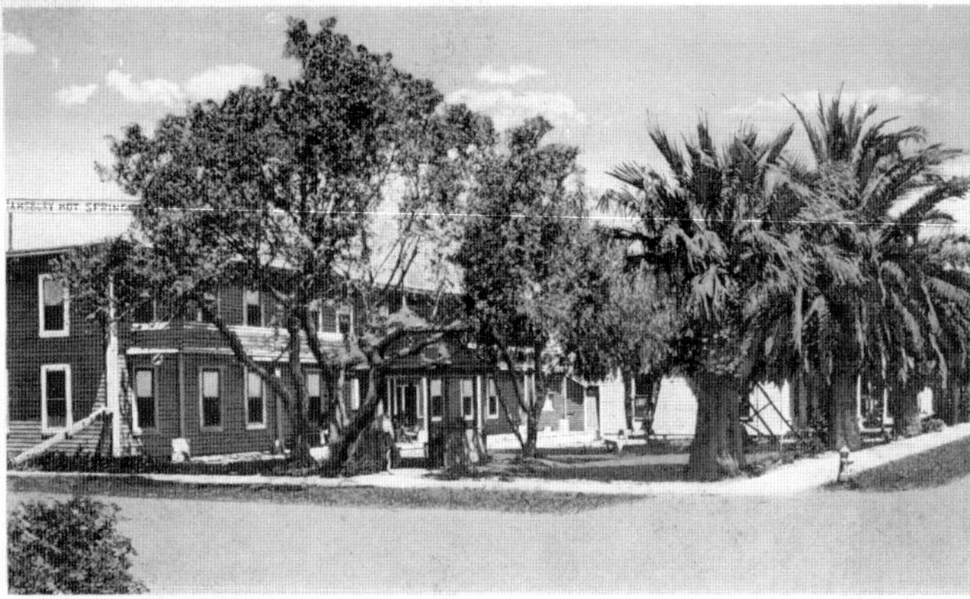


AMSBURY HOTEL, ELSINORE, CALIF.

This hotel facility was located at the corner of Spring Street and Heald Avenue. The rates were $2 to $3 per day or $11 to $17 per week. This included board, room, and plain mineral baths. The hotel was two blocks from the station, and the omnibus met every train. The baths were in connection with the hotel, so patients could pass directly from the bath room to their bedroom to rest. One could have hot baths, sweat baths, mud baths—in fact every form of bath conducive to health was given. Massage treatment was of great benefit in conjunction with the hot mineral baths. (Above, EP; below, CTA.)

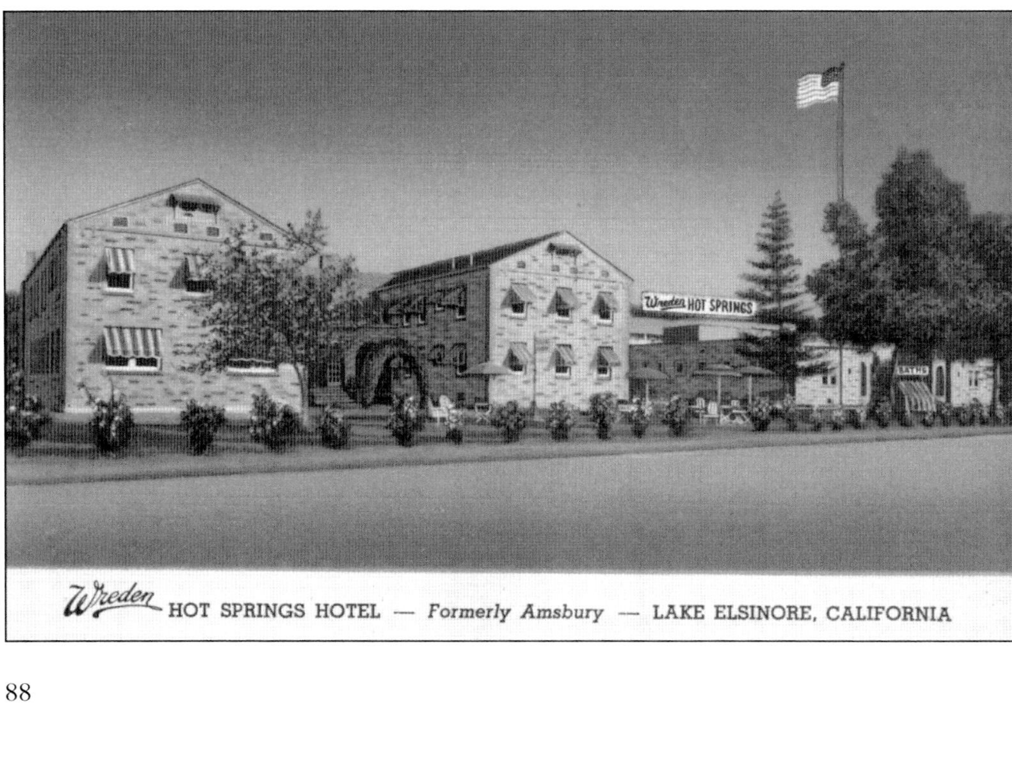


*Wreden* HOT SPRINGS HOTEL — *Formerly Amsbury* — LAKE ELSINORE, CALIFORNIA

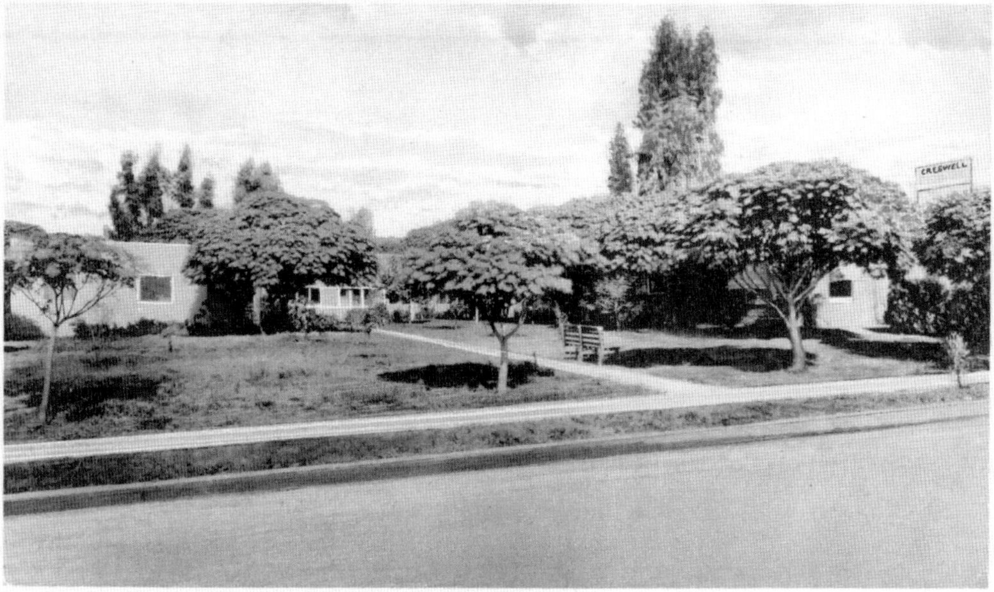


CRESWELL BATH HOUSE. ELSINORE, CALIFORNIA.

Capt. R. M. Cresswell of San Diego bought the hot well and two lots from Kate Coster opposite the Bundy Hotel. The new bathhouse would be a modern, one-story building constructed with cream-colored hollow tile. This tile was made from Elsinore clay shipped to Tropico and returned in the finished product. When the new building opened in June 1916, it was 102 by 20 feet with mission arches. In front was the hot well surrounded by a cement floor, and under a large rustic pergola both a pump and a drinking fountain invited the public to imbibe the hot medicinal waters. Three steps descended into the tubs, where one could recline at full length if desired. This facility is still in use today and is owned by the Nakai family. (Above, AC.)

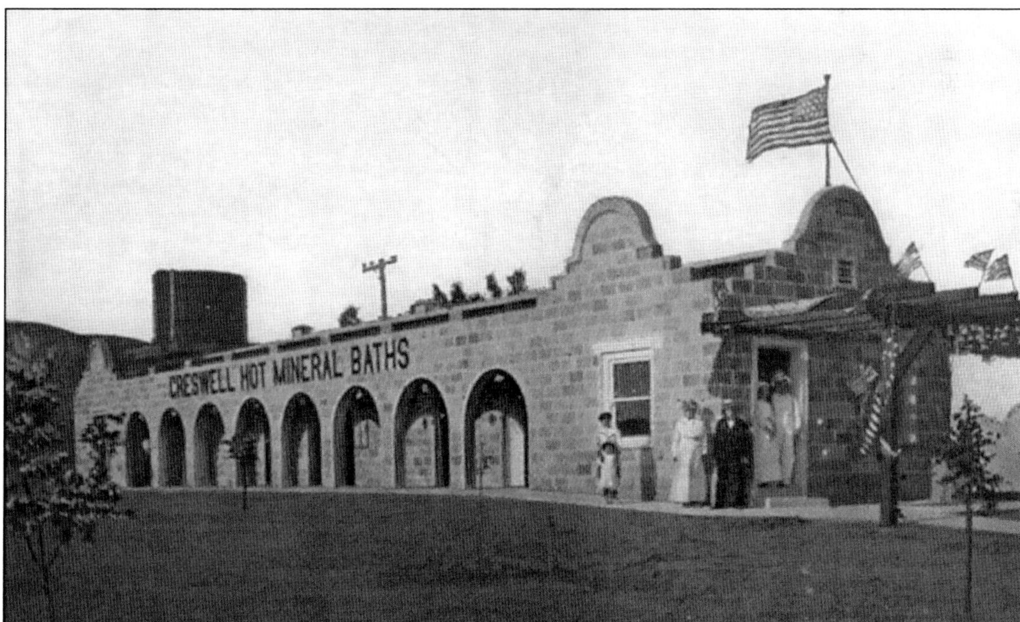

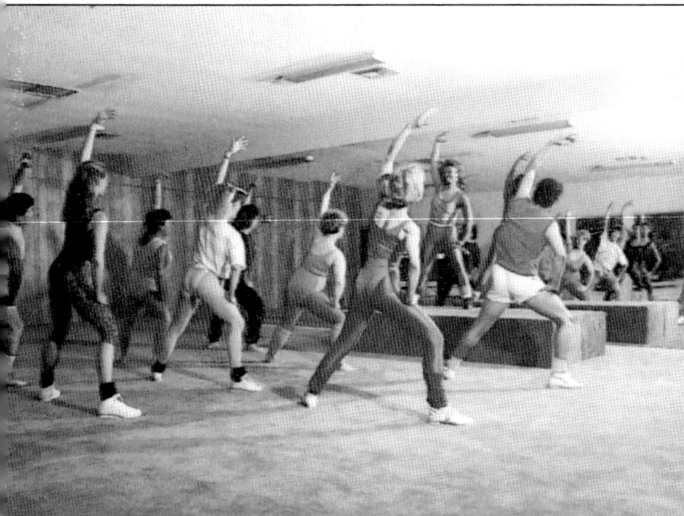

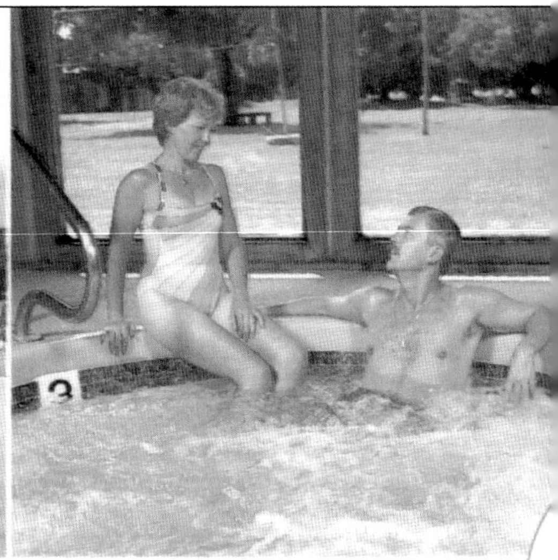

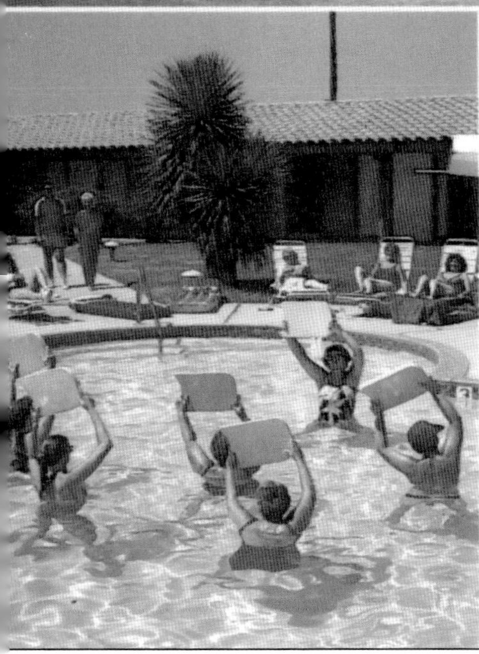

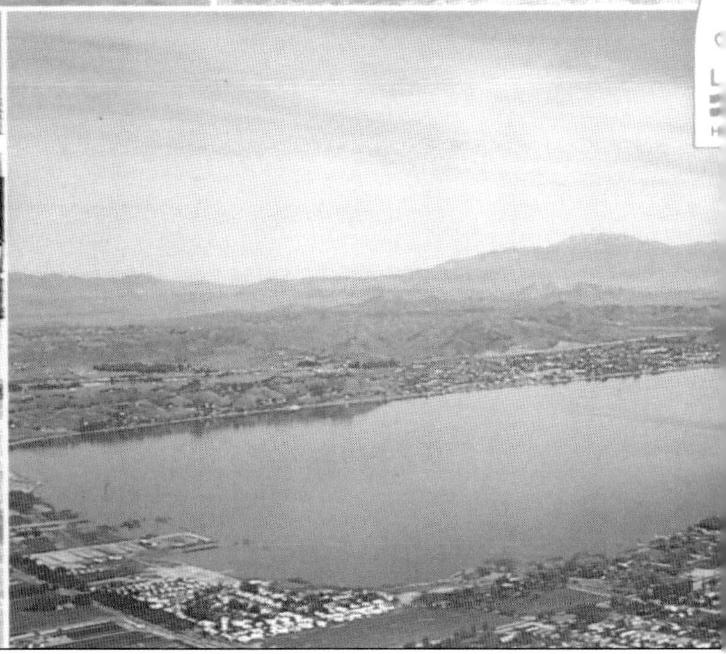

The Lakeside Spa was built by the laundry and dry cleaners' union on Riverside Drive. Becoming the Grove, it was touted as a reducing and conditioning spa where one could lose weight safely while vacationing in a luxurious resort. The spa offered it all: a medically supervised program of diet and an exercise program designed for anyone who wanted to look and feel better, regardless of age. According to the advertisement, "Unlimited activities here

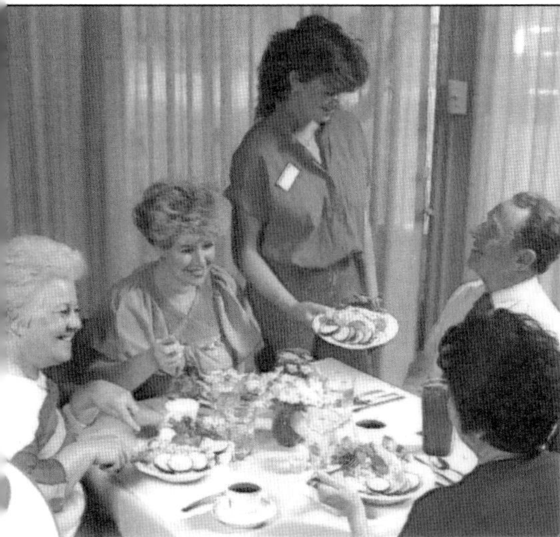
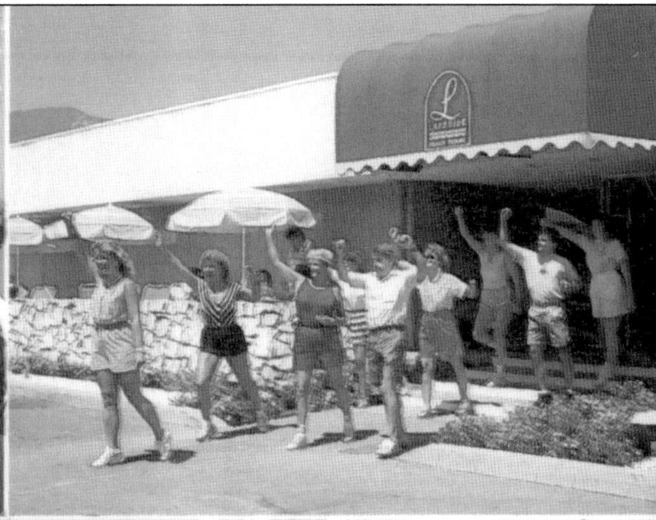
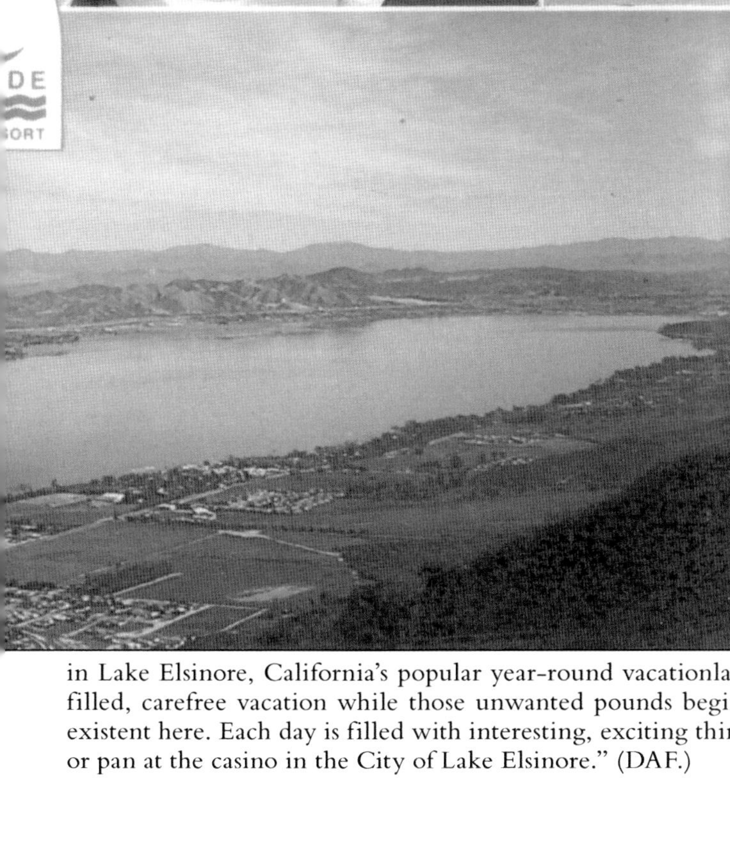
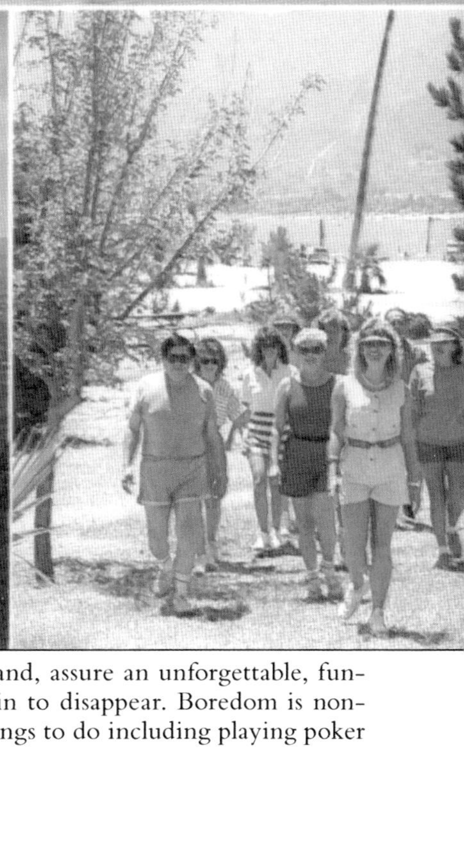

in Lake Elsinore, California's popular year-round vacationland, assure an unforgettable, fun-filled, carefree vacation while those unwanted pounds begin to disappear. Boredom is non-existent here. Each day is filled with interesting, exciting things to do including playing poker or pan at the casino in the City of Lake Elsinore." (DAF.)

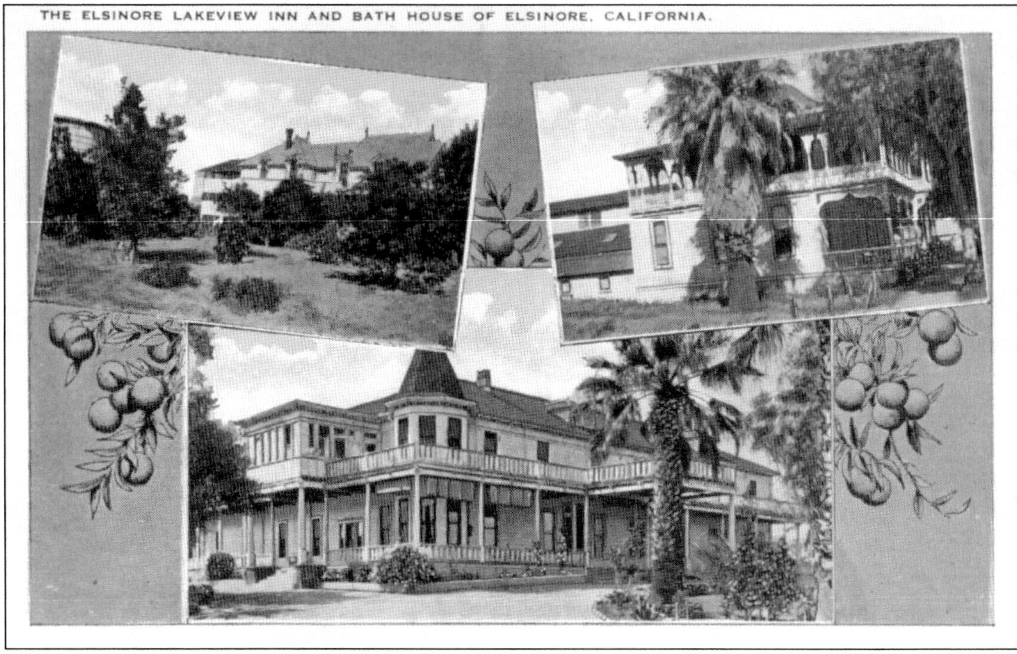


The Lake Dale Hotel, later called the Lake View (also Lakeview), opened on October 1, 1886. Its advertisement in the *Elsinore News* on March 5, 1887, was as follows: "This newly built and furnished hotel, opened October 1, stands on a beautiful knoll on the lakeshore . . . surrounded by mountains. In the distance are the snow-covered peaks . . . while the clear placid waters of Lake Elsinore reflect the mountains from the opposite shore. More beautiful scenery is not to be found this side of Switzerland. The hotel contains over 40 rooms with wide verandas. Large, airy rooms, open fireplace . . . reading room supplied with all the leading newspapers and magazines. Tables supplied with the best the markets . . . afford. Rooms Single or En Suite: Splendid accommodations for families wishing homes. Hack . . . to all trains, and special arrangements for driving or sailing." (Above, BRM; below, CTA.)

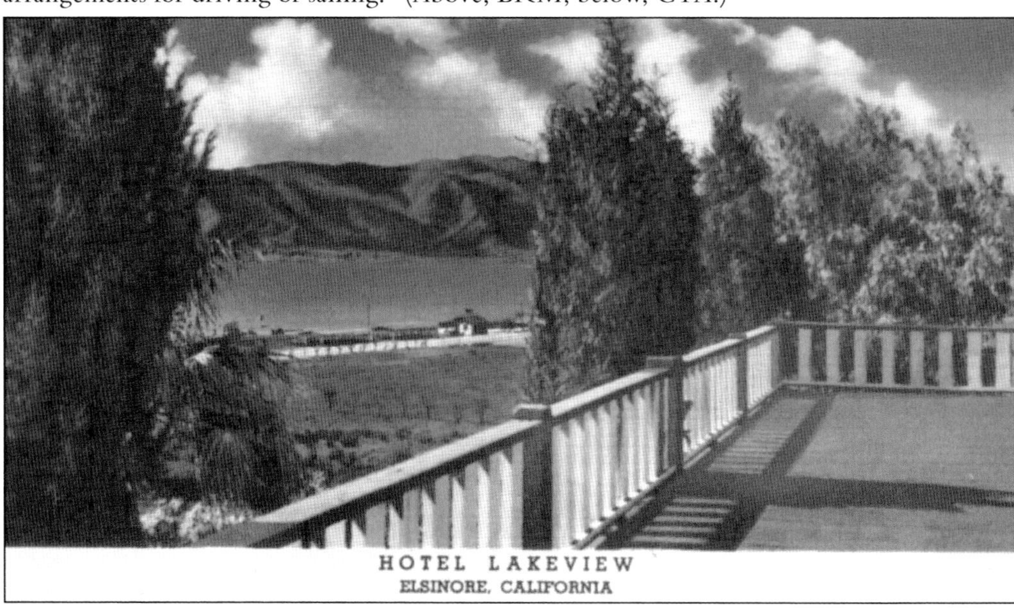

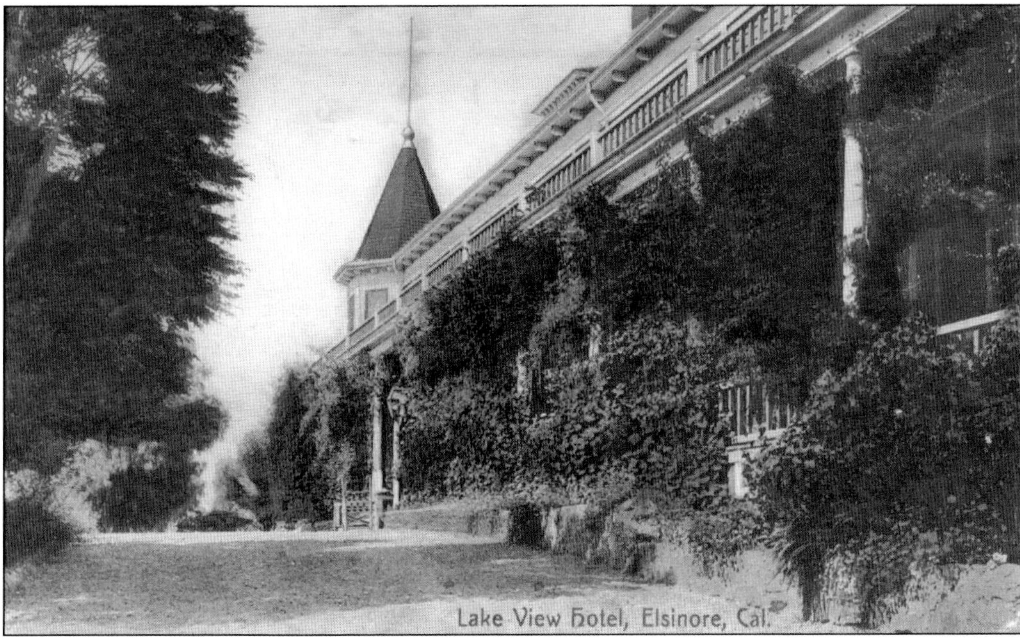


The Lakeview Hotel burned in April 1894 and was immediately rebuilt. The January 17, 1896, issue of the *Elsinore News* reported, "Lake View Annual Opening. Wednesday evening the second opening of the new Lakeview Hotel took place under the management of C. S. Traphagen & Co. . . . Note: The first passenger train came into town that evening." The January 7, 1898, issue stated, "Herbert Traphagen arrived late Sunday night with a fine three-seated carriage for the use of the Lake View guests. He made the drive from Los Angeles in 10 hours." After years of serving guests, an article in the newspaper reported that the hotel was being razed in 1970. The caption read, "The story has been told that President Grover Cleveland was once a guest there." (Below, MR.)

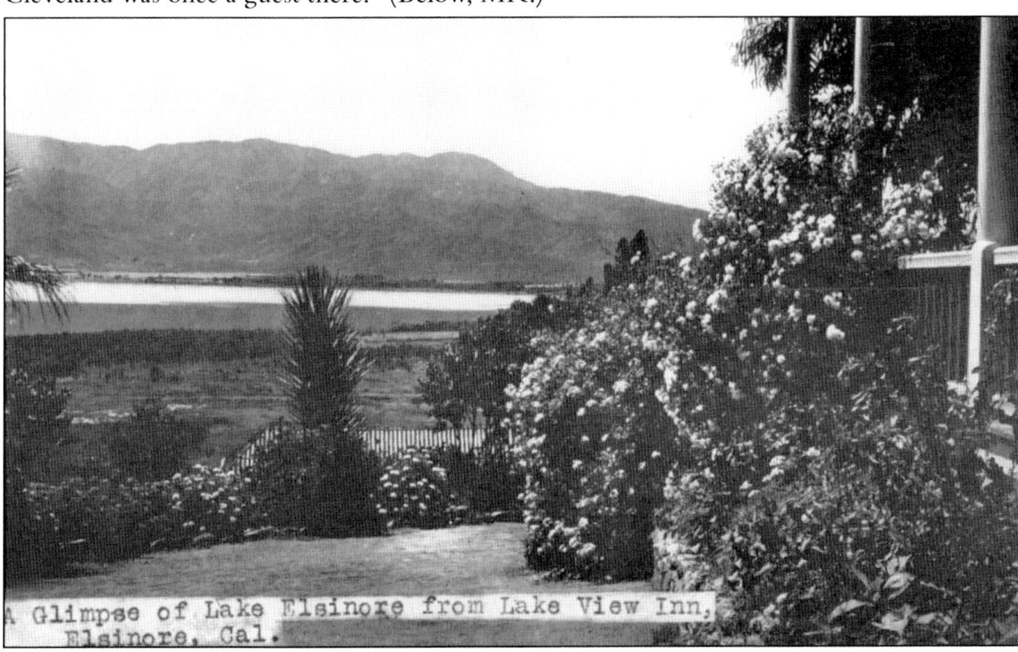

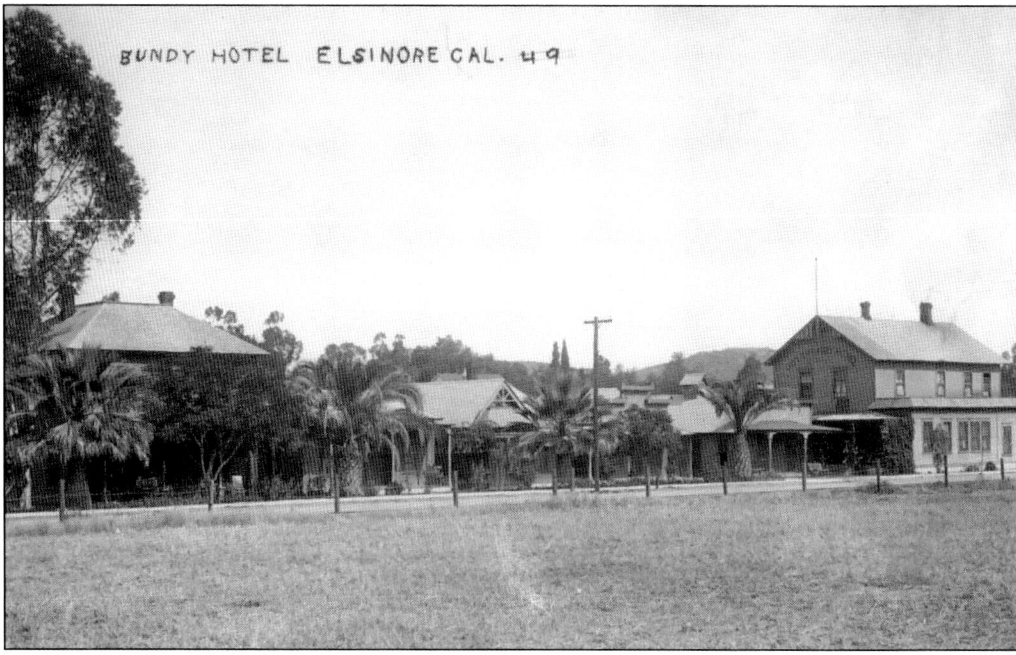


While the postcard indicates this scene is the Bundy Hotel, located at the corner of Spring Street and Heald Avenue, the notes on the back of the card indicate that these buildings were removed when a hotel was built across the street by the Amsburys.

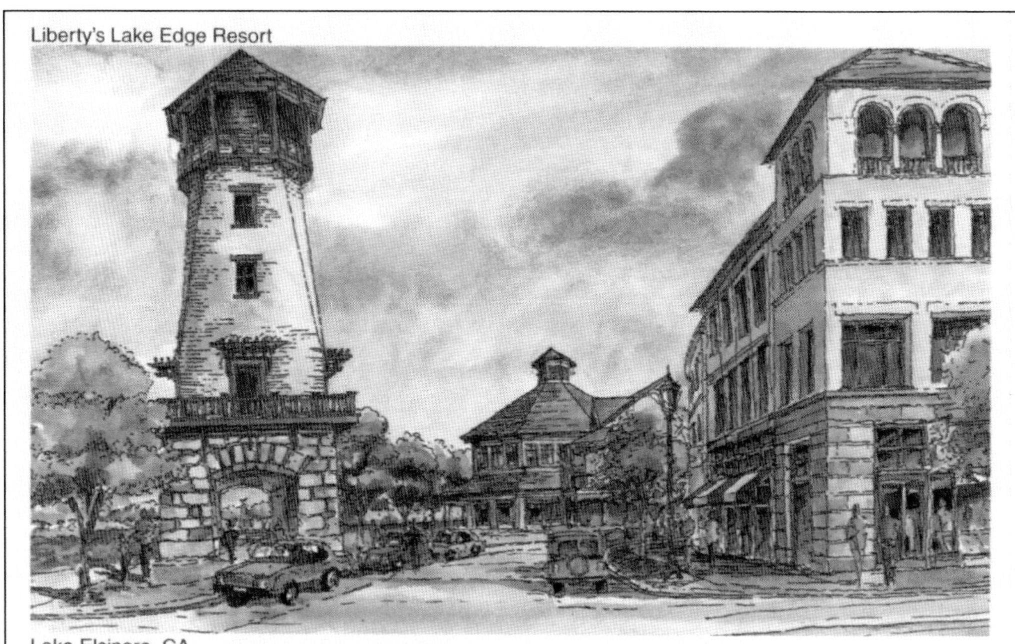


Liberty's Lake Edge Resort was a development proposed in 1999. The promotional materials included a postcard, stationery, and envelopes engraved with a pencil drawing of a community titled "Town." These samples were mailed to a local resident, the sender thanking her for sharing her Saturday and hoping she had fun at the ball game. (LF.)

# *Six*

# Recreation through the Years

For Southern California residents, Lake Elsinore has provided many hours of hiking, bike riding, swimming, sailboating, sky diving, speedboating, jet skiing, waterskiing, motorcycle racing, fishing, and years ago, duck hunting. Other activities involved the theater, skating rink, bowling alley, and the most popular place of the 1940s and 1950s, the Mava ice cream parlor. Teenagers headed each day to the Main Street shop to drink 5¢ Cokes and listen to the jukebox for hours.

Elsinore developed a ball field in 1940 on Poe Street between Limited Street and Lakeshore Drive. Probably the first one of its kind, it was named for Nick Matich, who was serving as mayor at the time. About 1971, the name of Swick was added in honor of Walt Swick, an active force in Elsinore youth sports programs. As children's sports became more popular, a need grew for additional parks, and today Lake Elsinore boasts 21 parks and recreational facilities covering 125 acres.

With the City of Lake Elsinore and the Elsinore Municipal Water District cooperating to improve the quality of water, Lake Elsinore has a bright future. Three wells off the levee are pumping reclaimed water into the lake constantly to replace the evaporated amounts during the summer. Aeration platforms have been installed in the middle of the lake, and under these platforms are giant fans to circulate the water at the bottom.

A beautiful new 18-hole championship golf course will open in fall 2007.

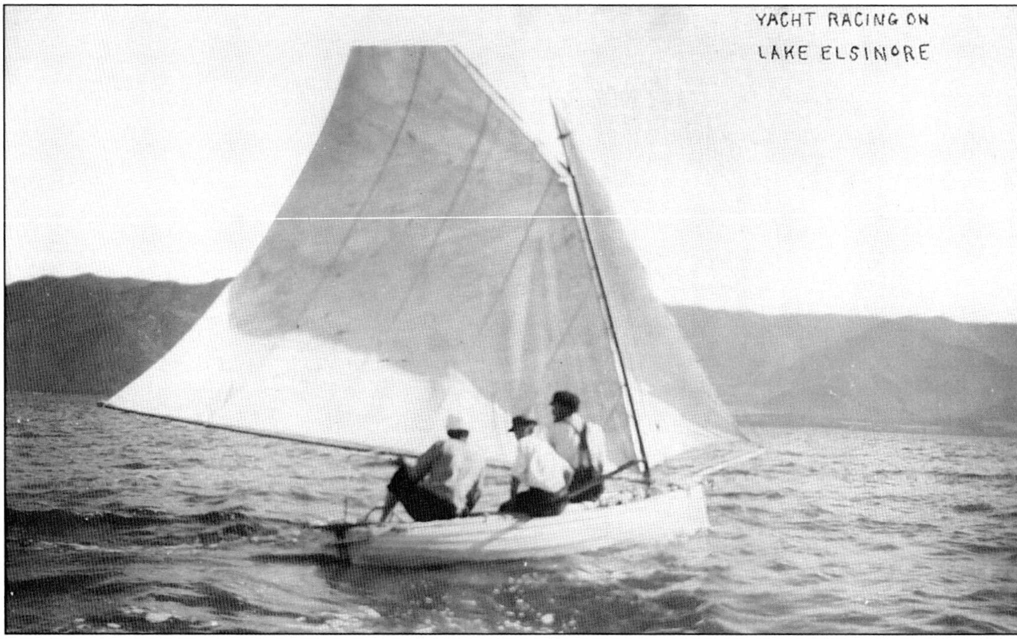


Boating has been—and continues to be—a favorite sport on Lake Elsinore. Yacht racing was popular in the 1920s, as was motorboat racing. Speed records were set at 33.74 miles per hour. Many boats sailed on the lake; however, only a few images exist of their outings.

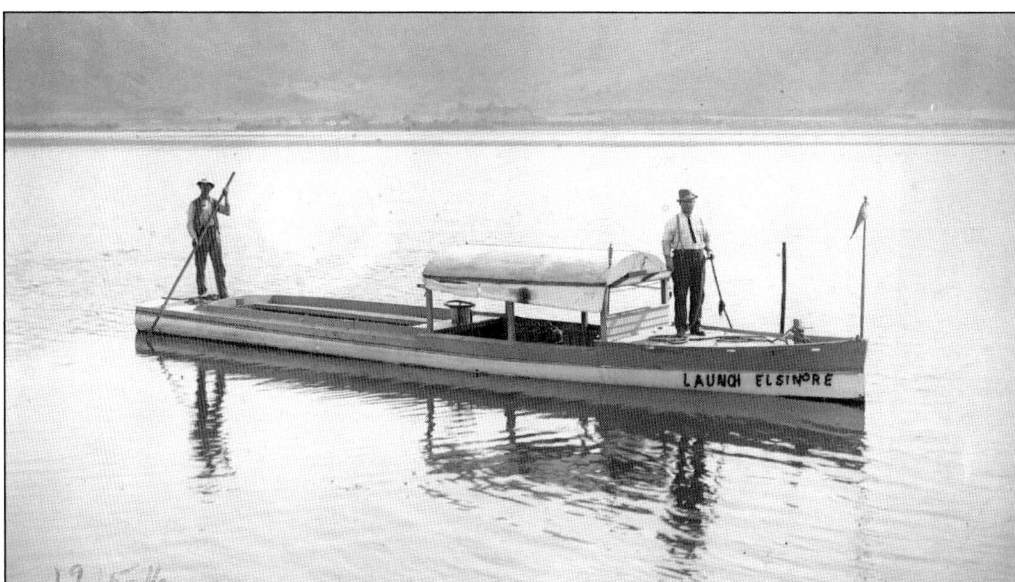


The *Launch Elsinore* and its occupants look to be posing for a photograph on the beautiful Lake Elsinore. Are they using the boat as a gondola, or are they going to have a relaxing day of fishing? The men are prepared for a warm, sunny day with their brimmed hats. This postcard is dated 1915–1916.

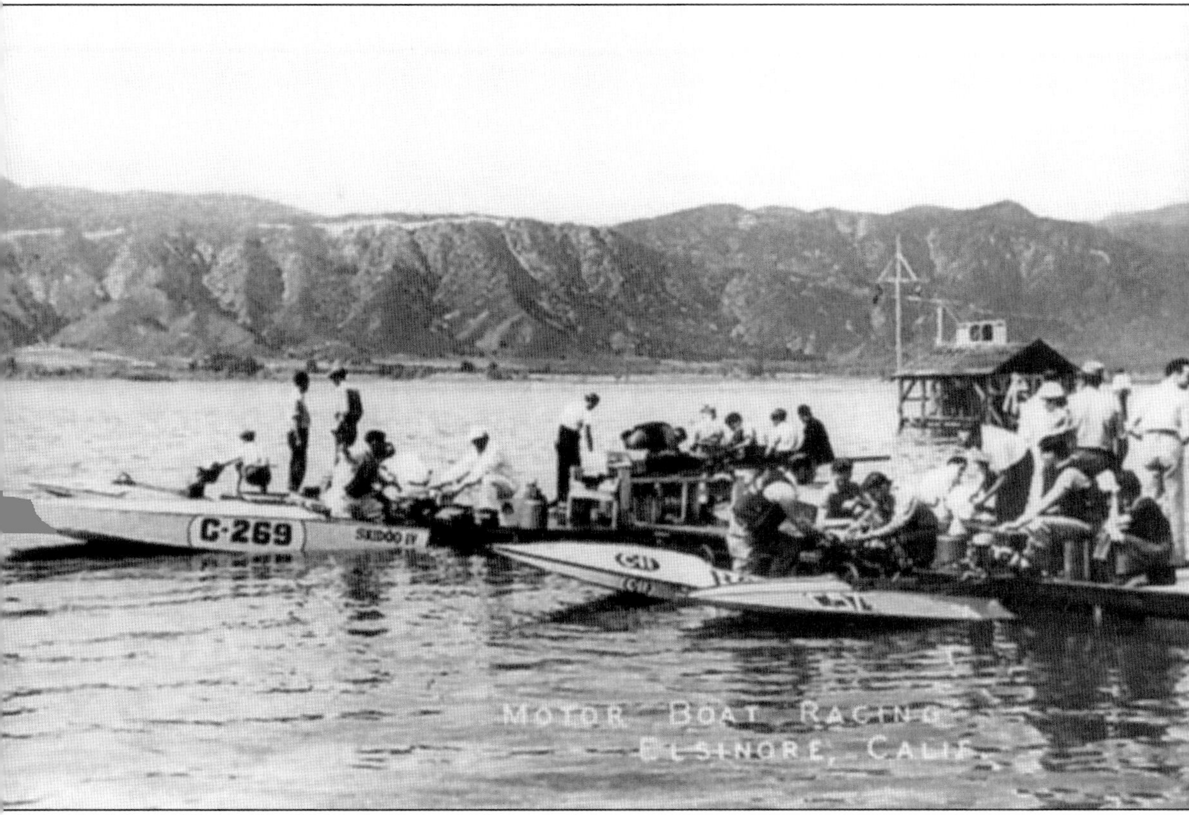


This group of boats is near the Aloha Pier. Many boating activities and speedboat records were set here in the 1920s. The Aloha Pier was built by the Clevelin Realty Company for the residents of Country Club Heights and was located across Lakeshore Drive from their hilltop homes. At the pier, there were swings for the children and a nice, sandy beach along Lakeshore Drive for those who wanted to relax in the sun. On the weekends, dances were held in the pavilion. When the lake's water level rose, a second floor was added to the pavilion. (OPC.)

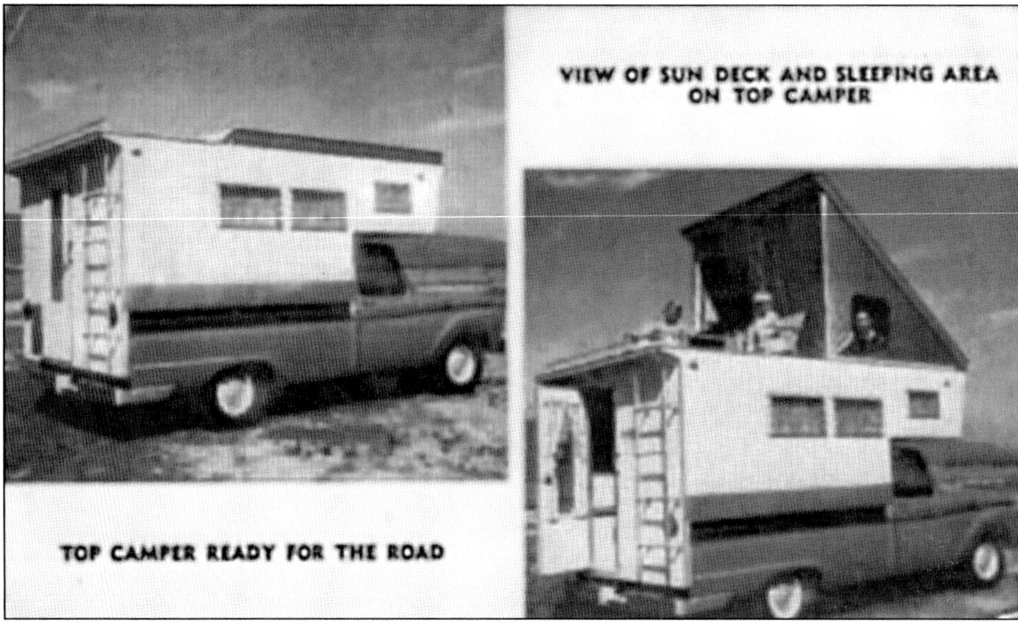


The back of this postcard reads, "The Unexpected is Here! It's New—It's Different—It's Top Camper. This unique camper is new in its field. For just a few more dollars here is plenty of room for sleeping eight people. Has all of the conveniences for making life easier for Mom, too." The camper was sold by the Hodges Ford Company of North Main Street.

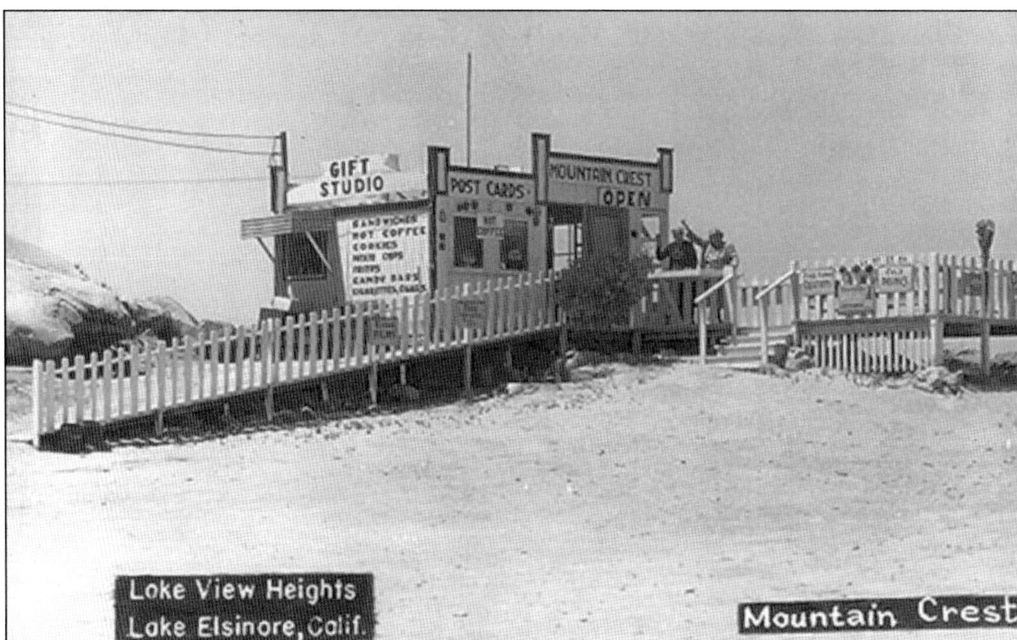


Mountain Crest, located in Lake View Heights, sold postcards, sandwiches, hot coffee, cookies, and other items to weary travelers on the Ortega Highway. Such little stores, popular in bygone years, provided travelers with necessities as well as souvenirs.

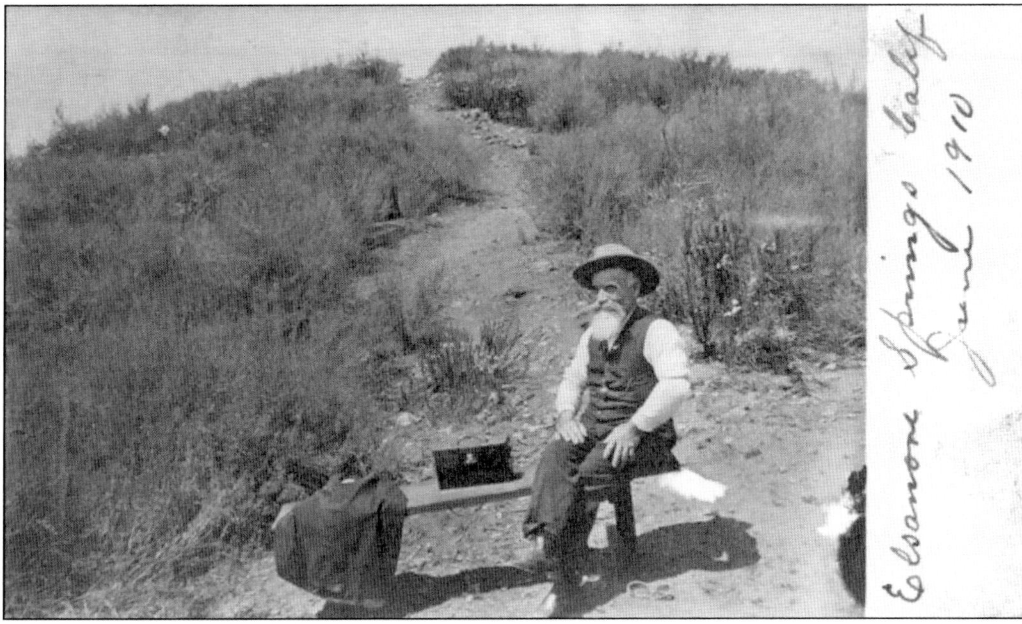

A man sits beside a road, probably the Ortega Highway. Is he posing or simply resting? A note on the edge of the photograph reads, "Elsinore Springs, Calif. June 1910." Of course, the box on the bench indicates that he may have stopped to enjoy his lunch in the Elsinore Mountains.

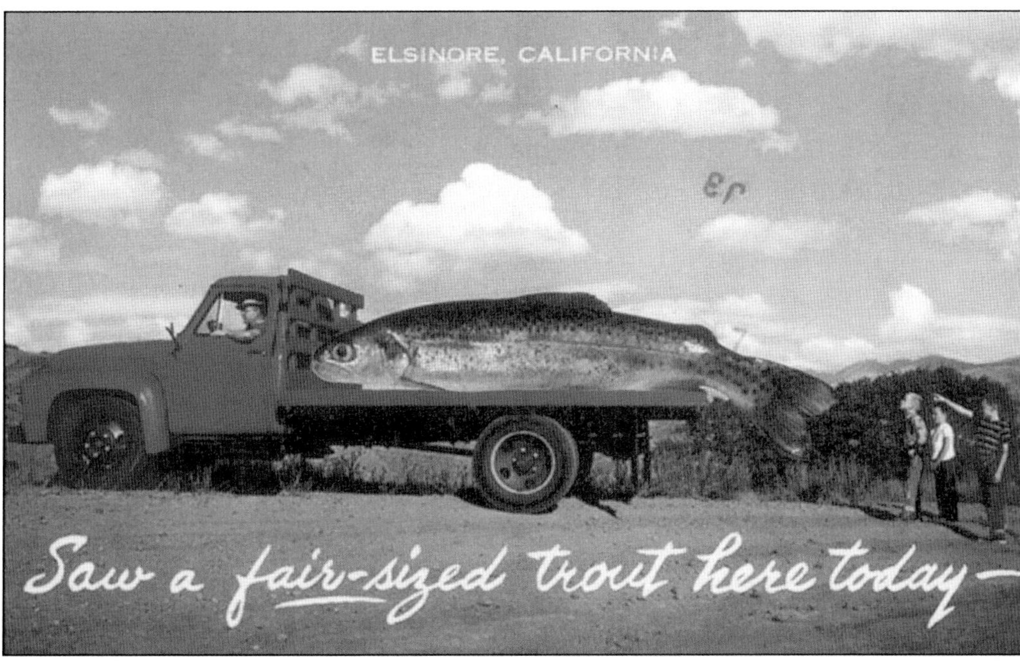


Funny postcards were always good for travelers to send home to friends and relatives to make them jealous of the sights. Indeed, many fishermen would have loved to see "a fair-sized trout here today."

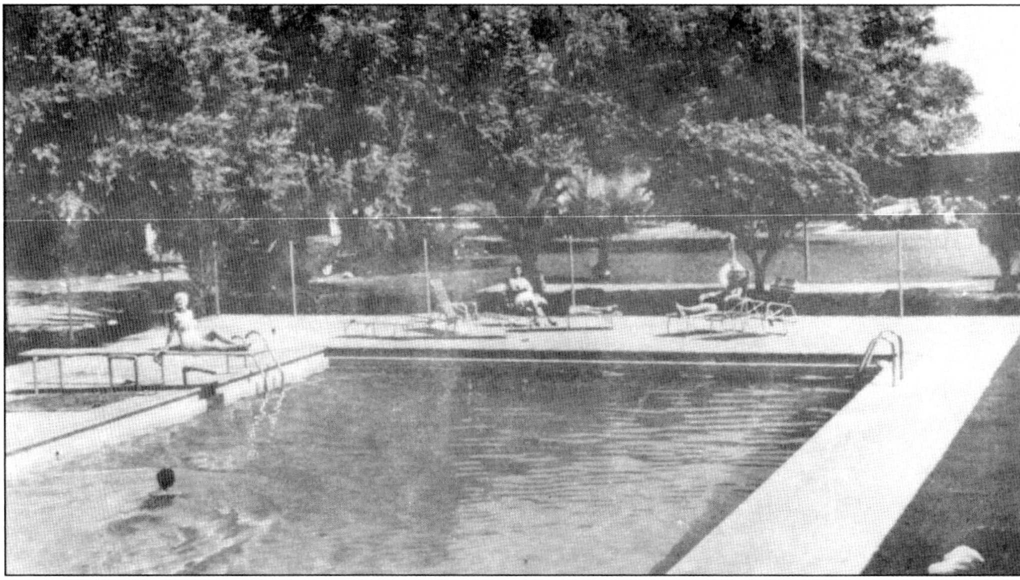

These photographs show two views of Kiowa Camp, which opened on Riverside Drive in 1949. It was originally a reducing center for ladies and was nicknamed "the Fat Women's Farm." During the 1950s, it became a summer camp for children with a nurse on duty. Today the site enjoys a good reputation as Lake Park. It is a favorite spot for camping with recreational vehicles.

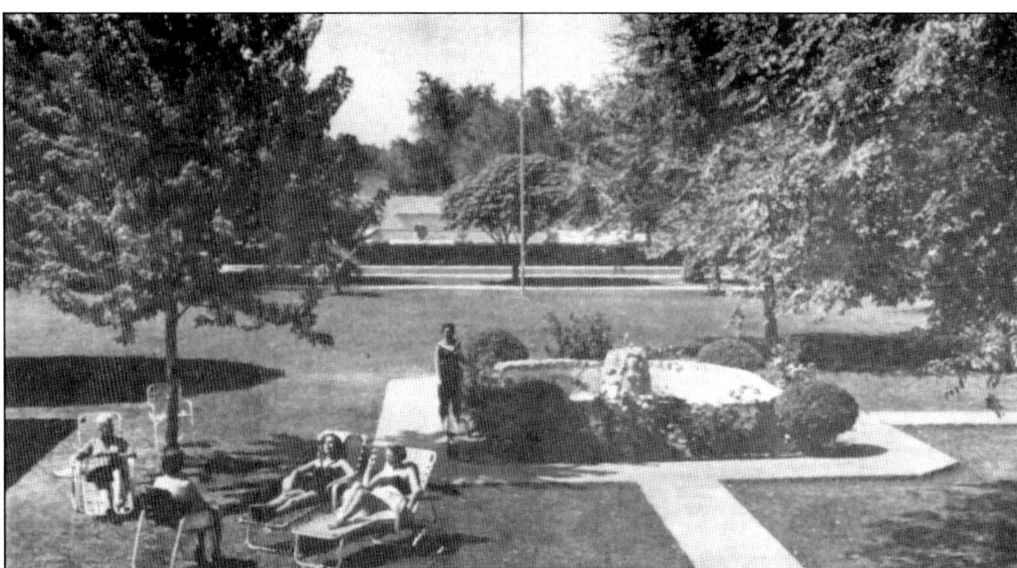

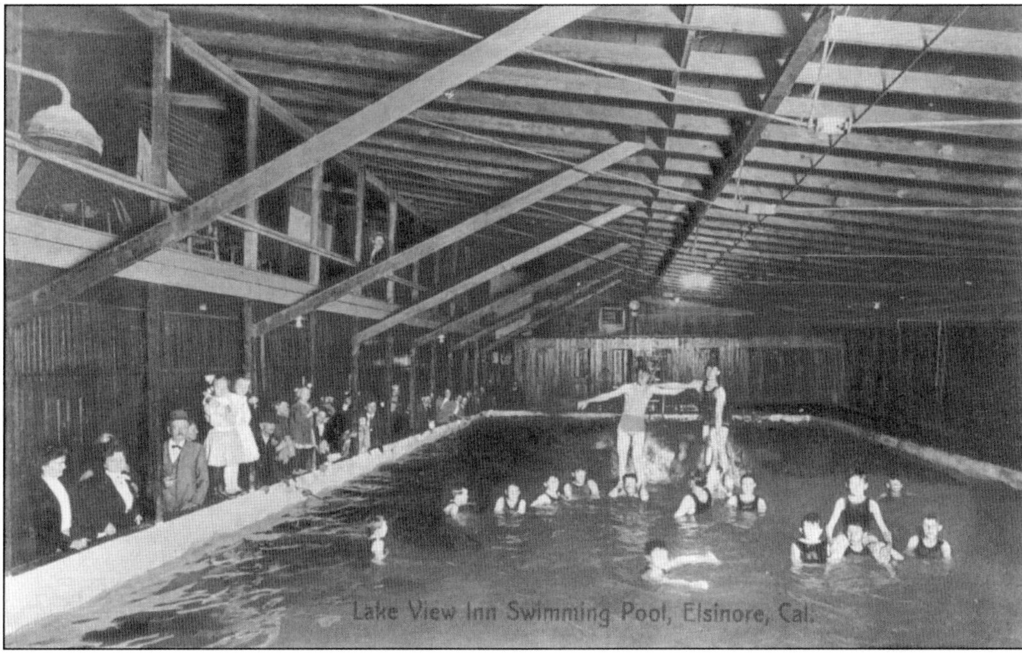


The indoor swimming pool at the Crescent Bath House was built for guests of the Lake View Hotel, located one block away. The pool provided enjoyment for young and old alike, but was closed and filled with dirt after a 12-year-old boy drowned in June 1935. (MR.)

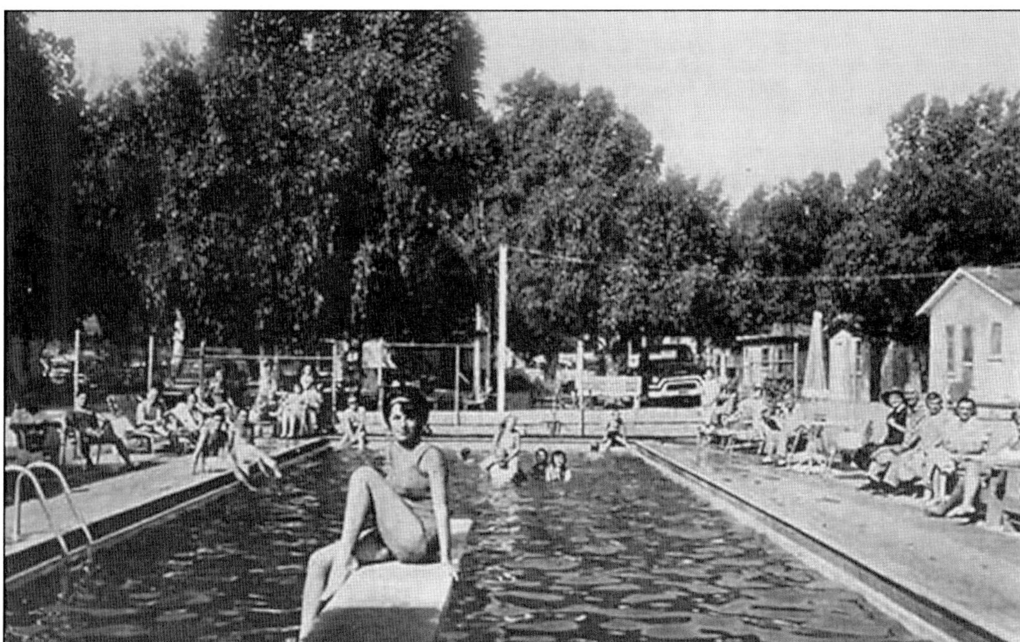

Shore Acres Lodge, situated at 15712 Grand Avenue, was a pie-shaped property extending down to the lake's edge. In the 1920s, it was a favorite of those camping with travel trailers and tents. Campers liked having access to the lake, as it was akin to having their own private beach.

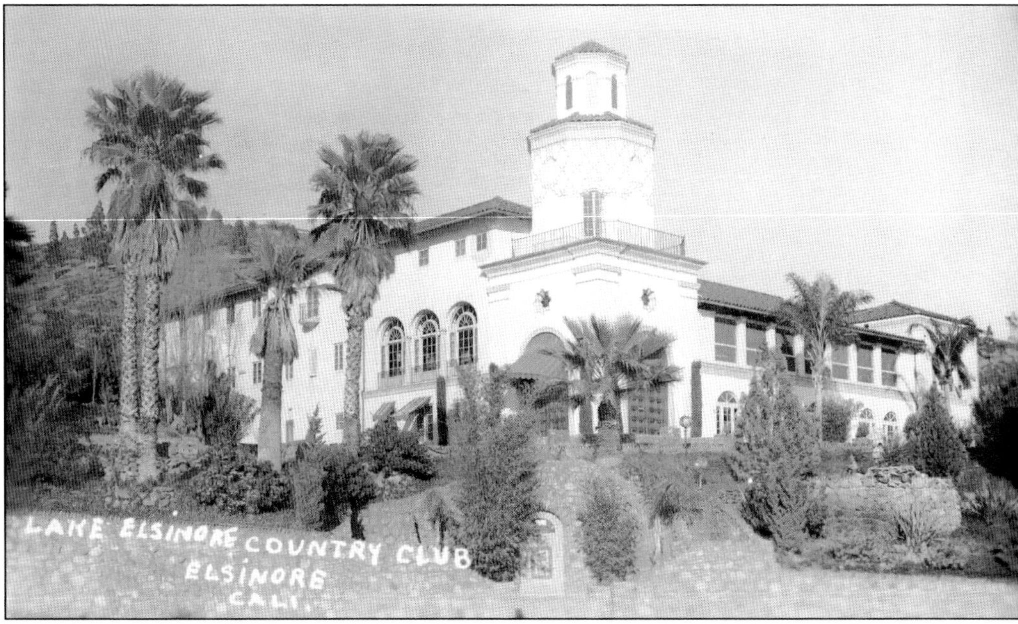


The Clevelin Realty Company built the country club in 1926 for the residents of Country Club Heights. The pier and country club were the site of many dances, boat races, group swims, and water sports. The Aloha Pier was so popular that parking space was at a premium. People would sit on the running boards of their cars and eat lunch so they would not have to leave their spots. The wooden pier was razed in 1950. The country club was renovated in 1951 and reopened to the public as the scene of many social events. Residents still talk of the activities they attended at the country club and how elegantly it was decorated. The building had been for sale for many years, and an offer was finally made in January 2001. Before escrow could close, an arsonist set fire to the structure and it burned to the ground in a few short hours.

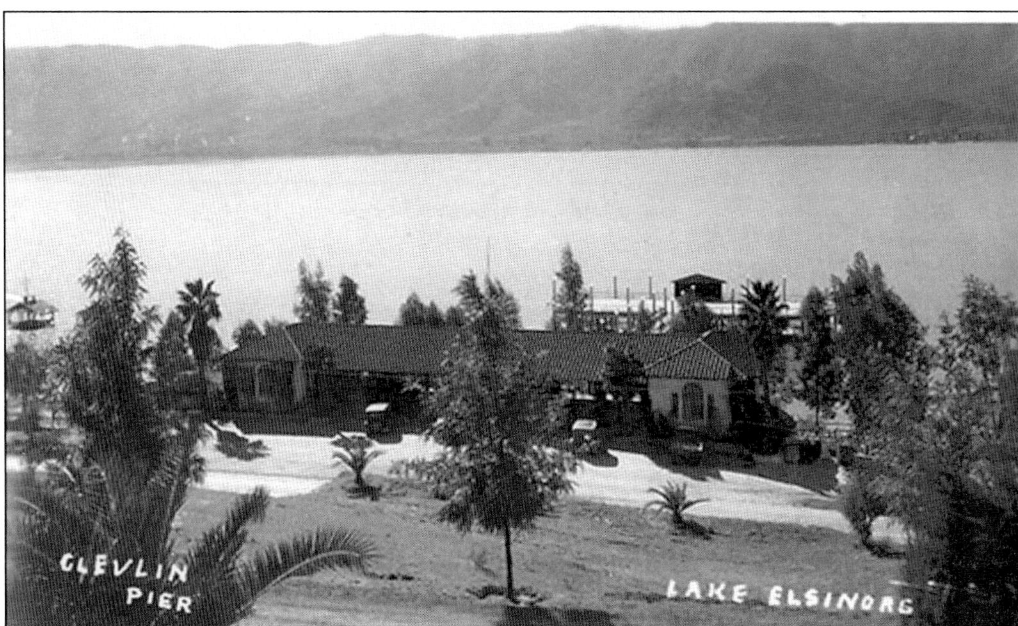

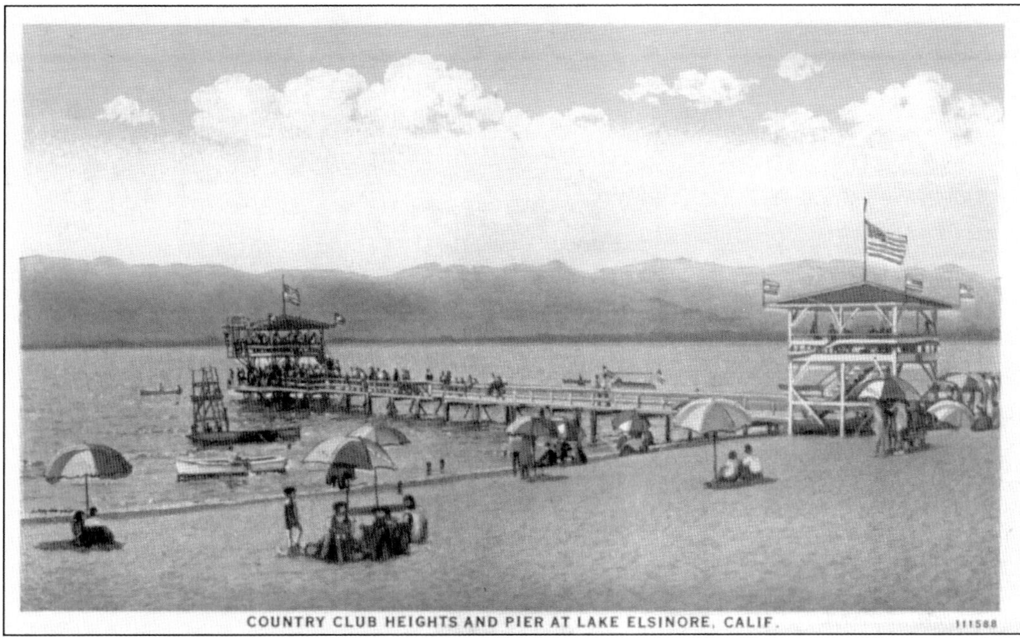


At times, this area was called the Clevelin Pier after the realty company that developed Country Club Heights in the largest real estate promotion ever conceived and carried out in the Lake Elsinore Valley. It brought fame, both good and bad, to the valley. The pier was built in 1926 with swings and playgrounds for the children. The pier and beach were popular for swimming and boating. The arched-roof pavilion was constructed adjoining the pier. When the rains of 1927 came, a second floor was added so the residents could continue to dance on the superb dance floor, where orchestras performed on weekends and holidays. The pier was demolished in 1950. (MK.)

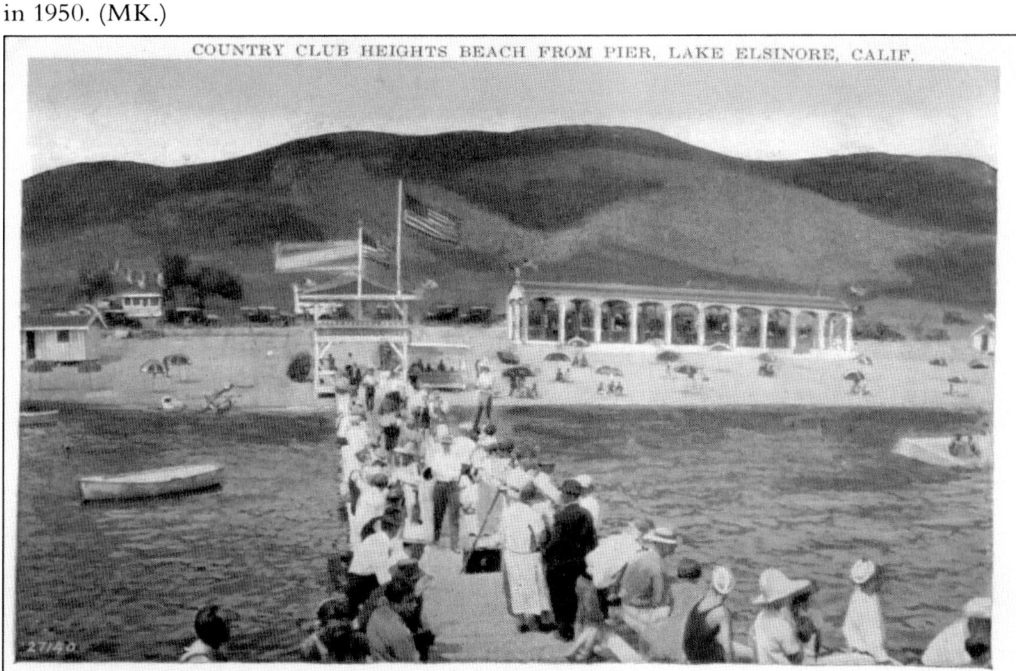

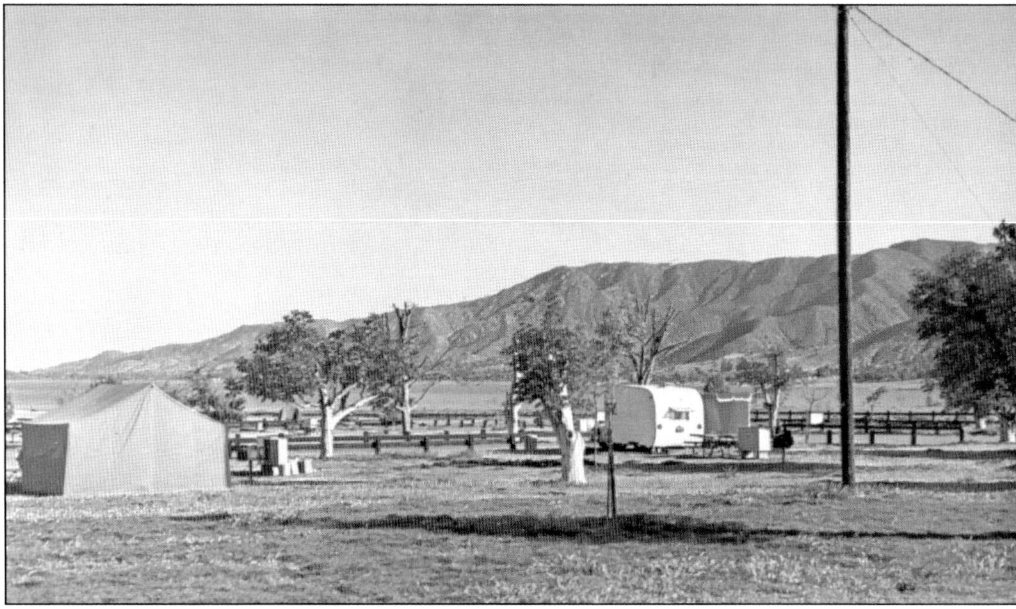

The State of California established a campground on the north shore of Lake Elsinore. The city's decision to sell the 2,900-acre lake to the state was a long time in the making. Finally, in 1955, the state took the lake and then gave it back in the 1960s. In 1972, Proposition II was approved and the site went back to the state as an official state park. Because of the floods of 1978 to 1980, the state lost a bundle and a lawsuit ensued. The state returned ownership to Lake Elsinore in the 1990s. A management company is currently renovating and upgrading the area, known as Lake Elsinore Recreation Park, to include a new boat launch and swimming area, upgraded camping spots, and a tenting area for campers such as the Boy Scouts. In these photographs, campers take advantage of the beautiful Lake Elsinore views. (Above, CWI; below, AP.)

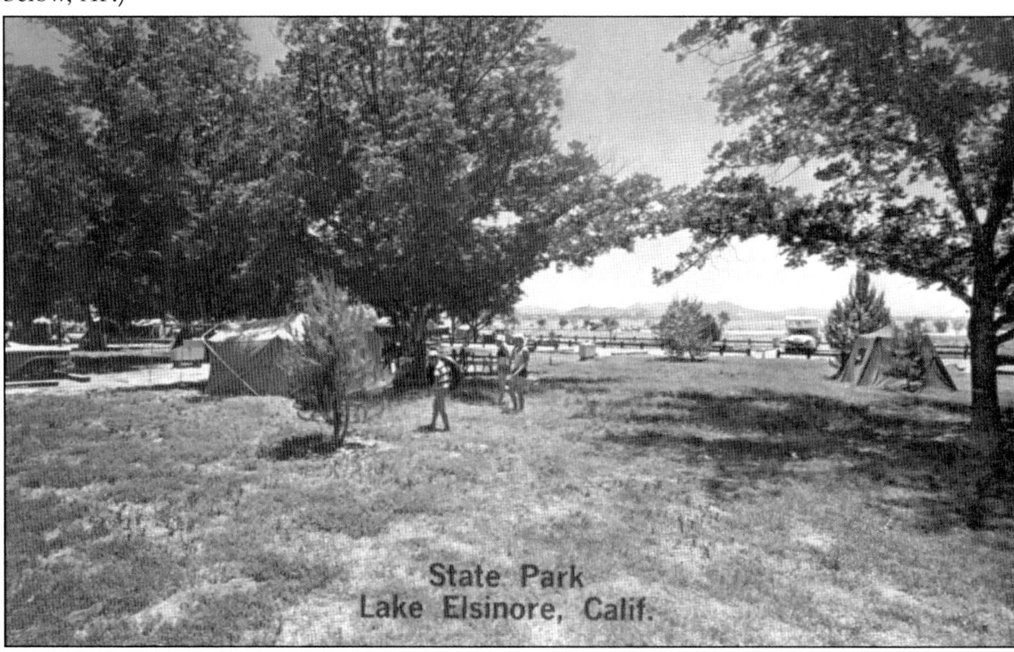

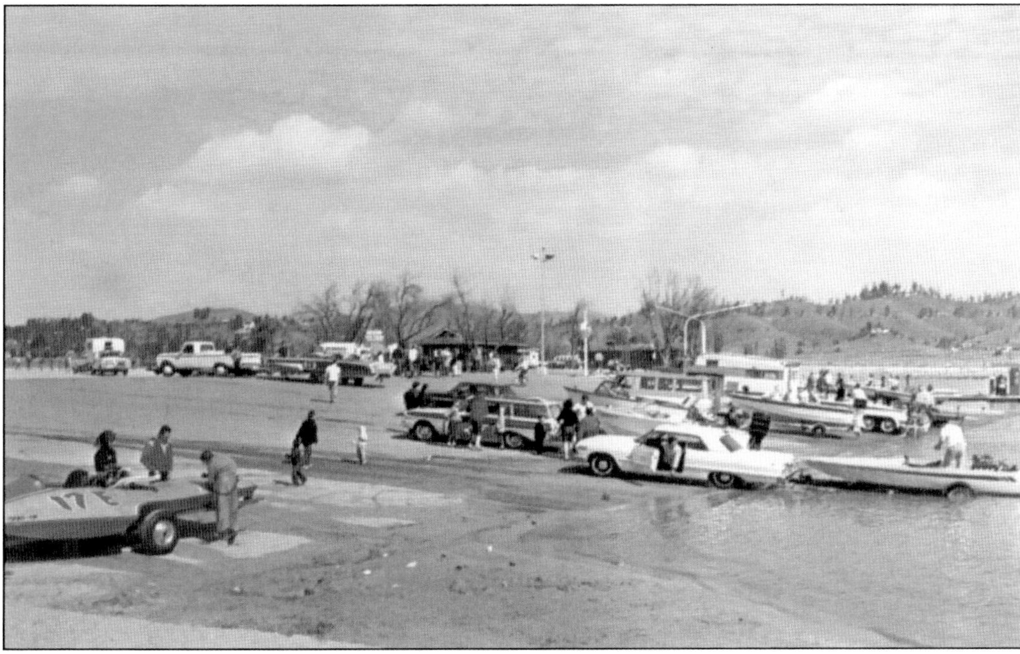

Speedboat racing is another popular sport on Lake Elsinore. With no launching facilities, the cars were backed down to the water and the boats launched into the lake. The above scene depicts the new state park marina, on Riverside Drive. In the image below, some upgrades have been made to the boat launch facility. During the 1930s, a racing record of 33.74 miles per hour was set on Lake Elsinore. The hills of Country Club Heights are visible in the center of the photograph. (Both CWI/ CG.)

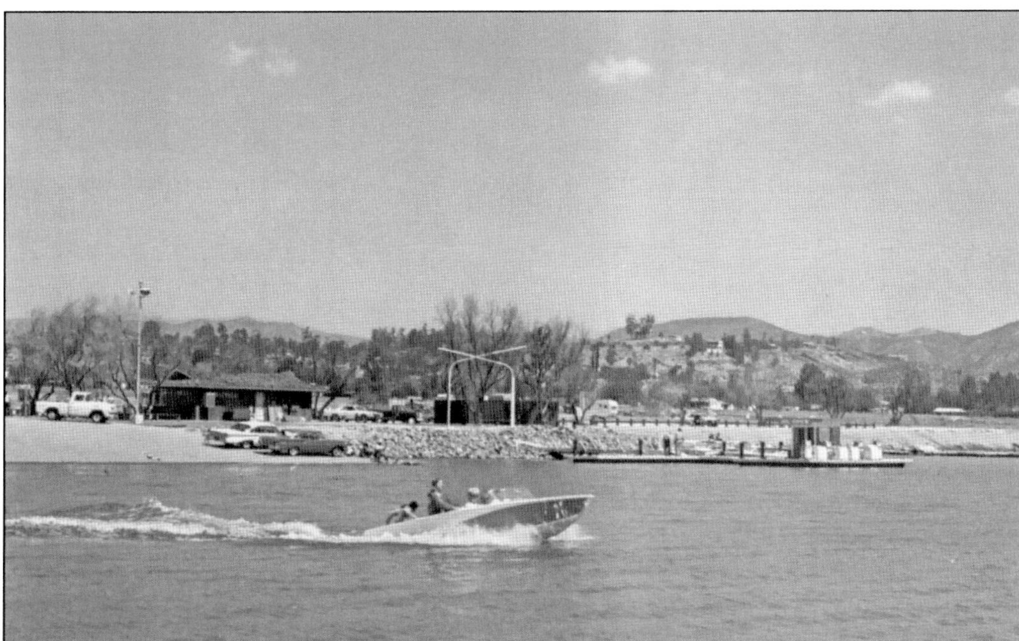

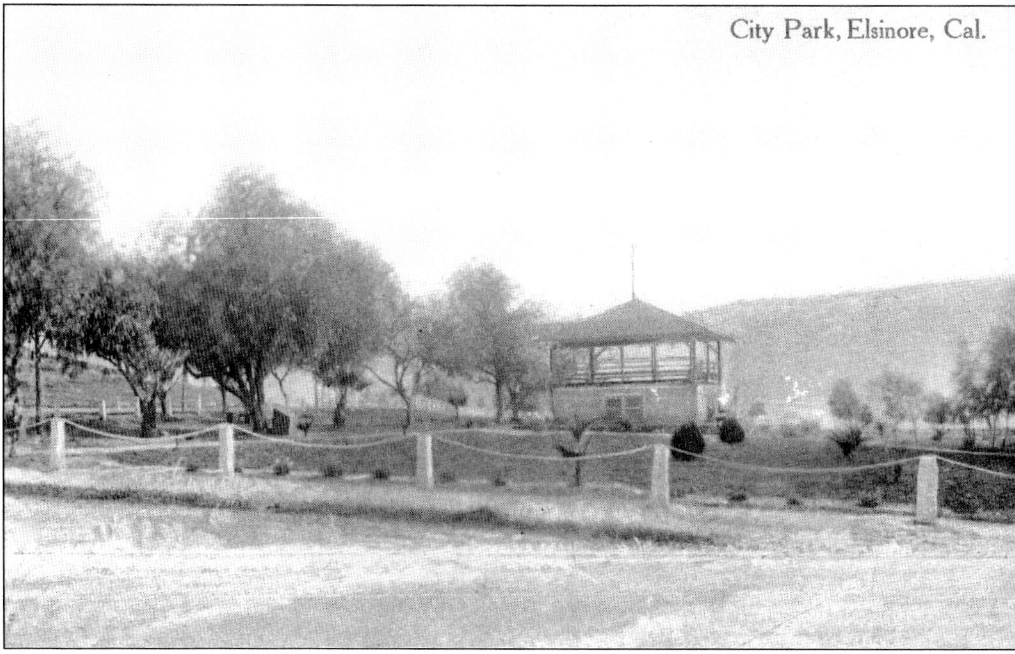


C. S. and Hattie Traphagen, owners of the Lake View Hotel, deeded seven parcels of land to the city, provided the land be used for park purposes, between March 2 and May 18, 1906. A year or two later, the Traphagens and others planted trees in the park and constructed the bandstand (above), which was the first gazebo and entertainment center. The pavilion building (below) looks much the same today. On the right side of the photograph is a gazebo that remains in use. (Above, MSL/ LC.)

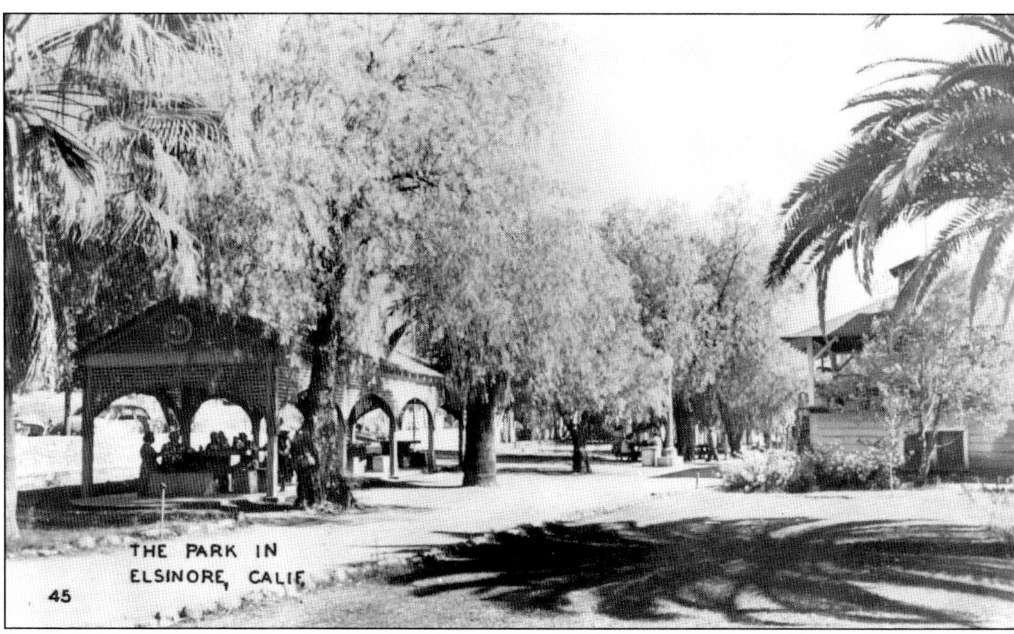

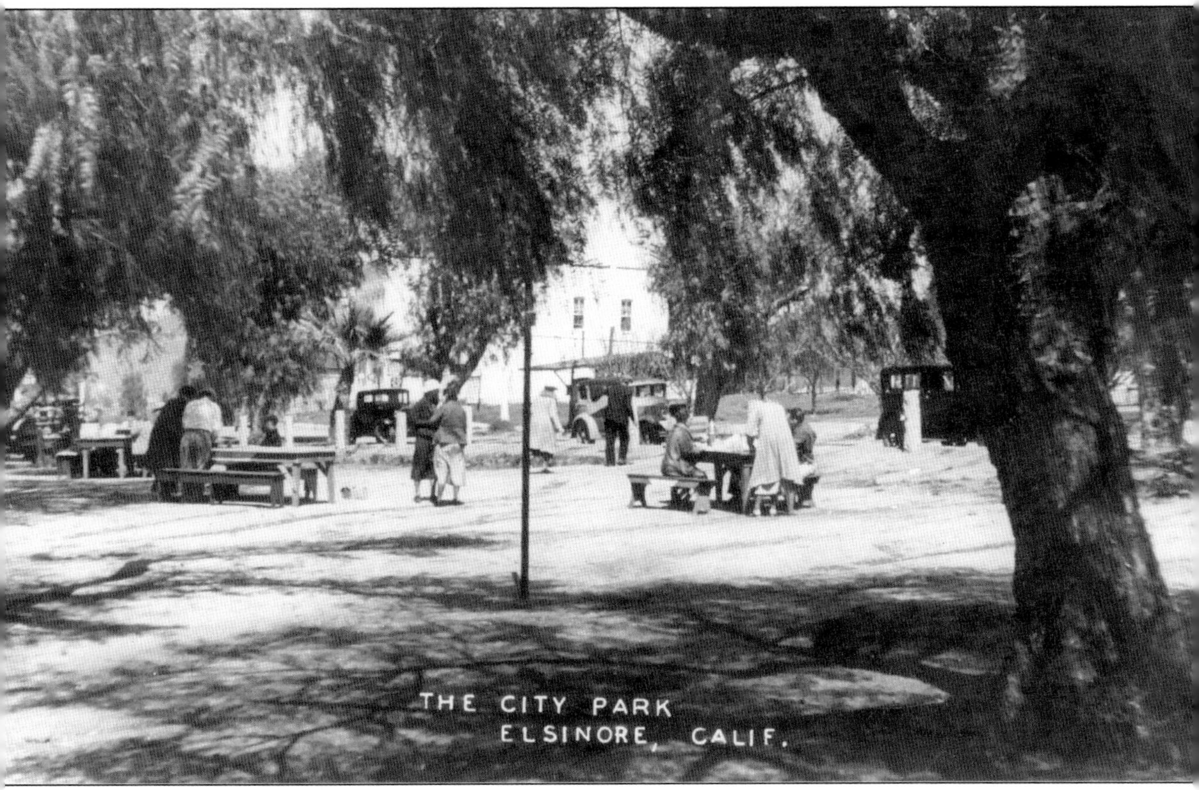


Cars sit at the Ambassador Hotel in this view through the park. The rock wall surrounding City Park was constructed by the WPA in 1938. A few years ago, it was suggested that the site be renamed in honor of a deceased citizen. The community objected, stating that it was donated as the City Park and therefore the name should not be changed. It continues as City Park today. (LC.)

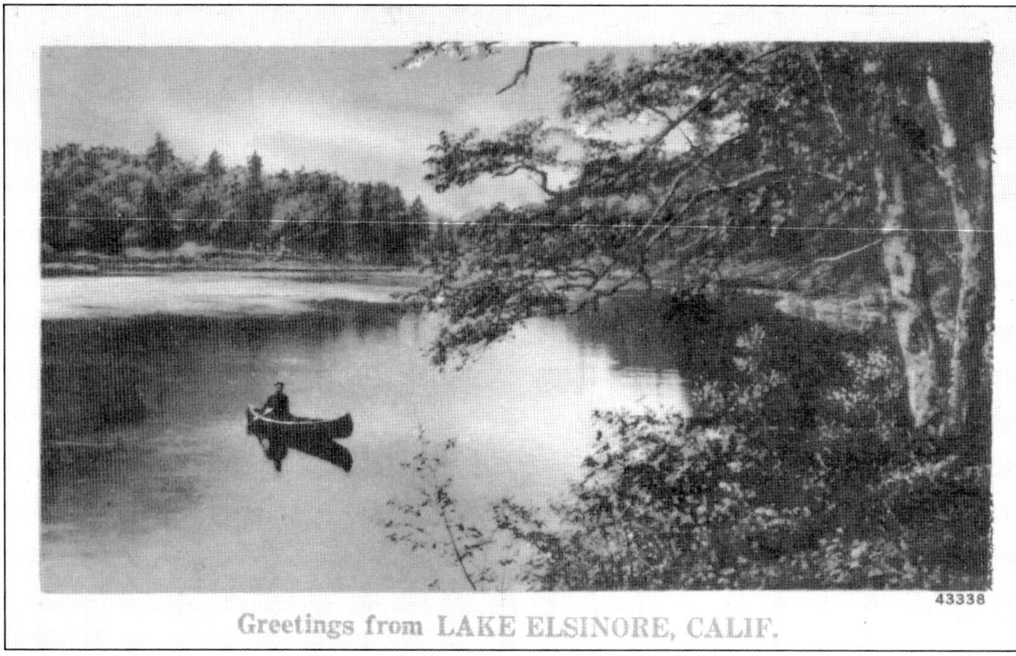


Lake Elsinore is a natural lake covering more than 2,900 acres. As the city's population grows, the new residents want to have access to the recreational activities involving the water. Watercraft companies in town use the lake for test runs of their new boats. A person can find all types of activities on the lake almost any time of the day. (NYCE.)

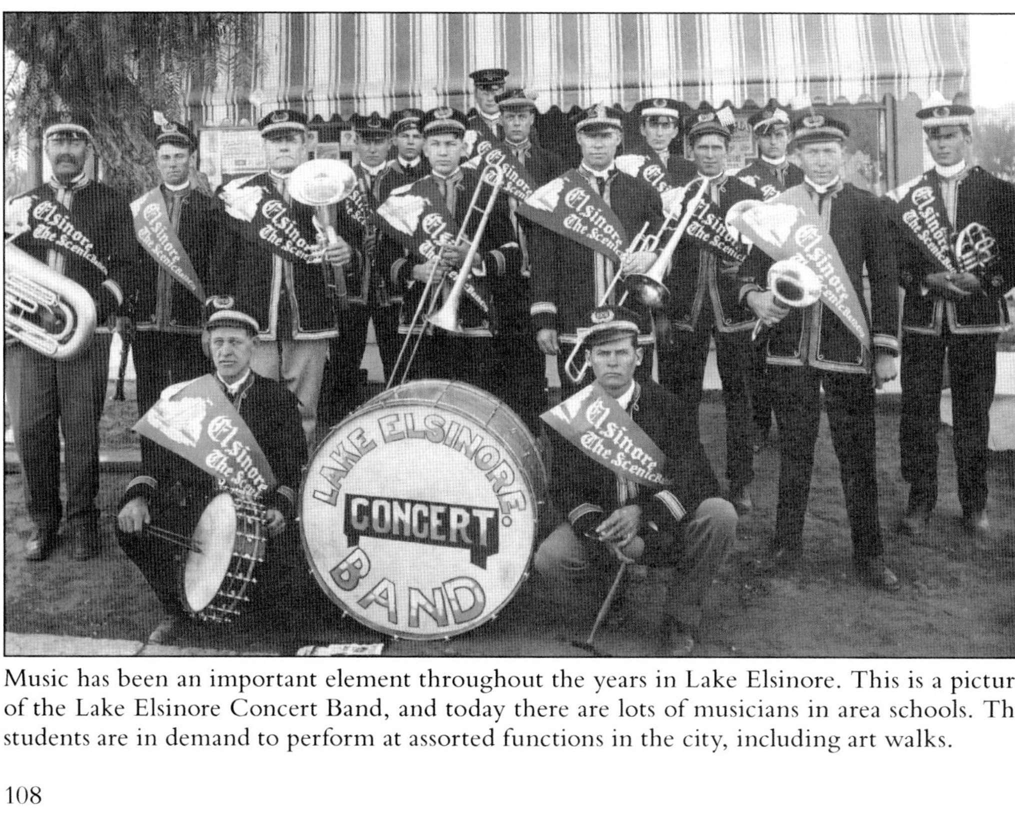


Music has been an important element throughout the years in Lake Elsinore. This is a picture of the Lake Elsinore Concert Band, and today there are lots of musicians in area schools. The students are in demand to perform at assorted functions in the city, including art walks.

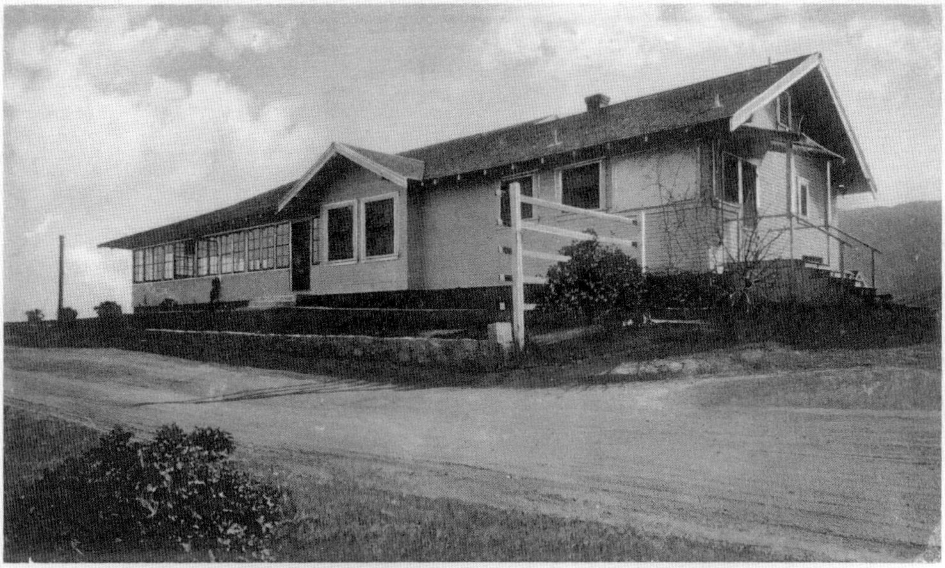

Golf Club, Southern California Athletic and Country Club

The Southern California Golf Course was built in 1924, and on May 30 of that year, the 18-hole championship course was opened to the public. Located on the west side of Corydon Road near Grand Avenue, it was developed by a group of Los Angeles business executives at a cost of more than $60,000.

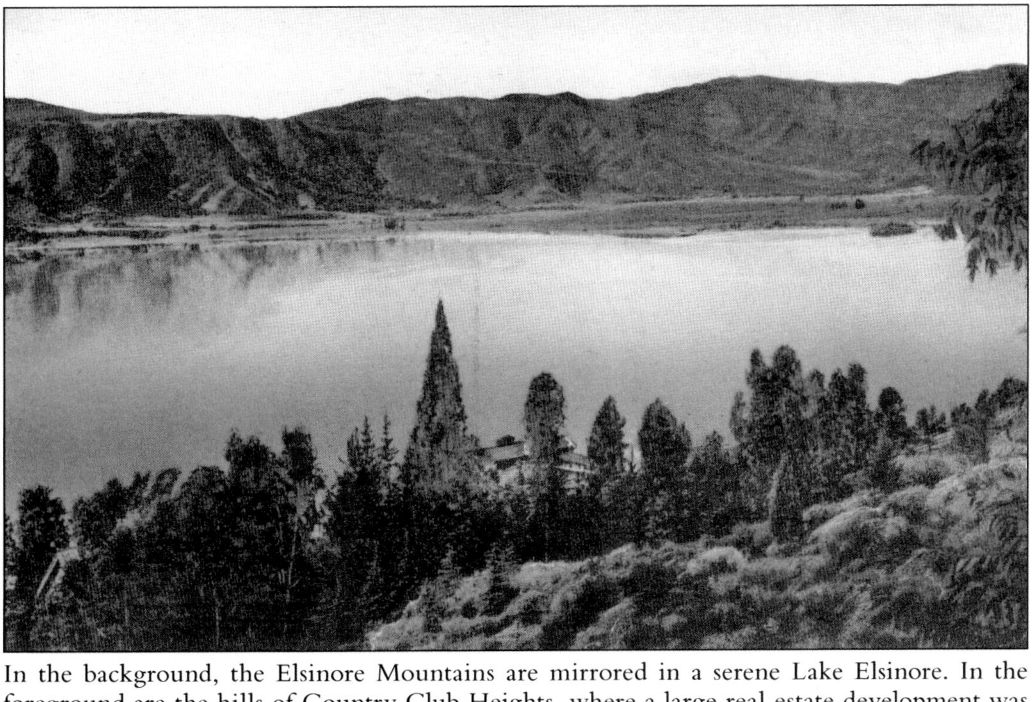

In the background, the Elsinore Mountains are mirrored in a serene Lake Elsinore. In the foreground are the hills of Country Club Heights, where a large real estate development was promoted in the 1930s.

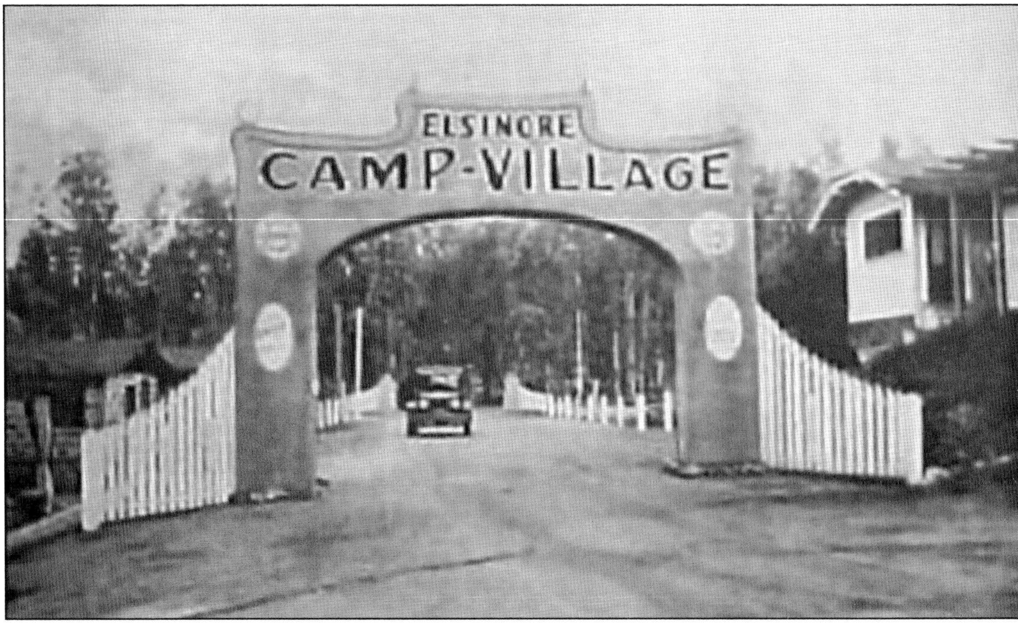


Motor courts, such as the Elsinore Camp Village and Elsinore Auto Camp Ground, were popular in the 1930s and 1940s. Families would pack their belongings and go to the lake, mountains, or their favorite location and spend a few days, a few weeks, a month, and in some cases the summer. These spots created great memories for children who spent their vacations in Elsinore. The courts offered cottages furnished with the bare essentials, and the occupants brought their own luxuries. The pictured campgrounds were probably on Grand Avenue near the lake.

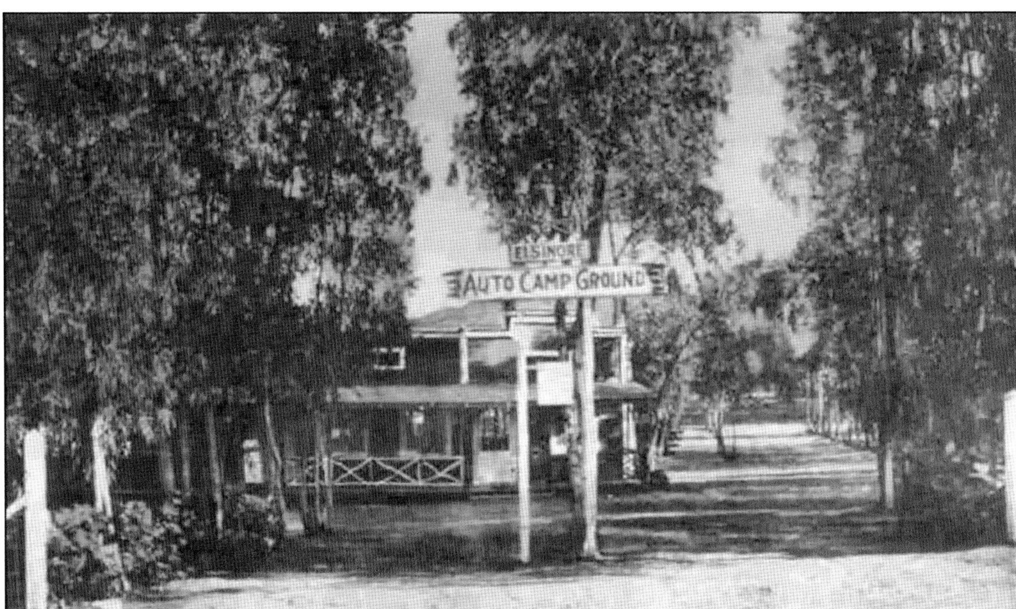

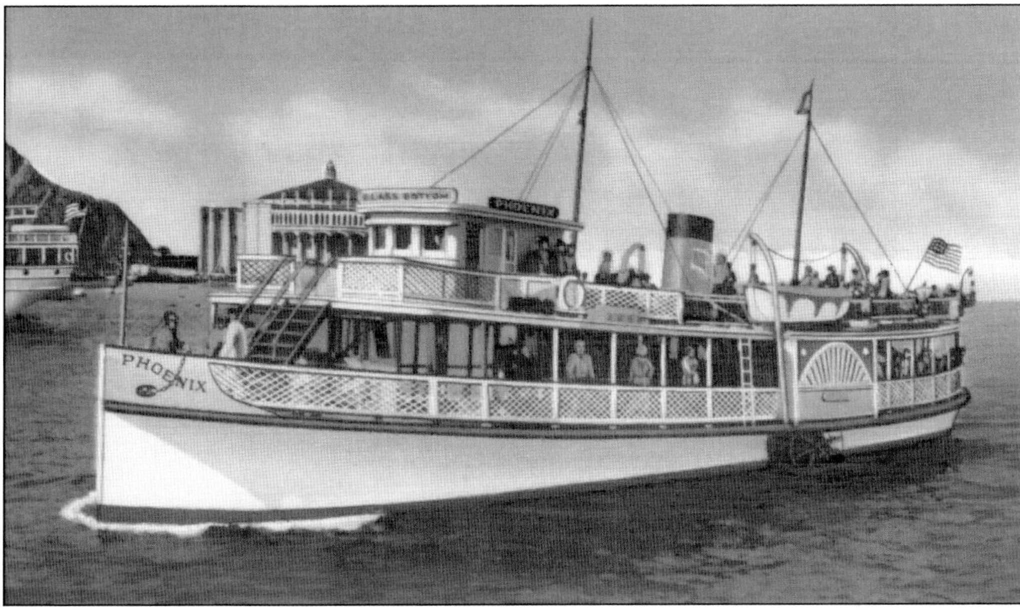


Five paddle-wheel boats were built in San Pedro for the William Wrigley family of chewing gum fame to use on Catalina Island. Below, people view the submarine gardens off Catalina Island. After service on Catalina, the *M. V. Princess* was moved to Long Beach, where it became a restaurant in Long Beach Harbor. The ship seen above was moved to Lake Elsinore and renamed the *Elsinore Princess* in 1999. The Lake Elsinore Citizens Committee has applied to Riverside County to have it listed on the National Register. In July 2007, the Riverside County Board of Supervisors unanimously approved the *Elsinore Princess* for a historic designation. When restored, it will have a berth in the Rivers Edge Marina on Lakeshore Drive. (Both WPNC.)

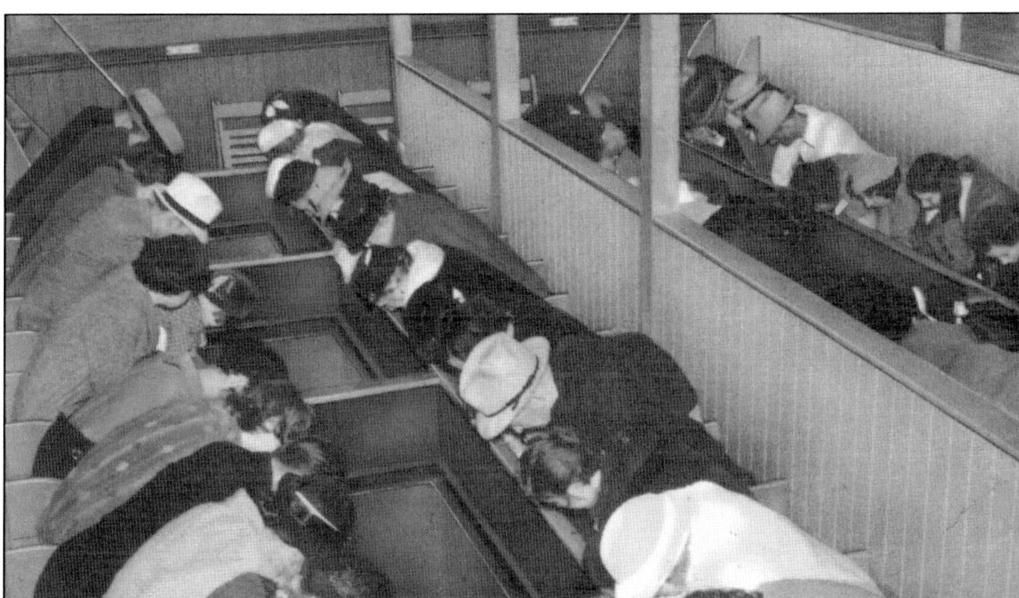

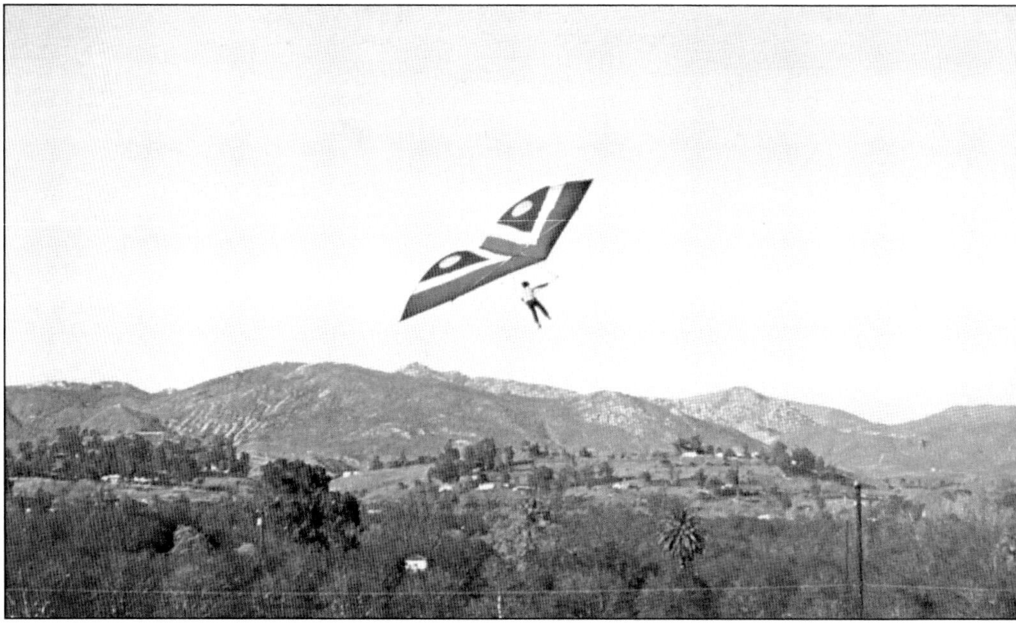

A lone hang glider floats through the thermal air over the mountains and lake. This is one of the few places in the world with the right air currents for gliding, hang gliding, and parachuting. A pilot takes people up in an airplane at Skylark Airport, and when the correct altitude is reached, the skydivers jump from the plane and come down at a landing spot near the Ortega Highway or some other designated area. (RB/ DA.)

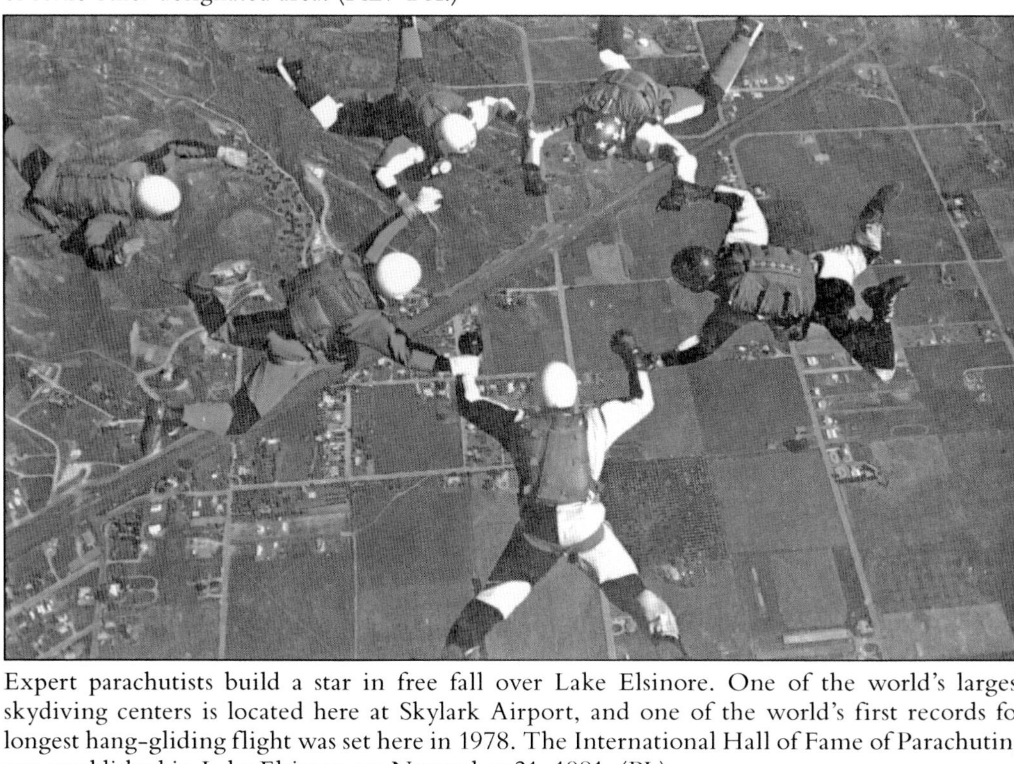

Expert parachutists build a star in free fall over Lake Elsinore. One of the world's largest skydiving centers is located here at Skylark Airport, and one of the world's first records for longest hang-gliding flight was set here in 1978. The International Hall of Fame of Parachuting was established in Lake Elsinore on November 21, 1981. (PI.)

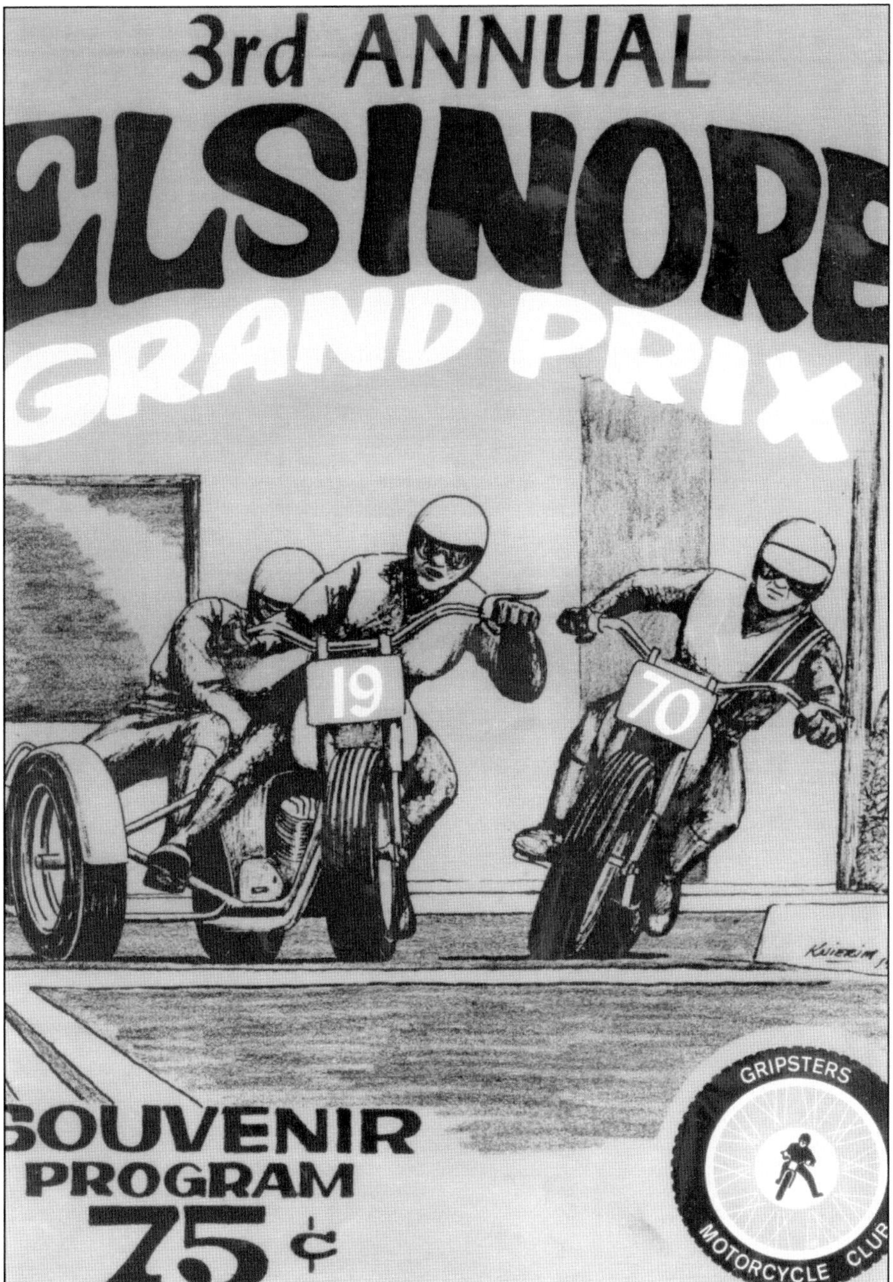


From 1969 to 1972, during the Elsinore Grand Prix, the city played host to the Gripsters Motorcycle Club, whose members raced through the streets and surrounding hills of Elsinore. One of the favorite racers of the day was Steve McQueen, whose movie *On Any Sunday* was filmed here. After a 24-year absence, the city council brought motorcycle racing back in 1996. When the events resumed, a race was named the Harvey Mushman (Steve McQueen's racing name) in his honor. The course continues today through the streets, hills, and countryside of our city. Excitement is in the air when the Grand Prix arrives because all of the area's facilities are used for registration, camping, and meeting old friends.

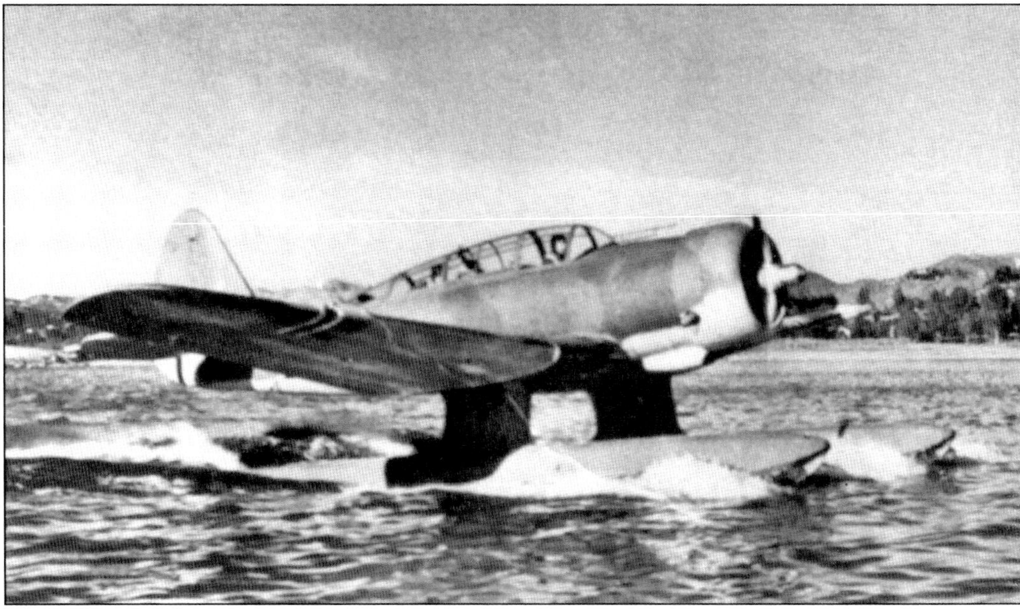

This N-3PB biplane completed a test flight on Lake Elsinore. These planes were dubbed the Northrops by the Norwegians. They were ferried up the West Coast to Canada, where a training base had been established by Royal Norwegian Air Force personnel. Elsinore's other contribution to the World War II effort was when the Douglas Aircraft Corporation leased facilities in the city for a machine shop designed to manufacture wings for B-17 bombers.

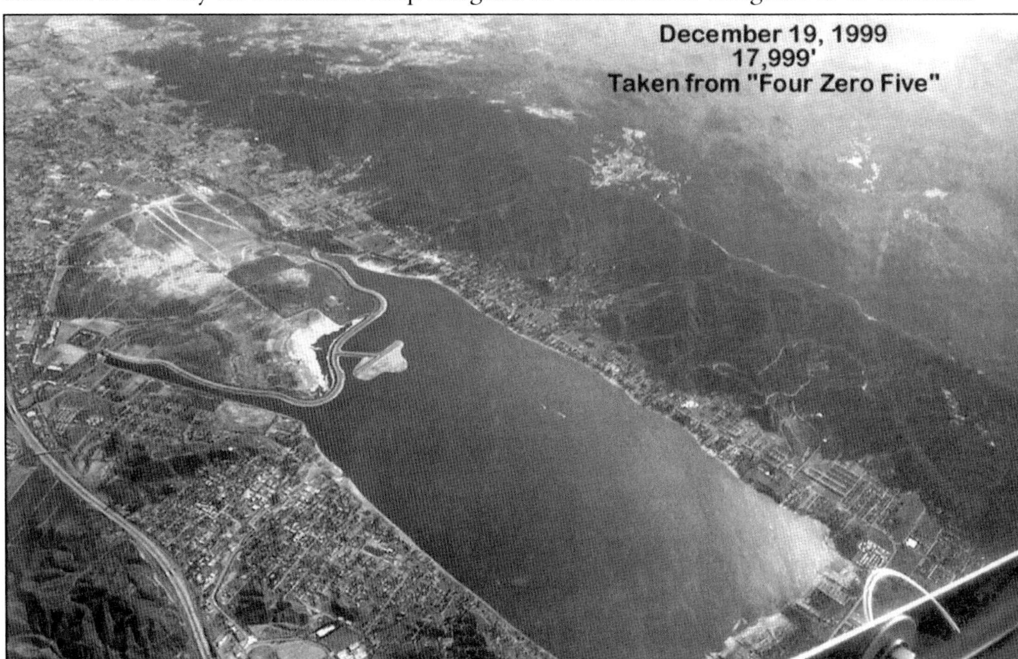


This aerial view of Lake Elsinore shows the entire area from the Ortega Highway on the left to the mountains on the right. The levee had been constructed in the middle. The aircraft from which this photograph was taken, tail number 405, is registered with the Federal Aviation Administration.

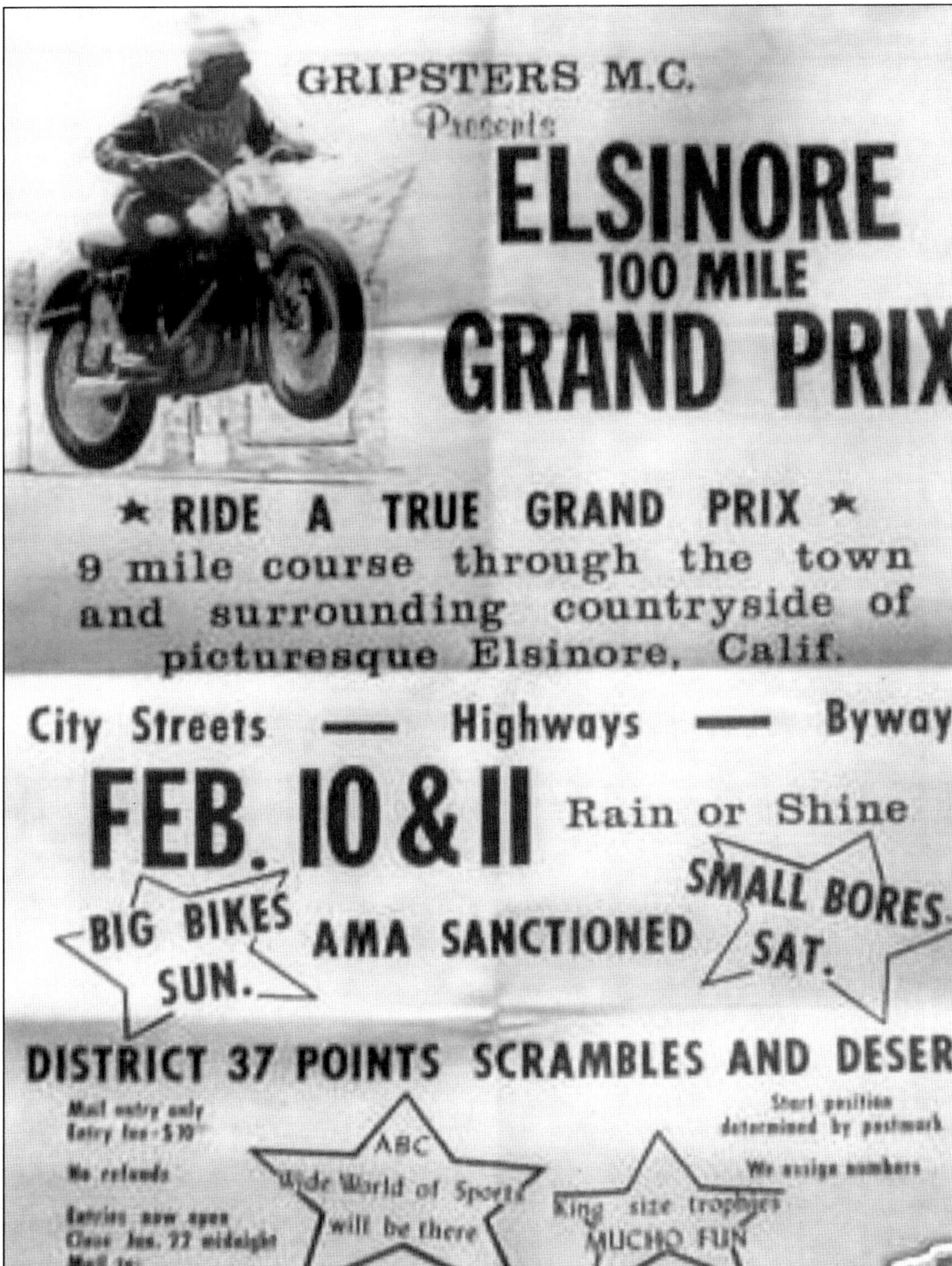


This handbill advertises the Elsinore Grand Prix. In the early days, the souvenir programs were full of information including lists of registered racers and last year's winners, advertisements for local businesses, and lots of photographs. The Gripsters Motorcycle Club of Southern California and the City of Lake Elsinore sponsored the event. The race, lasting two days, was sanctioned by the American Motorcycle Association. The program indicates the elements that make the Elsinore Grand Prix exciting: city streets of asphalt and curbs.

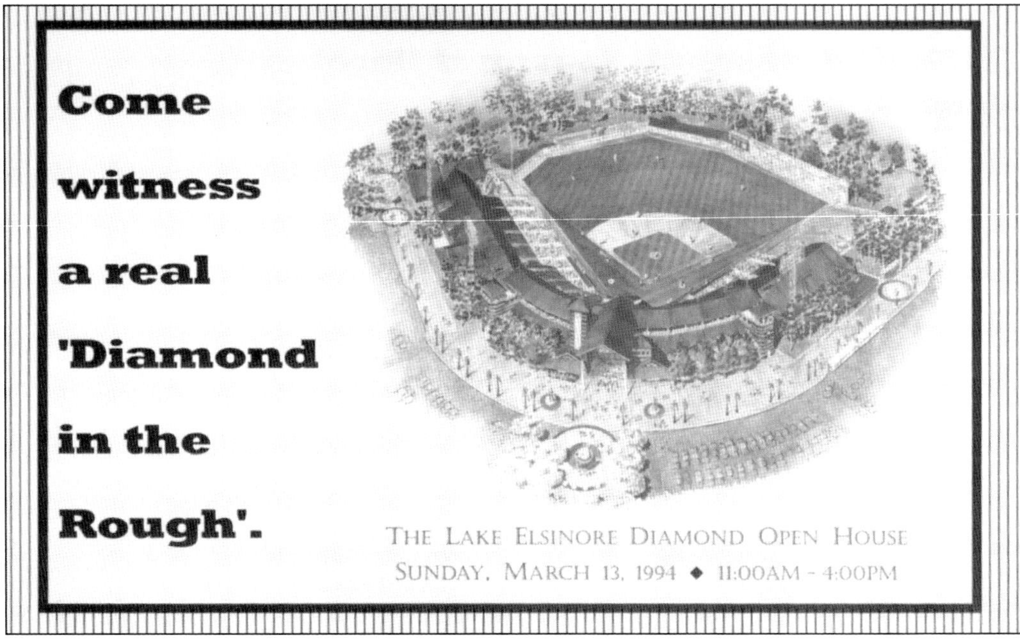


The Diamond Stadium was controversial during its construction, and the controversy has continued because of cost overruns. The stadium opened on March 13, 1994, as home to the minor farm team for the Anaheim Angels. The facility, a state-of-the art baseball field with seating for more than 6,000 guests, is rated the best Class A stadium in the nation.

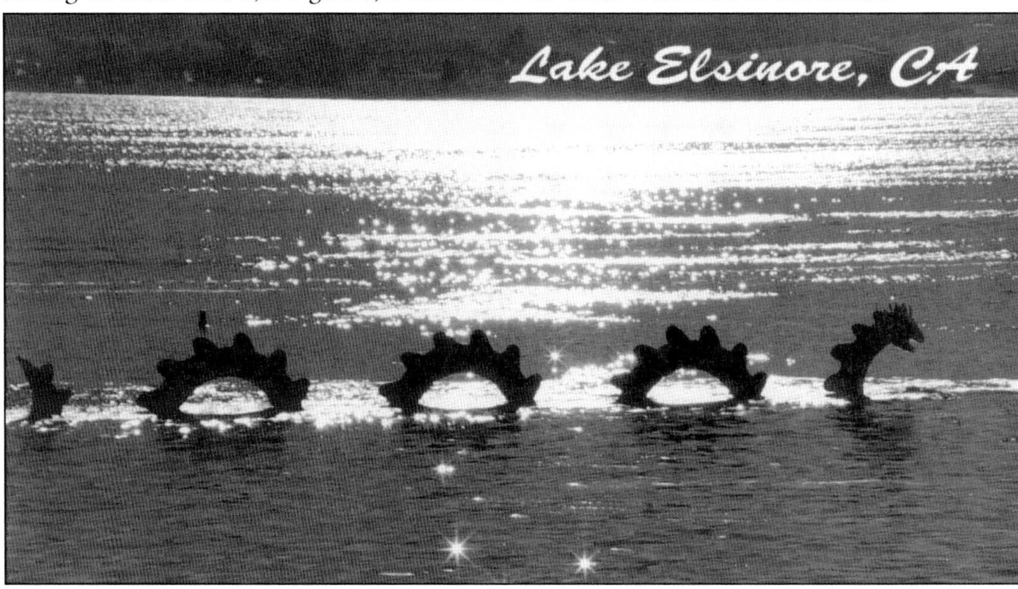


Elsie, the Loch Elsinore Monster, related to the famous Loch Ness Monster, came to life on April 9, 1988, on the city's 100th anniversary of incorporation. Elsie was planned as a centennial surprise by two local businesspeople who designed and created her out of chicken wire, wood pieces, rolls of black plastic, and rigid foam packing for fins. She did not fare too well in her first outing and was snagged by some lake debris. A new super-sized Elsie, made as an all-volunteer community project, has participated in many community activities to the delight of visitors.

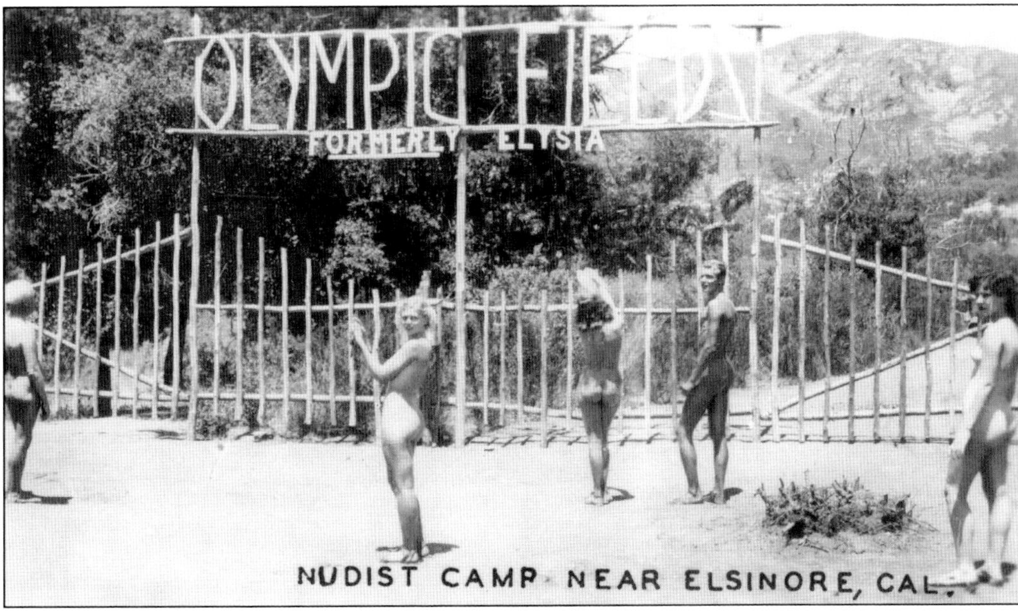

Olympic Fields Nudist Camp was established in 1933 and was located in the Elsinore Mountains off the Ortega Highway. Originally called Elysian Fields and founded by Mr. and Mrs. Hobart Glassey and Peter McConville, it was sold in 1952 to Mr. and Mrs. Wally Nilson, who changed the name to McConville. Subsequently, the camp was changed to Mystic Oaks and was operated by Mrs. Nilson and her son until early 2007, when it was sold.

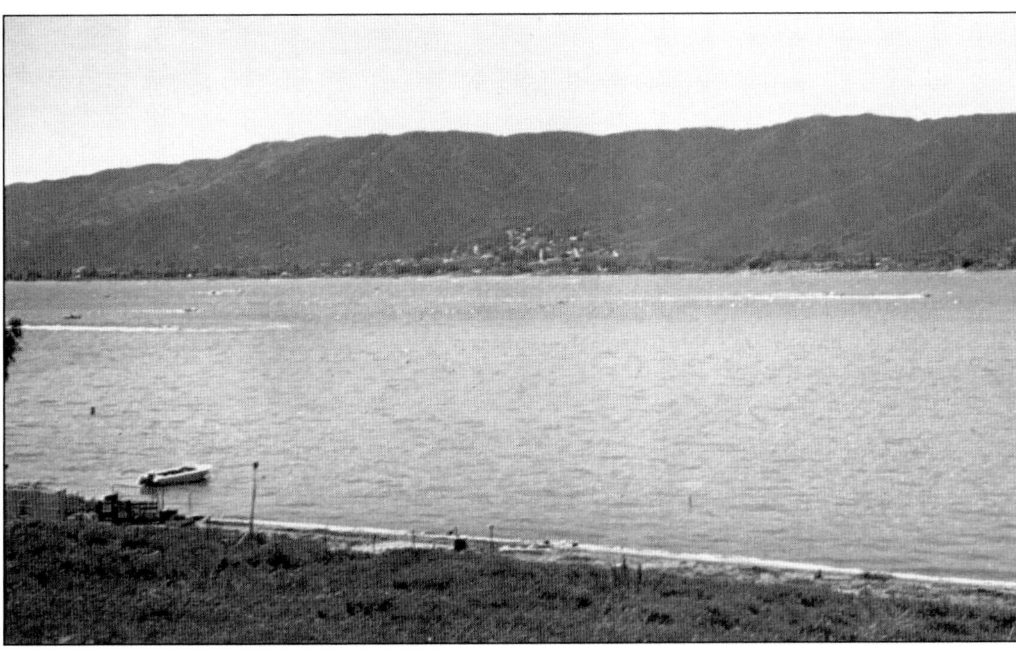
This scenic view of Lake Elsinore looks from the Grand Avenue side toward the Country Club Heights area, with the mountains in the background. The water is calm and makes one feel relaxed with the waves lapping the shoreline. On this day, a lone boat was anchored near the shoreline. (RB/ DA.)

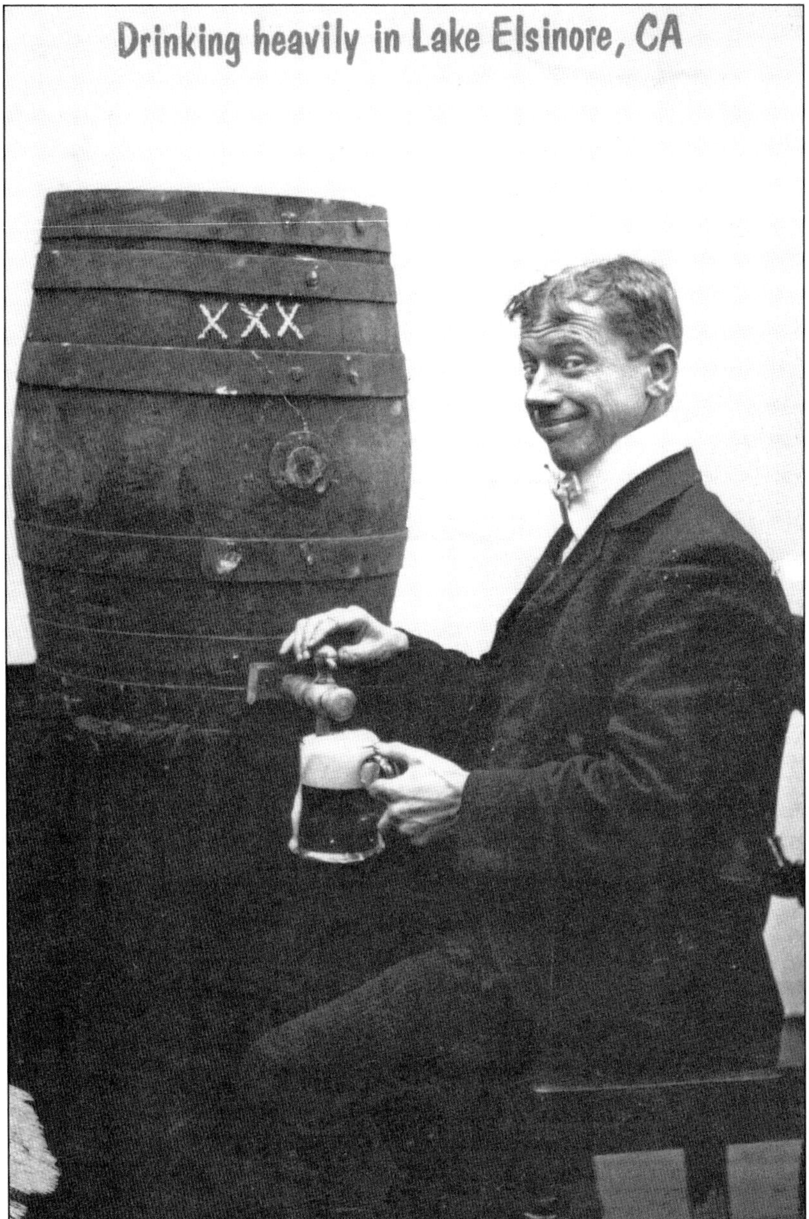


The following are postcard messages: "Hello Babe Went to ranch nobody home see you later Best Wishes.""Thank you much for remembering us at Christmas, come out and see us this year, the weather is great." "Here we are at Elsinore having a fine time—reading, bathing, writing, and visiting." "I certainly did enjoy visiting with you—and the auto ride was a treat—Also, Florence's nice music." "Am here visiting for a few days. Just like summer weather [written November 15, 1906]." "We have a little cabin on the lake and we take a dip every day. You better come and spend the day with us Sunday. It only takes three hours to get here and Lea is coming down Saturday afternoon. Come and join us at the cabin." "When I wrote your letter yesterday I forgot to thank you for sending the slip an stepins of Jonines Robert is sitting here by me an he told me to tell Uncle Chris the lollypops were ver good." (JC.)

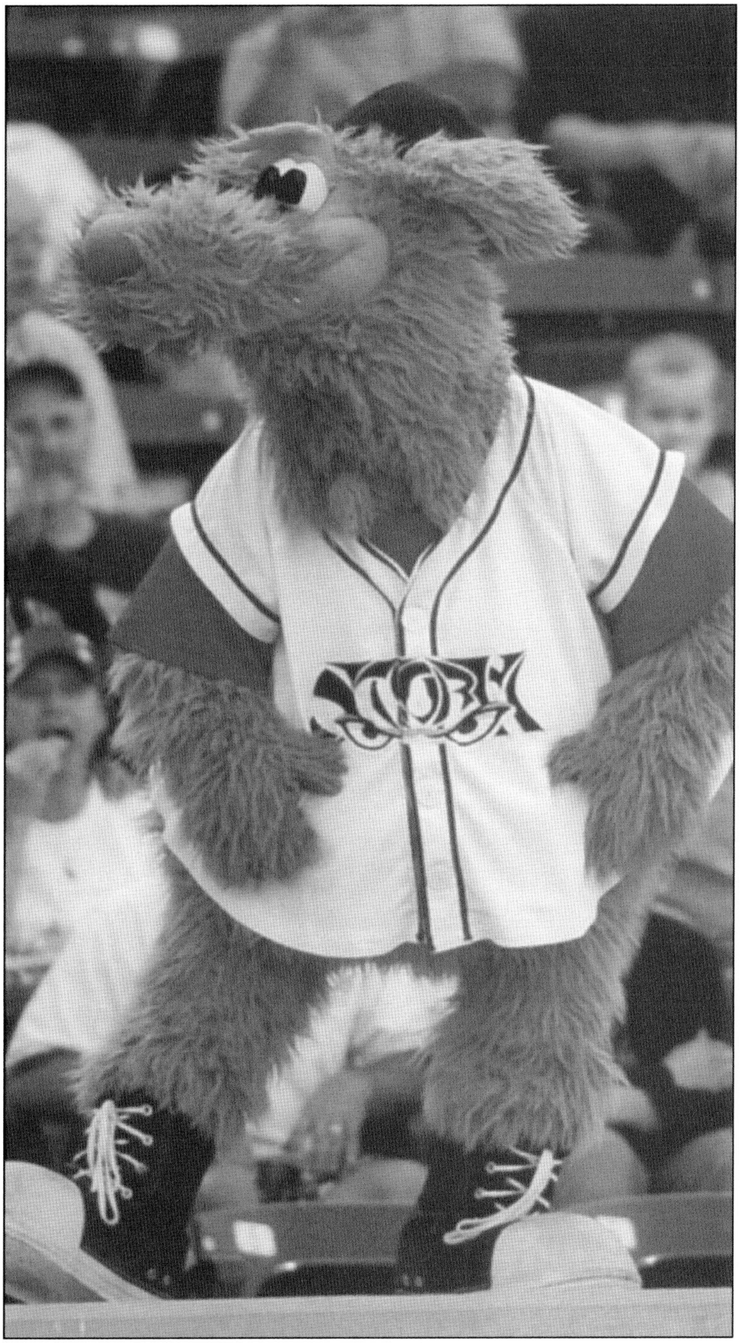

Thunder is a green, shaggy-haired dog who has been named the favorite mascot in California. He performs on the top of the dugouts, leads children across the field during "Thunder's Run," and wanders throughout the stadium. The children love to catch up with him while their parents take a picture. Occasionally, a child will be afraid of this big mascot. The Lake Elsinore Storm encourages people to invite Thunder to children's parties, and he shows up at lots of the civic activities in the city. When Thunder attends functions, you can count on him to smooch with the ladies and ruffle the men's hair.

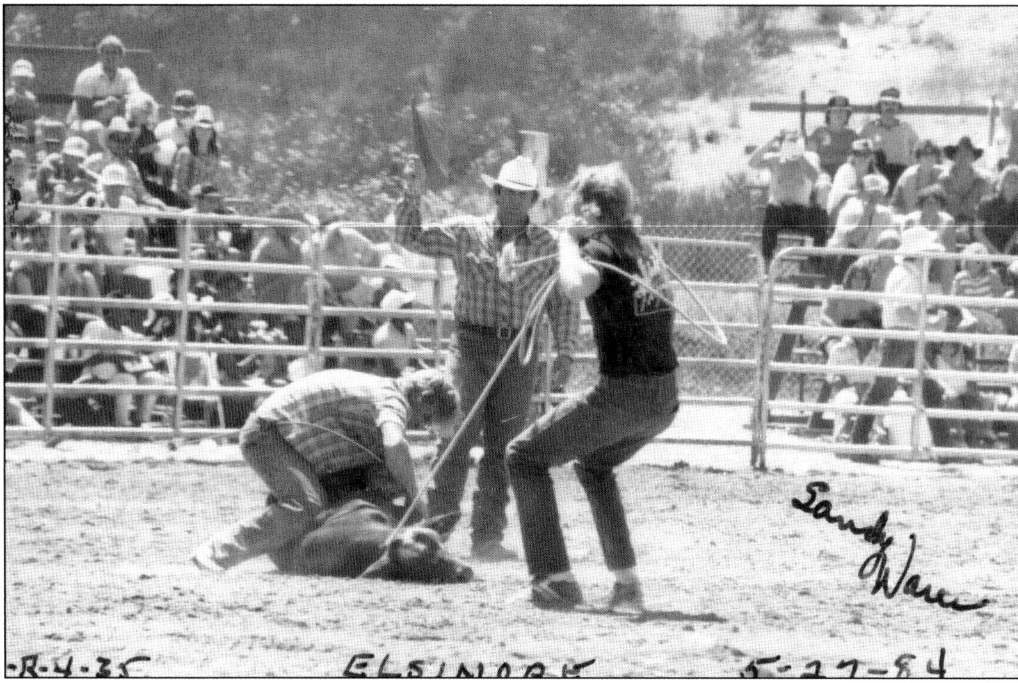

The rodeo in Lake Elsinore is a sport of the past and one in which the entire community participated, including the annual selection of the rodeo queen. While the grounds are still on Franklin Street, rodeos have not been held for more than 10 years. These functions were sanctioned by the official rodeo organization. The property is scheduled for development in the future.

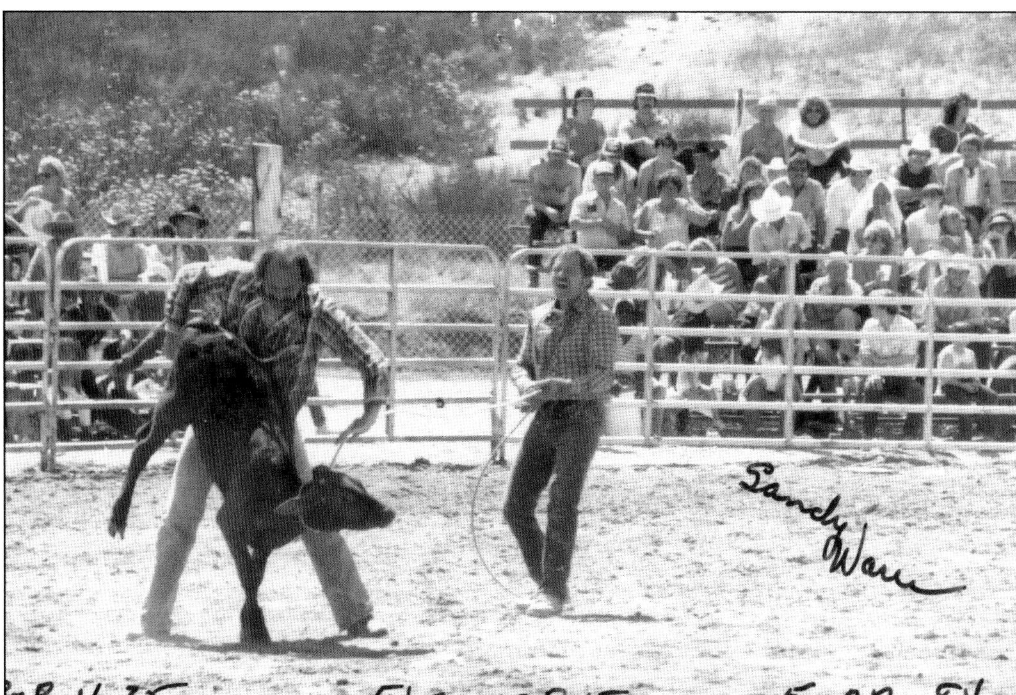

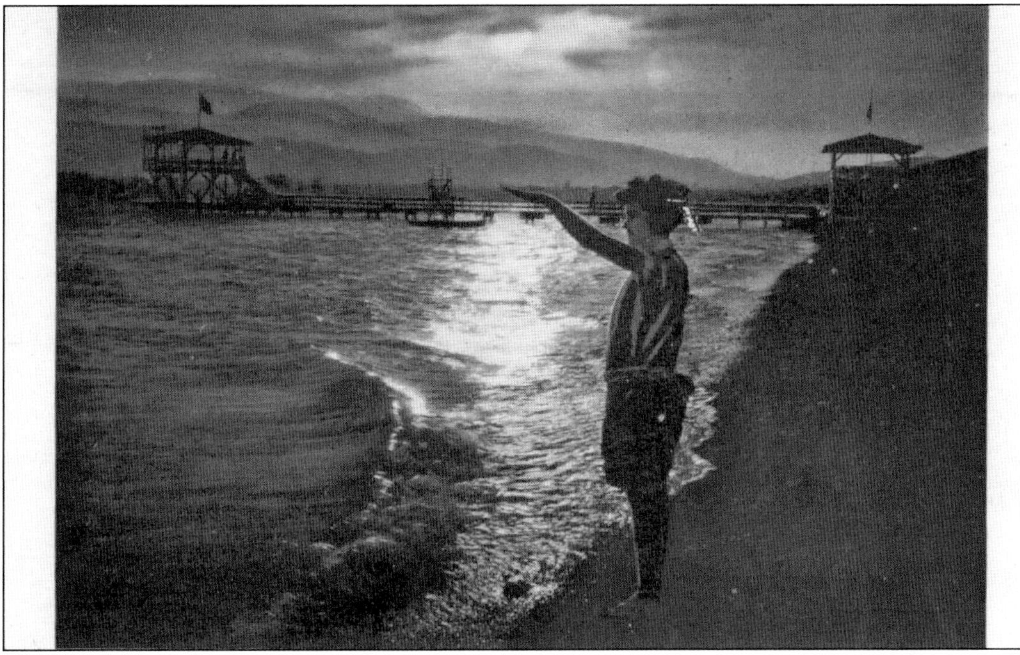

This moonlight scene on Lake Elsinore was taken from Lakeshore Drive and looks toward the location of the old Aloha Pier. Today 17 double-arm lamps line Lakeshore Drive, restored from Clevelin Realty Company days by the City of Lake Elsinore and providing a golden glow as motorists drive by. (CyG.)

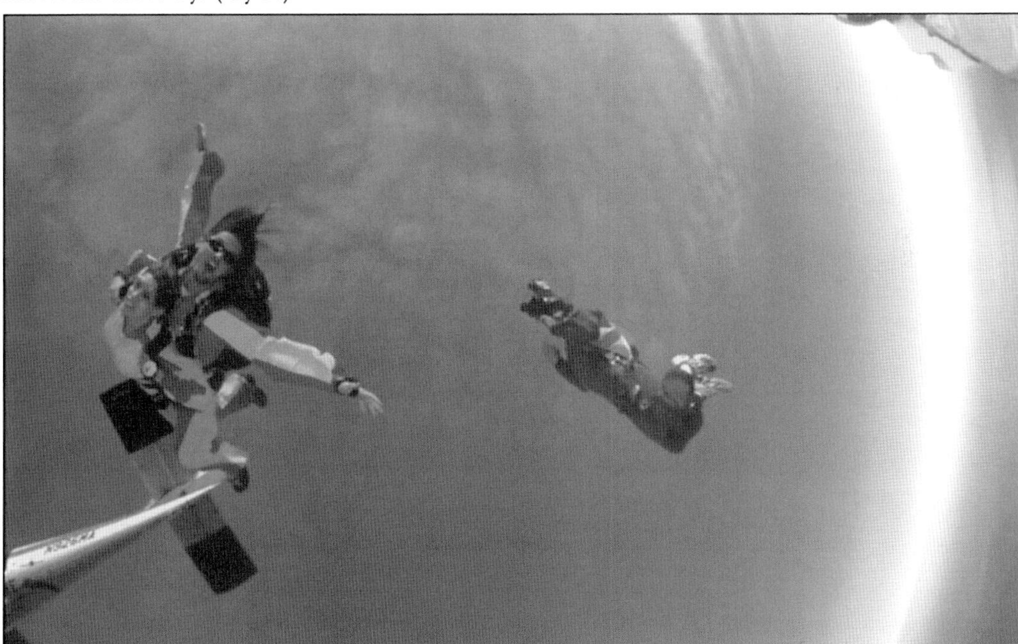

Skylark Airport has been in existence at its present site since January 1953. It is the home of Skydive Elsinore and is the headquarters for gliders and skydivers. On any afternoon, one may look up into the sky and see parachutists floating down through the air. To watch the parachutists come down is exciting and colorful.

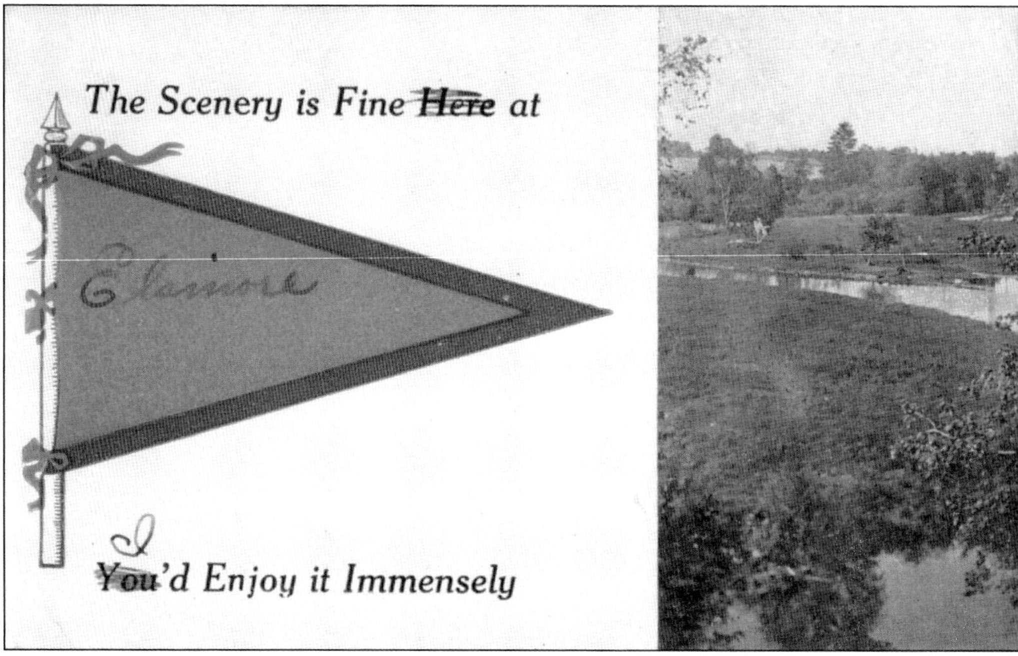


The following are additional postcard messages: "Here I am in a little jerk water town just about sweltering to death." "Did you ever see this place? Thought you might like to show it to the bunch." "The town and countryside is overrun with hunters from all over the country. Haven't heard from you yet. Don't expect many birds for they are hard to find." (JC.)

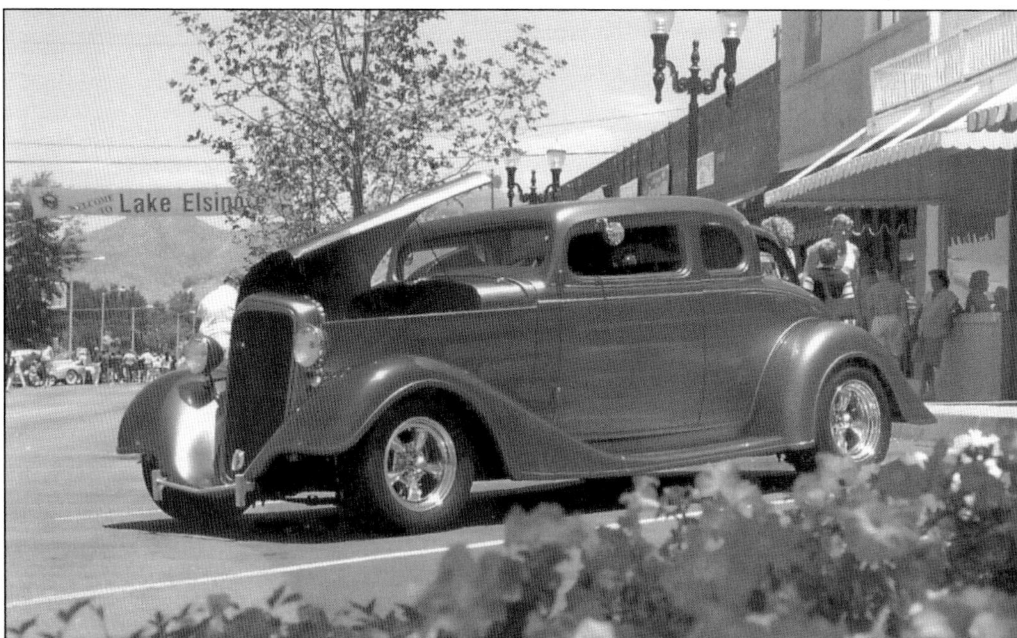

Car shows have been popular in Lake Elsinore for many years. This photograph depicts one held on July Fourth, along with all of the attendant celebrations for the holiday. Main Street in historic downtown is closed to vehicular traffic, and car enthusiasts are invited to park in the diagonal spaces. Visitors love to come, spread out their lawn chairs, and visit with friends.

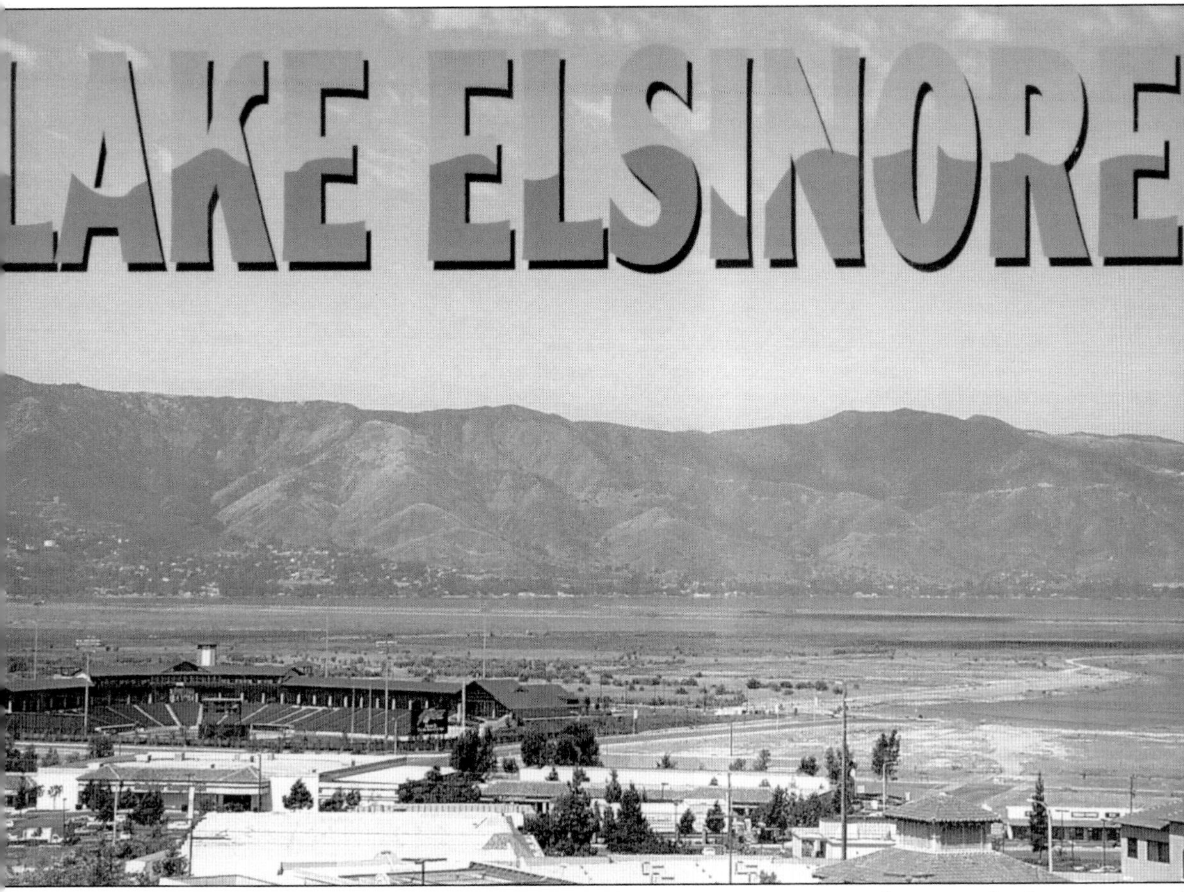


The city council built the beautiful Diamond Stadium in 1994 to serve as home to the Storm minor-league Class A baseball team, originally an affiliate of the Anaheim Angels. In 2001, the Storm's affiliation was changed to the San Diego Padres. The grassy knoll above first base is a great place for children to play and try to catch foul balls. Sean McCall, the Storm's radio announcer, says, "Only people under 48 inches tall should be allowed there—that's kid country!" The Storm management provides many events for the community, and the children have many *Field of Dreams* opportunities to go out on the ball field with the players of the future just before the game begins. The team's mascot is a green, shaggy-haired dog named Thunder who has been named the favorite mascot in California. The Storm's original mascot, Hamlet, was a lovable sea monster akin to Elsie—or Essie, as she was first named in the 1920s. (CP.)

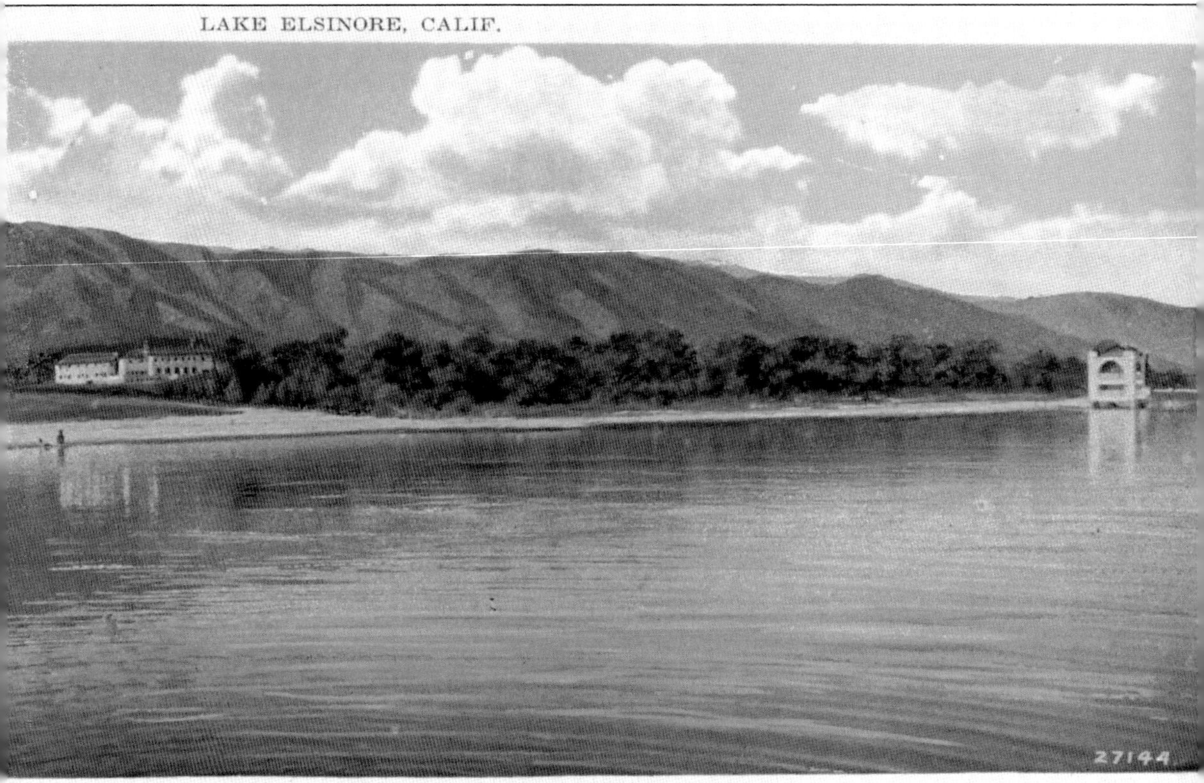


The lake looks serene in this image of the Elsinore Naval and Military Academy, with the pier at water's edge. The Elsinore Mountains are lovely as well. The photograph is so perfect it appears to have been staged. (MK.)

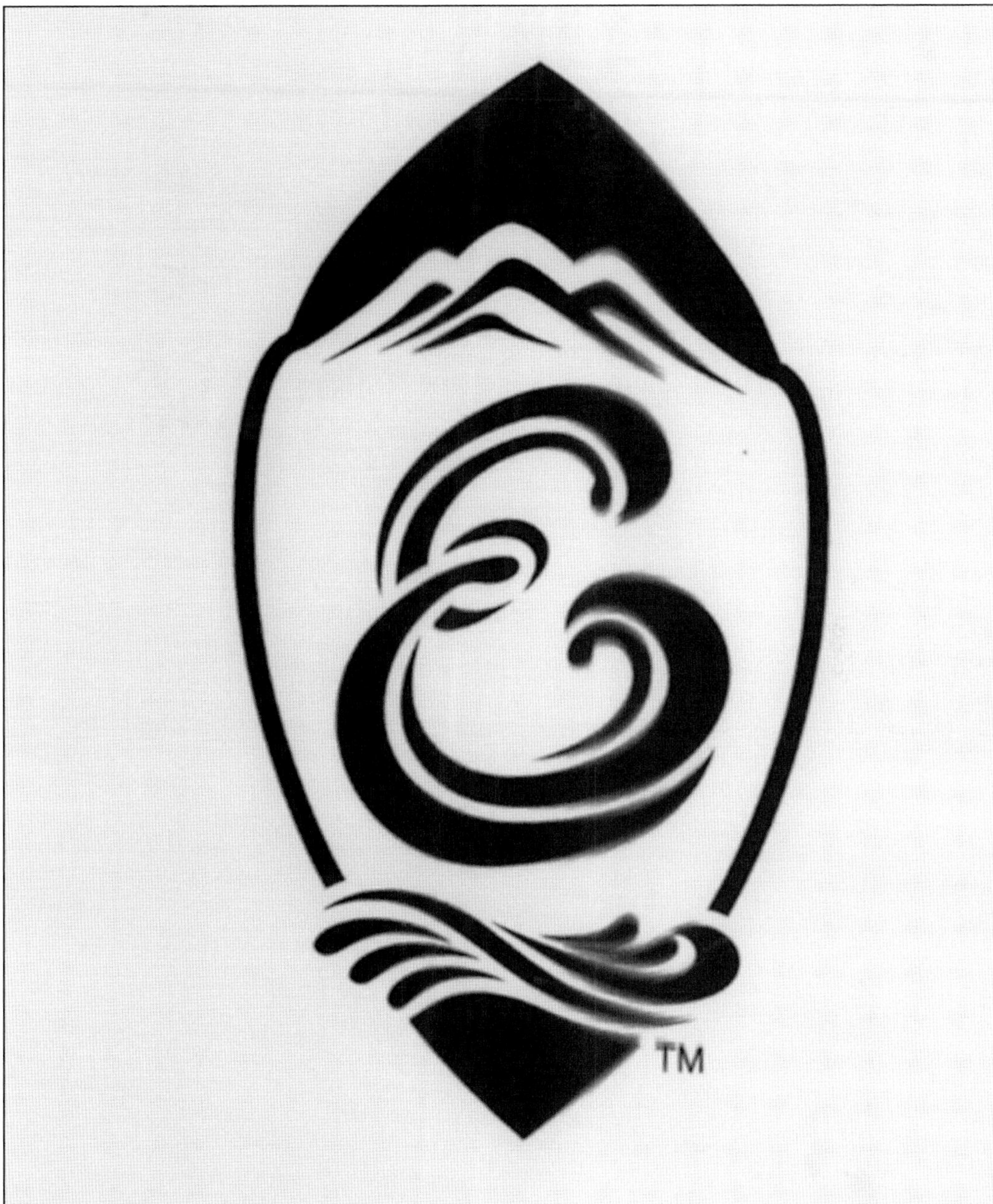


In April 2008, Lake Elsinore will be 120 years young—and the oldest city in Southwest Riverside County. With population approaching 50,000 comes a brand-new image to reflect its place among the fastest-growing cities in the Inland Empire region. "Dream Extreme" plays on the city's unique features, particularly its reputation for providing a wide variety of extreme sports venues, and communicates several concepts about the city. Lake Elsinore is a place to enjoy outdoor activities and realize the American Dream of owning an affordable home. The new logo depicts mountains on the top of a shield and waves on the bottom. Growth and business opportunities have increased dramatically, and the City of Lake Elsinore's new branding campaign reflects the attitude of the city for extreme sports, recreation, business and development opportunities, and lifestyles.

# Image Credits

## Postcard Collections

Claudia Goldberg (CG)
Cynthia Graves (CyG)
Jeanie Corral (JC)
John Gonzales (JG)
Linda Compos (LC)

## Postcard Companies

Albertype Company (AC)
Ames Advertising (AA)
Amescolor Publishers (AP)
Angeleno Photo Service (APS)
B. R. Montgomery (BRM)
Columbia Publishing (CP)
Columbia Wholesale Incorporated (CWI)
C. T. Art-Colortone Post Card (CTA)
David A. Fresh and Associates (DAF)
Ebert Photo (EbP)
Elsinore Pharmacy (EP)
Liberty Founders (LF)
M. Kashower Company (MK)
McGown-Silsbee Litho Company (MSL)
M. Rieder (MR)
Newman P. C. Company (NPC)
NYCE Quality Colored Landscape Locals (NYCE)
Old Photo Company (OPC)
Parachutes Incorporated (PI)
Photographs by R. Bennett, cards by D. Allen (RB/DA)
Picto Cards–Kaester and Blair (PCKB)
Post Cards of Quality–The Albertype Company (PCQ)
Tichnor Brothers (TB)
Union Oil Company of California (UOC-C)
United States Postal Service (USPS)
Western Publishing and Novelty Company (WPNC)
Wood's Post Cards (WPC)

# Bibliography

Hudson, Tom. *Lake Elsinore Valley: Its Story, 1777–1976.* Published for Lake Elsinore Valley Bicentennial Commission by Laguna House.

James, Elizabeth. *Elsinore History Vignettes*, Inland California Publishing Company.

Selected items from the files of Altha Merrifield Cauch.

Selected items from the files of Lilah Merrifield.

## Across America, People are Discovering Something Wonderful. *Their Heritage.*

Arcadia Publishing is the leading local history publisher in the United States. With more than 4,000 titles in print and hundreds of new titles released every year, Arcadia has extensive specialized experience chronicling the history of communities and celebrating America's hidden stories, bringing to life the people, places, and events from the past. To discover the history of other communities across the nation, please visit:

### www.arcadiapublishing.com

Customized search tools allow you to find regional history books about the town where you grew up, the cities where your friends and family live, the town where your parents met, or even that retirement spot you've been dreaming about.

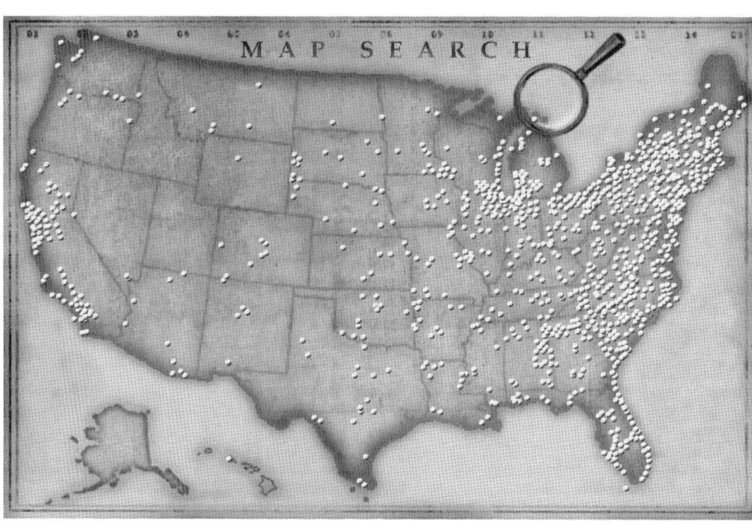